Tennessee Williams

Paradoxes of Nonconformism and Genre Recreations

Prakash Joshi

Foreword by

Amritjit Singh
Langston Hughes Professor of English and
African American Studies, 360 Ellis Hall
Ohio University, Athens, Ohio 45701

ATLANTIC
PUBLISHERS & DISTRIBUTORS (P) LTD

Published by
ATLANTIC
PUBLISHERS & DISTRIBUTORS (P) LTD
7/22, Ansari Road, Darya Ganj, New Delhi-110002
Phones : +91-11-40775252, 23273880, 23275880, 23280451
Fax : +91-11-23285873
Web : www.atlanticbooks.com
E-mail : orders@atlanticbooks.com

Branch Office
5, Nallathambi Street, Wallajah Road, Chennai-600002
Phones : +91-44-64611085, 32413319
E-mail : chennai@atlanticbooks.com

Printed in India at Nice Printing Press, A-33/3A, Site-IV, Industrial Area, Sahibabad, Ghaziabad, U.P.

Foreword

It has indeed been a pleasure for me during my Fulbright-Nehru year in India (2014-15) to renew several old friendships and to begin some new ones. Among the people I have enjoyed meeting most is Dr. Prakash Joshi, a man of impeccable manners, who exudes an unmistakable if quiet passion for his work as a teacher, scholar, and mentor. In fact, while Dr. Joshi is a new friend, he knew of my family and me in Jaipur during the early 1980s, when he was a young boy and his father was doing his Ph.D. in English at the University of Rajasthan. I encountered Dr. Joshi at first at two conferences in Jodhpur (October 2014) and Goa (December 2014). Slowly but surely, he used those two occasions deftly to persuade me to come to Sagar in March 2015 as a Resource Person for the five-day Workshop on the Literary and Cultural History of India that he and Dr. Nivedita Maitra, his Department Head, were organizing at Dr. Harisingh Gour Central University in Sagar. And now I have had the opportunity to review Dr. Joshi's book on a critically neglected aspect of playwright Tennessee Williams's writings, a project that has grown out of the doctoral thesis he did in Jaipur under the supervision of Professor Rajul Bhargava.

I have enjoyed reading Dr. Joshi's study in which he brings to surface a largely unexamined aspect of Williams's oeuvre—the high incidence of inter-genre and intra-genre textuality among his writings. Dr. Joshi notes how Williams's best short fiction belongs to the same two decades, the 1940s and the 1950s, which signal his best work as a playwright and then goes on to analyze the extent of the interrelationships between Williams's short fiction and drama. For example, *The Glass Menagerie*—a "memory play" and probably the most frequently anthologized of Williams's—has been developed from his short story, "The Portrait of a Girl in Glass." Similarly, another equally acclaimed play, *Cat on a Hot Tin Roof*, began as a short story titled, "Three Players of a Summer Game." In his wide-ranging analysis of this intertextuality across genres in Williams's writings, Dr. Joshi places the pre- and post-transformation stages in perspective to highlight the parallels, losses, and gains in transit. Williams's motifs and concerns—like those of William Faulkner, a fellow Mississippian—remain the same throughout his career, with understandable contextual variations. His characters from well-defined classes often gain an archetypal status within his canon. For Dr. Joshi, as Williams "moves from the preparatory stage, fiction, to the final stage of drama, his art moves upward and upland from Southern concerns and becomes more comprehensive in terms of regional literary traditions." Titled *Tennessee Williams: Paradoxes of Nonconformism and Genre Recreations*, Dr. Joshi's in-depth study of this particular aspect of Williams's work builds assiduously on the available Williams scholarship, even as he views the writer's later writings to have been shaped by postmodern influences.

Somc of Dr. Joshi's welcome research in this book would not have been possible twenty years ago. Although we knew plenty of Williams's writings before he died in 1983, so much more has come to light posthumously. Between 1995 and 2011, the Library of America published several volumes of plays that run into several thousand pages and include scores of plays that had never before been seen or read. Many of Williams's unpublished draft writings, sketches for later plays, and revisions and rewritings were also streamed through the successive issues of *The Tennessee Williams Annual Review* since its launch in 1998.

As a result of the availability of all these new materials, we are witnessing a rejuvenation of Tennessee Williams Studies, as evidenced in the September 2011 issue of the *American Theater*, which notes that "Tennessee Williams is being honored in the centennial year of his birth" in various ways, including "celebrities lining up to speak his word and sing his praises" (27). The same issue of *American Theater* also mentions "original

Tennessee Williams

Paradoxes of Nonconformism and Genre Recreations

Prakash Joshi

Foreword by

Amritjit Singh
Langston Hughes Professor of English and
African American Studies, 360 Ellis Hall
Ohio University, Athens, Ohio 45701

ATLANTIC
PUBLISHERS & DISTRIBUTORS (P) LTD

Published by
ATLANTIC
PUBLISHERS & DISTRIBUTORS (P) LTD
7/22, Ansari Road, Darya Ganj, New Delhi-110002
Phones : +91-11-40775252, 23273880, 23275880, 23280451
Fax : +91-11-23285873
Web : www.atlanticbooks.com
E-mail : orders@atlanticbooks.com

Branch Office
5, Nallathambi Street, Wallajah Road, Chennai-600002
Phones : +91-44-64611085, 32413319
E-mail : chennai@atlanticbooks.com

Printed in India at Nice Printing Press, A-33/3A, Site-IV, Industrial Area, Sahibabad, Ghaziabad, U.P.

Acknowledgements

I have incurred a sizeable amount of indebtedness to bring this study to its present form and shape. To begin with, I am especially indebted to Dr. Amritjit Singh, Langston Hughes Professor of English and African American Studies at Ohio University, the United States of America, for writing the Foreword which tersely captures the central theme of the book.

I acknowledge the support and affection of Professor Rajul Bhargava, my mentor in and outside this study, whose graceful manner of mentoring has gone deep into making this study worth what it is.

My thanks are due to Professor Jasbir Jain, my teacher and a former Head of the Department of English, University of Rajasthan, for her valuable suggestions. I had also benefited immensely from my discussions with late Professor Isaac Sequeira during my visits to the then IACIS (formerly ASRC), Hyderabad, while he was the Director of the Center. My gratitude and thanks are also due to the staff of AIRC (American Center) Libraries at New Delhi, Chennai and Mumbai for their characteristic promptness and help in tracing the recent developments and revival of research in Tennessee Williams Studies. I thank Ms. Angela Patrinos, a friend at New York and a former Fulbright Scholar at Banasthali University, for sharing her perceptions.

Of all the places I have worked, the most rewarding for the book has been the atmosphere and the culture and my colleagues at the Department of Comparative Literature at Queens College, the

City University of New York, USA, where I taught as a Fulbright Scholar. I mention my thanks to Professor Ali Jimale, Professor Clare Carroll, Professor Christopher Winks, Professor Caroline Rupprecht—all of the Department of Comparative Literature at the college—for our various interactions and conversations that gave me quite a good idea of the openness of the American attitude to arts. I am grateful for the cooperation I received at the Department from Mr. Sonny Hung and Ms. Cherishe Sookdeo and her good classmates taking my course on Modern Indian Drama. In and outside the Department, I acknowledge the cooperation of Dr. Helen Gaudette, Ms. Georgine Ingber, Dr. Nora Teikmanis, Ms. Rosa Amatulli and Dr. Lori Yamato.

Speaking of other places where I have taught, I record my thanks to Professor Aditya Shastri, the Vice Chancellor of Banasthali University for Women, and to Professor Nivedita Maitra, the Chairperson of the Department of English at Dr. Harisingh Gour Central University, for being supportive and kind in various ways.

To conclude, I acknowledge the blessings of my parents and the various petty secretarial kind of tasks that Anu and Joy, my wife and my son, did for me while I engrossed myself in work for and on this book.

Prakash Joshi

Foreword

It has indeed been a pleasure for me during my Fulbright-Nehru year in India (2014-15) to renew several old friendships and to begin some new ones. Among the people I have enjoyed meeting most is Dr. Prakash Joshi, a man of impeccable manners, who exudes an unmistakable if quiet passion for his work as a teacher, scholar, and mentor. In fact, while Dr. Joshi is a new friend, he knew of my family and me in Jaipur during the early 1980s, when he was a young boy and his father was doing his Ph.D. in English at the University of Rajasthan. I encountered Dr. Joshi at first at two conferences in Jodhpur (October 2014) and Goa (December 2014). Slowly but surely, he used those two occasions deftly to persuade me to come to Sagar in March 2015 as a Resource Person for the five-day Workshop on the Literary and Cultural History of India that he and Dr. Nivedita Maitra, his Department Head, were organizing at Dr. Harisingh Gour Central University in Sagar. And now I have had the opportunity to review Dr. Joshi's book on a critically neglected aspect of playwright Tennessee Williams's writings, a project that has grown out of the doctoral thesis he did in Jaipur under the supervision of Professor Rajul Bhargava.

I have enjoyed reading Dr. Joshi's study in which he brings to surface a largely unexamined aspect of Williams's oeuvre—the high incidence of inter-genre and intra-genre textuality among his writings. Dr. Joshi notes how Williams's best short fiction belongs to the same two decades, the 1940s and the 1950s, which signal his best work as a playwright and then goes on to analyze the extent of the interrelationships between Williams's short fiction and drama. For example, *The Glass Menagerie*—a "memory play" and probably the most frequently anthologized of Williams's—has been developed from his short story, "The Portrait of a Girl in Glass." Similarly, another equally acclaimed play, *Cat on a Hot Tin Roof*, began as a short story titled, "Three Players of a Summer Game." In his wide-ranging analysis of this intertextuality across genres in Williams's writings, Dr. Joshi places the pre- and post-transformation stages in perspective to highlight the parallels, losses, and gains in transit. Williams's motifs and concerns—like those of William Faulkner, a fellow Mississippian—remain the same throughout his career, with understandable contextual variations. His characters from well-defined classes often gain an archetypal status within his canon. For Dr. Joshi, as Williams "moves from the preparatory stage, fiction, to the final stage of drama, his art moves upward and upland from Southern concerns and becomes more comprehensive in terms of regional literary traditions." Titled *Tennessee Williams: Paradoxes of Nonconformism and Genre Recreations*, Dr. Joshi's in-depth study of this particular aspect of Williams's work builds assiduously on the available Williams scholarship, even as he views the writer's later writings to have been shaped by postmodern influences.

Some of Dr. Joshi's welcome research in this book would not have been possible twenty years ago. Although we knew plenty of Williams's writings before he died in 1983, so much more has come to light posthumously. Between 1995 and 2011, the Library of America published several volumes of plays that run into several thousand pages and include scores of plays that had never before been seen or read. Many of Williams's unpublished draft writings, sketches for later plays, and revisions and rewritings were also streamed through the successive issues of *The Tennessee Williams Annual Review* since its launch in 1998.

As a result of the availability of all these new materials, we are witnessing a rejuvenation of Tennessee Williams Studies, as evidenced in the September 2011 issue of the *American Theater*, which notes that "Tennessee Williams is being honored in the centennial year of his birth" in various ways, including "celebrities lining up to speak his word and sing his praises" (27). The same issue of *American Theater* also mentions "original works about Tennessee Williams being debuted" (27). Suitably and meaningfully entitled, "Williams Then & Now," a special section in the magazine underscores the enduring relevance of the author. The same issue also carries a review by Garrett Eisler of *Tenn at One Hundred: The Reputation of Tennessee Williams*, edited by David Kaplan, that includes 18 biographical essays on Williams by writers as diverse as Robert Bray, Barton Palmer, Vincent Brook, Thomas Keith, Claudia Wilsch, Albert Devlin, and John Lahr. Eisler highlights the essay titled "Tennessee Williams in Never Apolitical," by Amiri Baraka (formerly LeRoi Jones) in order to point out that Tennessee Williams the playwright is championing the oppressed and their struggle for power.

For the South Asian readers of Williams, Dr. Joshi's book is an affirmation of the need to re-examine our relationship to the playwright and his creative output—just as the playwright examined, time and again, with poignancy and sensitivity, issues surrounding the individual's relationship to social conventions and pressures. The hold of age-old attitudes and customs is a subject that is more pertinent than ever for South Asians, who continue to confront challenges of moving past casteism, communalism, and arcane notions of gender and sexuality. Tennessee Williams speaks to us at many levels and Dr. Joshi hopes we are ready to listen. I wish Dr. Joshi and his book the very best as they both go forth and flourish in the academy in the months and years ahead.

Amritjit Singh
Langston Hughes Professor of English
and African American Studies,
360 Ellis Hall,
Ohio University,
Athens, Ohio 45701

Preface

Eugene O'Neill, Arthur Miller and Tennessee Williams together form the trinity of the 20th Century American Drama. The three have had their well-deserved shares of the Broadway stage with their separate distinctions. Williams has the distinction of being designated the dramatist of lost souls, of fugitives. His plays are the genuine representations of the psyche and tragedy of the 'Fugitive Kind'. Since he identifies himself with this self-effacing victimized section of humanity—"I am Blanche Dubois", he has said on more than one occasion—his delineation of the individual yet collective tragedy of that section of humanity carries the stamp of authority. One of the remarkable features of his craft has been a combination of lyricism and experimentation. David Mamet, one of his great contemporaries, describes Tennessee Williams's plays as "the greatest dramatic poetry in the American language" (qtd. in Dean 50). To get a fuller sense of what Mamet means, we refer to Anne Dean's rendering of the quote: "He also considers that Tennessee Williams wrote the greatest dramatic poetry in the American Language [and dramatized] a kind people living in a cruel country [who] don't know how to show [their] love" (50).

A huge amount of research work on Williams exists; yet much still remains, as Philip C. Kolin terms it, the "undiscovered country". The resurgence of research on Williams—making discoveries into that "undiscovered country"—has generally ignored the phenomenon of the intense interrelationships between the author's short fiction and drama. It is so because the critical attention has usually and generally been directed to the dramaturgy of the author. Seven landmark works brought out in our own 21st century more than substantiate the point. The seven works in context, leaning heavily towards the drama of Williams are: *The Undiscovered Country* (2002) by Philip C. Kolin, *Magical Muse: Millennial Essays on Tennessee Williams* (2002) by Ralph F. Voss, *Tennessee Williams: A Case Book* (2002) by Robert F. Gross, *Hollywood's Tennessee: The Williams Films and Postwar America* (2009) by R. Barton Palmer and Robert Bray, *The Late Plays of Tennessee Williams* (2009) by William Prosser, *Tennessee Williams: Mad Pilgrimage of the Flesh* (2014) by John Lahr, and *Tennessee Williams and the Theatre of Excess: The Strange, the Crazed, the Queer* (2015) by Annette J. Saddik.

A keen preliminary survey of Williams's art leads one to the fact of the enduring importance of the fictional side of his creative genius. The fact can be substantiated and proved by a simple analysis of his creative career as a writer. All of his artistic and commercial successes on stage belong to a period of around fifteen years—from his grand opus on Broadway with *The Glass Menagerie* in 1945 to *The Night of the Iguana,* his last artistic and commercial success on stage in 1961. Apart from a few promising pieces written earlier, the best of Williams's short fiction also belongs to the same successful period of his creative career—1940s and 1950s. The study in the book makes an endeavor to closely analyze the extent of the affinities and interrelationships between Williams's short fiction and drama. Many of the author's plays have sprung from his short stories. The list of such pairs of short stories and plays includes many interesting cases of transformation. Here is a cursory view of the plays evolving from the short stories of the author: *The Glass Menagerie* from "The Portrait of a Girl in Glass", *27 Wagons Full of Cotton* from a story with the same title except the numerals put in words, *Summer and Smoke* from "The Yellow Bird", *Cat on a Hot Tin Roof* from "Three Players of a Summer Game", *The Milk Train Doesn't Stop Here Anymore* from "Man Bring This Up Road", *The Night of the Iguana* from a story with the same title, *The Strangest Kind of Romance* from "The Malediction", and *The Kingdom of Earth* from a story with the same title.

It would not be out of place to mention here that many of these plays have earned a general critical acclaim with scant thought ever accorded to their geneses in fiction. All these instances of inter-genre transformation apart, there are quite a few unstated cases and strands of recreations flowing from the fiction of the author to his drama. The study makes exclusive and comprehensive analyses of these fiction-to-drama transformations.

Further, the study also probes exclusively and comprehensively the revisions and reproductions within the genre of drama. The oeuvre of Tennessee Williams has quite a few important instances of the revisions and adaptations of plays into later versions. Consolidating the theory of revisions, the research on Williams discovered one-act versions of *The Night of the Iguana* and *The Rose Tattoo* not very long ago. The one-act versions of the two plays have been published, respectively, in the 2001 and 2003 issues of *The Tennessee Williams Annual Review*. The theory of revisions gets a very recent reiteration through the recent discovery of *The Reading*, a one-act play first published in the 2010 issue of *The Tennessee Williams Annual Review*. The one-act becomes, to quote Robert Bray, a "part of a larger scheme..." of "the full length *Vieux Carré*" (3).

This study in the book places the pre- and post-transformation stages in perspective to investigate the parallels, losses and gains in transit. The crux of the study is borne by the intense textual study of these parallels and replications, along with the investigations into the losses and gains. The basic themes and concerns remain the same, with slight changes at every stage. Even Williams's characters fall into certain well-defined classes that can be designated the status of archetypes within the creative canon of the author. As he moves from the preparatory stage of fiction to the successive stages of drama, his art moves upward and upland from Southern concerns and becomes more incorporative and comprehensive in terms of 'territorial' literary traditions.

The magnitude and importance of some early influences on Tennessee Williams have reckonable expanse and significance. Coming mostly from the family members and the immediate surroundings, these influences grow into permanent experiences and shape up the psyche and the creativity of the author. Apart from his early childhood at Clarksdale, which forms an immaculate and almost a proverbially idyllic background to the bleak experiences in his adolescent and post-adolescent years, all that gets transcribed in Williams's writings is a litany of shattering experiences suffered by a person sensitive to the verge of neurosis. In fact, the biographers of the author suggest that the catharsis of creative writing saved him from going the way his sister, Rose, went. In the realm of Williams's creative world the biographical points of view cannot at all be ignored, because Williams the artist is inseparable from Williams the man. Williams the victimized 'Artist Figure', Williams the 'Fugitive' and Williams the susceptible being is throughout a key character in his writings. He learnt very early in his life the art of transcribing the humiliation, the bitterness and the confusion he suffered. At the concluding points of this transcription, we have a long series of writings starting with the narrative of a psychopathically vengeful sister in "The Vengeance of Nitocris" (an early short story) and coming to an end with the claustrophobic cries of a brother and his sister in *Out Cry* (a late play). The world that we encounter and experience in these writings evinces the artistic and creative influences of Ibsen, Strindberg, Chekhov, D.H. Lawrence, O'Neill and Hart Crane.

There are various elements that contribute to create a specific kind of atmosphere in the fictional and dramatic writings of Williams; and those elements call for a close analysis. The external atmosphere in his writings is marked by apathy, victimization and some convoluted varieties of violence. More remarkable, however, is the internal atmosphere, which is characterized by complex states of the mind and emotions. This complexity, beyond alleviation, is the result of contradictory passions afflicting the protagonists. As can be noticed in the case of all his representative writings, the protagonists are torn between repressed desires on the one hand and some varieties of sincerity and devotion on the other. This psychological torture, partially self-imposed, is noticeable in both the versions of the plot in the events of transformations from fiction to drama, and then from drama to drama. Tom and Laura, Brick Pollitt, Alma, Hannah Jelkes, Mrs. Goforth and Chicken have their tragedies stemming from the conflicting passions, devotions, sincerities rooted deep in their personalities. Williams's later writings—plays in particular—outline a new theology of sorts combining intense religious and physical passions. Shannon in *The Night of the Iguana* and Doc in *Small Craft Warnings* are the messiahs of that comprehensive theology. His late writings combine a heavily emphasized religiosity and inescapable physical desire. Though the proposition of this new theology comes much earlier in his career in *Battle of Angels*. Apart from this somber internal atmosphere of psychological suffering, most probably caused by the combining of two irreconcilable passions, the author's writings in both the genres exhibit a definite 'Southern-ness'. The Southern atmosphere functions at both the internal and external levels. At the less complex external level, the Southern atmosphere emerges through situations and settings that serve as the contrasting background to put in sharp relief the darker aspects of life. Though a fiercely contested term, 'Gothic' is sometimes applied to such situations in Tennessee Williams. At the complex internal level, the 'Southern' character of Williams's writings is manifested through the many permeating paradoxes.

Whatever has been artistically, thematically and structurally memorable in Williams, has essentially been grounded and reared in the South. One of the employments of Southern paradoxes by the author is available in one of his very early short stories, "The Vengeance of Nitocris", where the life-giving waters of the river Nile have been converted into an instrument of a blood-chilling massacre. "The Portrait of a Girl in Glass" (story) and *The Glass Menagerie* (drama version of the plot in the story) exploit and thrive upon the paradoxical opposites represented in Laura and in Tom. Such defining paradoxes determine the tension, the bleakness and the somberness of atmosphere in the writings of Tennessee Williams. The thematic and structural elements in Williams's writings have a corresponding and vibrant relationship with the general hostile atmosphere therein. He has so arranged his creative material, and so structured it, as to bring out the inanity of several of our taboo infested systems. One of the issues of importance here is a strong current of nonconformism flowing through Williams's works, which in many obvious and subtle ways has been the source of the atmosphere and paradoxes in his writings. Many of the author's early works like "The Vengeance of Nitocris" and *Battle of Angels* are virtual conflagrations. In these two cases, the taboo infested communities are consigned, respectively, to water and fire, which by their use in the two works get established as regenerative symbols.

The nonconformist protagonists in Williams are destined to fight two simultaneous battles. One of the two battles is an inner and psychological struggle against the inherited and deep rooted puritanical values, and the other is an external struggle against all that is decayed in the society. The structural pattern in his stories depends upon the sparseness of characters and is conducive to the twin struggles at the two fronts. A key structural element in Williams's fiction and drama is memory, usually mythicized and re-enacted during the time period captured in the work. Thus, we have Mr. Gonzales in "The Mysteries of Joy Rio" reliving the routine and perversions of his dead mentor, Mr. Kroger. On a couple of occasions, we may have the cases of lost memory and thwarted re-enactment, as in "Something by Tolstoi". The role of mythicized memory and its re-enactment is far too obvious in the *The Glass Menagerie, Summer and Smoke, The Streetcar Named Desire, Cat on a Hot Tin Roof* and *The Night of the Iguana.* In *Suddenly Last Summer* and *Orpheus Descending* and the works of that kind, a proper and established myth replaces mythicized memory.

As the cases of stated fiction-to-drama transformations and the contours of the parallelism between them constitute the pivotal purpose of the argument here, the study in the book attempts to individually and textually analyze all these cases of transformation to find out the patterns of replications and evolutions. These individual analyses also attempt to discover and discuss whether the short stories involved are simply preparatory works for the later drama versions or they have enough structural mettle and thematic substance to be considered and remembered as the masterpieces of the genre of fiction. In all the cases, the stories have been closer to the crude experiences, the unrefined pains (and pleasures) of the author. So, if the naked crudity of experience be seen as a mark of the authenticity of art, the stories of Williams would earn that status of authentic art earlier than his plays. Writing stories had been primarily and basically cathartic to him. The plays emerging from these stories very often assume an artistic distance from the crude and basic experiences of their author. The crucially interesting fact about these situations of transformations is that the stories constitute the base of the genesis of this process of artistic creation, and, simultaneously, are beautiful representatives of the art of Williams in the genre of fiction while they also function admirably well as the pre-text for his drama.

A frenetic and compulsive writer, Williams had the dissatisfaction characteristic of an artist. It happened very often that before reaching the final draft of a play, he would produce several preparatory drafts running through all sorts of stages—from individual pieces of conversation—to one-act plays and then to full-length plays. Quite a number of his plays have well delineated histories running through several years. Connected with their original versions, these plays constitute a good list of pairs: *Battle of Angles* and *Orpheus Descending; Summer and Smoke* and *The Eccentricities of Nightingale; Il Cane Incantato della Divina Costiera* and *The Rose Tattoo*, the One-Act and full length versions of *The Night of the Iguana*; *Confessional* and *Small Craft Warnings; Two Character Play* and *Out Cry;* and *The Strangest Kind of Romance* (with *The Lady of Larkspur Lotion* and the newly discovered *The Reading*) and *Vieux Carré.* The study in the book puts all these pairs (and, probably, trios or even a quartet) under close scrutiny for the changes made and for the realization or failure of the objective in transformation. An interesting aspect of these inter- and intra-genre recreations/ transformations in Williams is the presence of several free-floating strands creating a broad spectrum of interconnectivity among his short stories and plays.

Tennessee Williams can very well be placed in perspective with the postmodern approach of literary interpretations. In his later dramatic repertoire, the author actually experimented with such non-realistic styles as expressionism, surrealism and the absurd—all of which he arranged under what he called "plastic theatre". Towards the close, and very briefly, the study also looks into the possibility of the application of Jungian and Existential theories to the writings of Tennessee Williams.

The book is intended as a contribution to Tennessee Williams studies, especially in relation to the extensive intertextuality that is at work within the creative world of the author—an aspect of his work that still requires a lot of critical attention. The book endeavors to study the full range of the spectrum of interrelationships through inter- or intra-genre transformations to arrive at appropriate conclusions. The goal in the study has been to make the readers of Williams's writings more aware of the author's complex world, ridden as it is with paradoxes, conflicts and with situations of transience and liminality. In doing so, it also deploys the traditional biographical approach to prepare grounds for a better understanding of the author's art.

The character of the book has been primarily and largely textual. Ostensibly biographical in nature though, even the first chapter incorporates quite a few pieces from the writings of the author to demonstrate his lived experiences going almost unfiltered into his creative world. Many stories and plays come up for repeated references in different contexts as the study moves through the chapters. A special feature of the study has been tracing the (cross) genre recreations from the traceable points of the earliest beginnings. From the formative influences to the building up of and getting settled nonconformist thematic patterns to the inherent (thematic and other) paradoxes to transformational elements, the study attempts to meticulously note down the thematic and structural reorganization/reformations in the process of the transformation first from fiction to drama and then from drama to drama. As it does so, the study tries to follow the steady sequence and development from the former to the latter. There is a heavy reliance on profuse quotations and citations generally from the texts of the author and particularly from critical sources, either to provide a hands-on evidence or to prove the arguments or to bring in critical perspectives to validate the analyses. Often, the quotations from the fiction and drama texts (usually longish) have been placed in close proximity to analytically prove the elemental closeness and relationships between the thematic, structural, ideological and other patterns of the writings in the two genres. Wherever applicable, the study also refers to and takes up the recently discovered and previously unpublished manuscripts of the author coming up for first publication in the successive issues of *Tennessee Williams Annual Review* in order to create a comprehensive picture of genre recreations.

A NOTE ON REFERENCING AND CITATION STRATEGY

The book ostensibly uses the MLA citation style for in-text and end-text references. However, there have throughout been made some deviations from the recommended citation pattern to accommodate and simplify extensive references to the author's works and some canonical biographical and critical texts. The in-text references to the works of Tennessee Williams use the titles of the texts for citation rather than the last name of the author. The listing of the titles does not follow the alphabetical sequence. Individual works have been listed individually. The collection of stories and collections of plays reproduce all the titles that make up the collections. For reference in the Bibliography, therefore, the reader will look for the title of the work, individual or in a collection. It is for this reason along with that of the textual character of the study that writings of Williams have been placed separately as 'Primary Sources' in the Bibliography at the end.

In the course of the chapters, often there is the use of short handles for long titles. For example, *The Glass Menagerie* is identified as *Menagerie* in the in-text citations, *Cat on a Hot Tin Roof* as *Cat*, *Sweet Bird of Youth* as *Sweet Bird*, *The Milk Train Doesn't Stop Here Anymore* as *Milk Train*, and *The Strangest Kind of Romance* as *The Strangest*. Since there are no lists of works cited following the chapters, some more modifications have been done in some in-text citations for a precise reference in the Bibliography. The stories taken up for analyses of the genre recreations to drama are all from a single volume, *Collected Stories*, and have all been referred in the in-text citations by *Collected Stories* followed by the page number(s) of their occurrence in the volume. For plays, the entries in the 'Primary Sources' section put the names of the plays in the sequence of their occurrence in the respective collections.

To add a word about the Index, the entries there only mention the works of Tennessee Williams that have come up for reference in the course of the book. Keeping in mind and highlighting the textual character of the study in the book, the entries in the Index include the titles of the occasional prose pieces (essays) of the author, his fiction and his plays.

Prakash Joshi

Contents

1

The "Shadow of the Episcopal Church": Formative Relationships and Influences

> I've literally grown up right in the very Shadow of the Episcopal Church.
>
> (*Portrait of a Madonna*)

Almost at the risk of finding himself in the eye of the storm of a controversy, Roger Boxill calls Tennessee Williams "perhaps the only genuine writer in the history of American theatre" (21). All scholarly debate apart, the bold statement heavily underlines the immense significance of the profusely prolific writer in the context of Twentieth Century American Literature. During his lifetime, at least sixty-three of Tennessee Williams's "plays and playlets were published or given a major professional production or both" (Boxill 21). Apart from this huge theatrical material, he also published two books of poetry, two novels, four books of short stories, a book of essays, and his autobiography. And all this doesn't include the plays and other works that are getting their first publications in the successive issues of *The Tennessee Williams Annual Review*.

Out of this massive mass of writing emerge such unforgettable personae as Nitocris, Jacob Brodzky, Amanda Wingfield, Alma Winemiller, Baby Doll, Blanche DuBois, Maggie (the Cat), Alexandra Del Lago, Karen Stone, Stanley Kowalski, Jim O'Connor, Val Xavier, Tom Wingfield, Chance Wayne, Sebastian, Big Daddy, Shannon, Doc, Felice and Fräulein. The same great mass of writing also brings into focus a writer obsessively and frenetically at work (as if to escape from some torment). All this verifies the contention that writing for Tennessee Williams was "both home and healing, a way of making order out of disorder" (Weales 8). Much of the "disorder" which he suffered and which became the source of the special character of his writings, was brought to him through heredity. He carried in his blood two irreconcilable patterns of genes which formed his system of response to whatever he experienced in his childhood. He proclaimed and proved himself a "rebellious puritan". The discordance of the constituents of his personality can be traced back to the discordant marriage of his parents—"Edwina was as much a puritan as her husband was a Cavalier" (Tischler 16). The marriage between the rowdy traveler and the pampered "southern belle" had clearly been a "terrible mistake" (Spoto 8). A child of this marriage, Tennessee Williams sought a reconciliation between two contrary streams rooted in his being. Writing, therefore, became a psychological, emotional and even a physical compulsion for him.

There is a good justification for making a limited foray into Tennessee Williams's biographical details. Apart from demystifying the author for whom writing was a therapeutic escape, the exercise would also foreground the social milieu and the family environment out of which "he constructs a microcosm crystallizing all human experience" (Tischler 15). The author's personal life, particularly early, gains an additional significance in the context of the present study. It is so because the author almost invariably enters his own work as the perennial "fugitive", and reminisces about his life as a universalized pattern for the frustrations and satisfactions of individuals through generations of man. "The fugitive kind turns out to be mankind, after all" (Hoffman 404).

The childhood of Tennessee Williams has two distinctly set-apart phases. The first relates to his early childhood spent in a succession of Southern Episcopal rectories; and the second to the unhappy experiences at St Louis. The first part of his childhood has the idyllic background of Columbus and Clarksdale, Mississippi, and is characterized by his physical, psychological and emotional dependence upon the women around him. (Apart from himself and his grandfather, it was an all-women family he grew up in.) Clarksdale, a city of two rivers (the Mississippi and the Sunflower), turns into a nostalgic symbol for lost beauty, innocence and happiness. The loveliness of the place becomes a recurrent and inviolable piece of memory for the author; much the same way as Myra in "The Field of Blue Children" (a short story) and Amanda in *The Glass Menagerie* have their private treasures of memory to cherish and fall back on. For Myra, the field and the blue flowers are the witnesses of her brief consummation of relationship with Homer, the archetypal itinerant in Tennessee Williams: "The field was exactly as she had remembered it. She had walked quickly out among the flowers, then suddenly fell to her knees among them, sobbing" (*Collected Stories* 78). Amanda's memory of her gentleman callers has the rich fringe and frill of Mississippi Delta plantations: ..."My callers were gentleman—all! Among my callers were some of the most prominent young planters of the Mississippi Delta—planters and sons of planters" (*Menagerie* 238). The wistfully happy memory of the gentlemen callers—those "planters and sons of planters"—partially forms the background against which she places the tragedy of her daughter, though without fully appreciating the nuances of it.

An important event in Tennessee Williams's Clarksdale years was the severe attack of diphtheria that confined him to bed and drained all his strength rendering him physically incapable of moving out of the house for several months. The disease also damaged his vision for life and significantly changed his personality. The changed personality was an indirect outcome of the disease that kept him physically and emotionally dependent on three generations of women in his family—his grandmother, his mother and his sister. The "overly solicitous attention" of his mother during this period injected in his personality a certain amount of femininity that kept him uncomfortable all his life. As he looked back upon the event through the haze of years while writing his *Memoirs,* Tennessee Williams could see the two tones of his own personality before and after the event of the long disease: "Prior to it, I had been a little boy with a robust, aggressive, almost bullying nature. During the illness, I learned to play, alone, games of my own invention" (*Memoirs* 11).

Speaking from the vantage point of advanced years, Tennessee Williams ascribed this duality of personality on his mother's over attention:

> During this period of illness and solitary games, my mother's overly solicitous attention planted in me the makings of a sissy, much to my father's discontent. I was becoming a decided hybrid, different from the family line of frontiersmen—heroes of east Tennessee. (*Memoirs* 11-12)

Any attempt to trace the genesis of the 'fugitive', the perennial itinerant in Tennessee Williams, would bring us to "this period of illness and solitary games". The 'fugitive' in Tennessee Williams is a romantic misfit with a variously formed hybridity rooted deep in his nature. He is a man rendered misfit by his vulnerable sensibilities. At the receiving end of the brutalities of an insensitive world, he also has to suffer a struggle within his psyche. Destiny has charted out for him an end either like that of Tom in *The Glass Menagerie* or Lucio in "The Malediction" (short story). While Tom opts out to an itinerant existence free from the exigencies of reality, Lucio finds death as the single route to escape open to him. It is some worth to pause here and listen to Tom the inveterate, itinerant romantic:

> ...I left Saint Louis. I descended the steps of this fire escape for a last time and followed, from then on, in my father's footsteps, attempting to find in motion what was lost in space—I traveled around a great deal. The cities swept about me like dead leaves, leaves that were brightly colored but torn away from the branches.... (*Menagerie* 313)

Quite like Tom, Lucio takes his exit out of functional life; but quite unlike him, he prefers to get clear out of existence. He doesn't go alone; he takes along his sole companion, Nitchevo the cat:

> He carried her down the steep, cobbled street toward the river. It was an easy direction. The whole town slanted

> that way...Lucio spoke to the cat as the stream climbed about them.
>
> "Soon", he whispered, "Soon, soon, very soon". Only a single instant she struggled against him: clawed his shoulder and arm in a moment of doubt. My God, My God, why last thou forsaken me? Then the Ecstasy passed and her faith returned, they went away with the river. Away from the town, away and away from the town, as the smoke, the wind took from the chimneys—completely away. (*Collected Stories* 161-62)

The two manners of exit, one escapist and the other desperately hopeless, adopted by Tom and Lucio have a strange but real replication in their author's life. He lived like Tom of *The Glass Menagerie*, and died somewhat in the manner of Lucio in "The Malediction".

The seclusion that the disease imposed upon Tennessee Williams was just a variant of the social seclusion which was imposed upon him due to the religious calling of his grandfather. The grandchild of an Episcopal minister, he was always treated with a certain amount of deference by other children and parishioners. The situation naturally drew him towards his sister, Rose, who was senior to him by two years. The two siblings became great friends and playmates. Their games were different and incorporated the rich imagination of Rose. Playing in the large backyards of rectories, separate from other children, this rich imagination must even have been a necessity. Speaking to an interviewer, Jean Evans, years later as a new celebrity, Tennessee Williams remembers the time with a definite amount of nostalgia:

> ...we lived in small Mississippi towns. We always had a large backyard. My brother didn't figure in my childhood because he was a baby so long. But my sister and I played together. We invented games. The poor children used to run all over town, but my sister and I played in our own backyard. We were reclusive. (in Devlin 16)

The fertile imagination in his drama and non-drama has a beginning in this period of his childhood. The hyper religiosity, the dream like structure and the distinctly southern atmosphere so frequently available in his works would also have this period as their points of beginning. Tennessee Williams makes an acknowledgement of this fact to Jean Evans in the interview cited a few lines above: “Life was pleasant—gracious, full of imaginings. Perhaps that’s why, when writing, I nearly always return to South” (16).

The creative imagination, which the author in all probability learnt by responding to his sister’s incredible imagination, settled permanently with the being of Tennessee Williams while he was confined due to illness. Coupled with his keen observation, the imagination of the author developed into the potent concoction out of which emerged the material for writing about the travails of man. A singular instance of the author’s sensitive observation is available in his response to the plight of Laura Young whom he met while accompanying his grandfather on his parish calls. Though still effete, Tennessee Williams had sufficiently recovered to undertake these walks. The glass pendants in her white house near an orchard have an explicit resemblance to the glass animals of Laura Wingfield in *The Glass Menagerie*. Highlighting the significance of Laura Young in Tennessee Williams’s creative world, Nancy Tischler writes:

> Laura (whose name was given to the daughter in *The Glass Menagerie*) was the first to associate the qualities of music, glass, orchards, and love in an impressionable young mind that later was to find glass and music further associated with his beautiful sister, whose name became another symbol—Rose.... The shadowed personality of Laura turns into that of the heroine in *Battle of Angels*. Her orchard became a confectionery and a setting for love. (23)

As a delineator of several shadowed characters from real life, Tennessee Williams maintains a sympathetic objectivity rather than the cold finality of a judgment. Perhaps, his sensitive and sympathetic observation of Laura Young had taught him to appreciate the true dimensions of “sorrow and disgrace and to hold out compassion rather than judgment to the sufferer” (Tischler 24).

Two apparently unimportant but vital influences that Tennessee Williams carried right into his creative career as story-teller and dramatist, were Grandfather Walter Dakin and the maid nurse Ozzie. There are many an incident explaining the extent to which Ozzie's stories had stretched the imaginative power of the lisping toddler Tennessee Williams. One, of particular significance, is recalled by Edwina Dakin Williams, the author's mother, in *Remember Me to Tom*. The incident occurred at Nashville. Completely mesmerized by a tale of Ozzie about the Devil and his kingdom, Tom was spotted by his mother feverishly digging a large hole in the backyard. Surprised, she asked him about the purpose, and he replied, "I'm 'diggin' to de debbil" (12). The lisping response, though child-like, almost announced the lifelong obsession of Tennessee Williams. Nearly carving out a philosophy out of the child-like obsession of her son, Edwina says, "you might say Tom went on 'diggin' to de debbil' the rest of his life, trying to discover where the devil lives inside all of us" (12). Ozzie accompanied the family to Clarksdale where Grandfather Walter Dakin had a new parish to serve. Till she quit, her stories continued to be a permanent fixture of Tom's bedtime. She may have quit for any reason, but Tom always held himself guilty for her quitting. Just before she left he had called her a big black nigger; and, though the damage could hardly be undone, the incident kept rankling in the conscience of Tennessee Williams all his life. "This handsome young woman with the bearing of an Indian princess remained fixed in his memory, as did the terrible plight she suffered only for being born black" (Leverich 43-44). With Edwina mentioning and corroborating the theory of Ozzie's significant influence on him in his childhood and formative years, it becomes less of a conjecture and more of a fact that the frequent Gothic in Tennessee Williams's stories has an important source in Ozzie's bedtime stories.

Grandfather Reverend Dakin's influence on Tennessee Williams in his childhood has a definite subtlety about it. Though it can't be raised to the level of a theory, yet this influence cannot be ruled out altogether. The observant and impressionable mind of young Tom did receive vibes from the suave histrionics of Grandfather Dakin as preacher from the pulpit. What he imbibed from his grandfather, he exhibited as speaker from stage later on. Lyle Leverich finds a certain connection between Walter Dakin's histrionics at the pulpit and Tennessee Williams's mannerisms on lecture platform:

> It was generally conceded that the Reverend Dakin was something of a performer himself, much admired not only by his parishioners but also by a grandson who would someday exhibit a distinctly theatrical flair on the lecture platform. (Leverich 18)

His first encounter and introduction to theatricality and drama was in certain ways brought on by his grandfather and the essential dramatics of the Episcopal system of public worship. The substratum and skeleton of Tennessee Williams's drama had begun to take shape; and, as he grew up, circumstances and personae came along to form specific plots and characters.

The second formative phase of Tennessee Williams's childhood began with his unhappy migration to St. Louis in 1918. The migration was occasioned by his father's promotion to a non-travelling managerial position in the International Shoe Company. The promotion was not so much on account of merit as the shortage caused by the conscription of several managers. Cornelius Coffin Williams, his father, must have read a rather painful message in this promotion, which implied that he was not fit for military services. For a man who had always taken immense pride in having cavalier fighters of Tennessee as ancestors, the prohibitive handicap of a damaged eye must have been mortifying. There is every reason to believe that his violence at home was an unconscious manifestation of a frustration born of an insinuation of incapability. The proof of Cornelius's cynical obsession with the military and cavalier past of his ancestors is available in his reaction to his son's performance in a military training program by the name of Reserve Officers Training Corps (ROTC) at the university. The time in context here is 1929-30, when Thomas Lanier Williams was a student at the University of Missouri, Columbia. Dismayed that "his son, the son of a Spanish-American War Veteran, was not on his way to military commission", Cornelius cut off funds to him (Spoto 33). As if prophetic and indicative of the character of the relationship between himself and Cornelius, Tennessee Williams suffered his first experience of violence at the hands of his father on his very arrival at St. Louis. The experience in vividly recounted in *Memoirs*:

> He met us at Union Station. We had scarcely left that curiously designed structure of gray stone, now threatened with demolition, when we happened to pass an outdoor fruit stand. In passing it, I reached out and plucked a grape. Dad delivered a stinging slap to my hand and boomed out, never let me catch you stealing again! (13)

Since Rose, his sister, was still at Clarksdale, Tom became the first witness and victim of domestic violence between the mother and the father. It must have been a traumatic climb down for a child who had just come out of a protected life in spacious rectory residence in the calm and sophisticated supervision of an affectionate grandmother. The incident about the "stinging slap" immediately set off an estrangement between the father and the son. Though not so consciously, Edwina too drove a wedge between the two by incessantly presenting herself as the hapless victim of the brutalities inflicted upon her by CC (Cornelius Coffin, as known in his circle of employees at the International Shoe Company). To a casual observer, Edwina would appear the victim of a manifest domestic violence inflicted on her by her booze addicted husband; but even a slightly serious observation of their relationship would show CC at the receiving end of a subtle psychological violence. Edwina was an "indomitable mate" and "stood up to her husband's bullying tantrums" (Leverich 47). She was an annoyingly incessant talker; and, in her fights with CC, "she used words as her weapon. Always the salesman, though, CC, too, could talk up a storm. The result was her lighting and his thunder, which made Tom's new home, after his serene existence in a rectory, a terrifying place in which to live, and outside he found city life every bit as frightening" (Leverich 48). But for CC, the most shattering thing must have been the mortifying awareness that Edwina never loved him, and that she was still romantically fixated upon John Singleton, the brother of Claire Singleton (Edwina's lifelong friend), who is known to have proposed to her at a very young age. Years later, after CC's death, Edwina made the confession of her unfulfilled desire of marrying the handsome young John Singleton. In spite of this growing discord towards a failure of marriage, Edwina became pregnant a third time and gave birth to Walter Dakin Williams, to whom CC grew much closer in the course of time. However, CC and Tom remained distant and drifted further apart. Some amount of unconscious sibling rivalry did contribute to Tom's psychological problems. But it was the irreconcilable war between the parents that took a heavy toll on his psychological makeup. The horrible trauma of Tom is brought to us by Walter Dakin Williams in his biography of brother Tennessee Williams:

> The effects of this destructive home life on the children must have been traumatic. Tom, already a neurotic and introverted child, was having all kinds of psychological problems. He was even terrified to go to sleep at night, because he thought sleep was similar to death. (24)

The estrangement from his father created a void in Tennessee Williams's life that he could only undo in the imaginative theatrical world of his drama. The affection and the concern of Big Daddy for Brick in *Cat on a Hot Tin Roof* is, by many logical means, a representation of what the author craved and yearned for in real life. The legitimacy of the argument springs from the theory about Brick being a self-portrait of Tennessee Williams:

> Big Daddy: If you ain't careful you're gonna crawl off this plantation and then, by Jesus, you'll have to hustle your drinks along Skid Row!
>
> Brick: That'll come, Big Daddy.
>
> Big Daddy: Naw, it won't. You're my son and I'm going to straighten you out; now that *I'm* straightened out, I'm going to straighten out you. (*Cat* 53)

It is no secret that the author of this poignant conversation suffered a complete psychological disorder that his father could have (but didn't) volunteered to root out. The affectionate concern of a father for his son is an element and experience that Tennessee Williams was destined not to enjoy and live. Barring the early years of his life, he always looked upon his father as a pitiable person deserving sympathy rather than hatred. Being a writer with unmatched sympathy for victims of psychological complexes, he could understand and feel the complex predicament of his father.

The freewheeling and aggressive character of CC (Cornelius Coffin) had suffered equally painfully at the workplace and at home governed by a woman with unrelenting sophistication. In one of his declared autobiographical stories, Tennessee Williams tells us that he had "curiously mixed feelings of disgust and pity" for his father, "Cornelius Coffin Williams, the Mississippi drummer, who was removed from the wild and free road and put behind a desk like a jungle animal put in a cage in a zoo" (*Collected Stories*, Preface, ix-x). The autobiographical account titled "The Man in the Overstuffed Chair", which constitutes the "Preface" of *Collected Stories*, also carries a touching account of Tom's failed attempts to dismantle the barrier of alienation between the son and the father:

> The thing I most want to tell you about is none of this, however; it is something much stranger. It is the ride downtown that my father and I would take every morning in his Studebaker. This was a long ride, it took about half an hour, and seemed much longer for neither my father nor I had anything to say to each other during the ride. I remember that I would compose one sentence to deliver to my father, to break just once the intolerable silence that existed between us, as intolerable to him, I suspect, as it was to me. I would start composing this one sentence during breakfast and I would usually deliver it halfway downtown. It was a shockingly uninteresting remark... And looking back on it, now, I feel that he understood my fear of him and forgave me for it, and wished there was some way to break the wall between us. (*Collected Stories* xiii-xiv)

As the account reveals, the sparks of sympathy did exist between the two; but it did not have the potential to grow powerful enough to "break the wall" that had been steadily constructed by Edwina. Since the "wall" could not go, the author was left with the dream world of his drama, and other varieties of writing, to make up for an absent relationship. For once, in *Cat on a Hot Tin Roof,* he does exploit that world of creative imagination to undo the otherwise insurmountable distance between himself and his father. Walter Dakin Williams approves of Tennessee William's appreciation of his father's predicament, and his consequent sympathy for him:

> Cornelius had had a miserable childhood. His mother, Isabel Coffin Williams, was very beautiful. She died at twenty-eight from tuberculosis. Cornelius's father, Thomas Lanier Williams II, seemed to care mainly for other women and for his relentless and futile pursuit of the governorship of Tennessee.... Later he studied Law at the University of Tennessee. But before he could win a degree he was shipped off to the Spanish-American War, where he caught typhoid and lost all his hair.... (14-15)

Tennessee Williams's relationship with his father (more precisely, the absence of it) had a significant formative influence on him, and became a latent creative material for him later. But the most significant formative relationship with respect to the fiction and drama of the author was the one between him and his sister. More than any other, this relationship made and marred the author's creative psyche. Tom and Rose, his sister, shared a wonderfully comprehensive friendship during their early childhood in the Mississippi Episcopal rectories where they did not have a peer group of children to play with. Their friendship firmed up as they moved to St. Louis to live with their father. At St. Louis, too, they missed a peer group, though for different reasons. In the Mississippi towns, Tom and Rose were kept at a deferential distance by other children; but at St. Louis they were put in an isolation of sorts because of their Southern mannerisms. For the extra-ordinarily sensitive Tom, the fall from respectful recognition to a situation of insignificance was a wrecking experience not very different from the experience of victimization. Warring parents at home and condescending children outside—Tom and Rose had to either negotiate or suffer these two hostile situations. Since the two had only each other to look up to, a friendship was inevitable to develop between the two. By and by, without their knowing, the relationship grew into an urgent need for both. The need and emotional dependence on both sides had grown to inestimable proportions. Since the human world is incapable of holding anything sublime, this near sublime relationship had only one probable culmination to reach—a catastrophe. While combating and repressing her maddening urges, Rose could rely on the sympathetic understanding of Tom. Already a psychic case, allegedly because of repression, the final strand of her precarious mental balance snapped when Tom, in a fit of exasperation, scolded her in more than usual strong words. For Rose, who had played mother to sonny Tom, it was more than intolerable. She was lost forever in the oblivion of lunacy. For Tom it was an irreparable and compounded loss of a friendly and motherly sister. In his own manner, he tried to apotheosize Rose in his creative world. The world of Tennessee Williams, therefore, carries myriad images of Rose and her predicament.

"The Vengeance of Nitocris" is an early short story by Tennessee Williams that graphically portrays his feelings towards his sister on the canvas of a Gothic and violent atmosphere. The story also manifests the overwhelming significance of the author's lost relationship with his sister. The bare minimum of the plot of the story is the narration of the revenge that Nitocris takes upon the noblemen and priests who had decreed the killing of the late Pharaoh, her brother, for his wilful desecration of the holy altar of Osiris. Nitocris in the story is the sister who turns a mother figure with her aggression and violent vengefulness that is characteristic of mother that has lost her child. Her revenge does not come in a fit of passion; it comes in a slow, studied and well-brooded manner:

> When she was borne down the steps of the place in her rich litter after the elaborate ceremony of coronation had been concluded, she responded to the cheers of the multitude with a smile which could not have appeared

> more amicable and gracious. None might know from that smile upon her beautiful carmined lips that within her heart she was thinking, "These are the people who slew my brother. Ah, god Issus grant me power to avenge his death upon them!" (*Collected Stories* 04)

She carries out her dark, gruesome plan with a meticulous zeal. Not for a moment does she deter during the months of preparation for the execution; not for a moment does pity enter her heart as she watches the gathering of her brother's killers to be drowned in the waters of Nile brought through a tunnel into the subterranean banquet hall. Her poise moments ahead of the impending tragedy adds immense horror to the manner and character of revenge:

> The queen alone, seated upon a cushioned dais from which she might overlook the whole room, remained aloof from the general hilarity. Her thick brows twitched; her luminous black eyes shone strangely between their narrow painted lids. (*Collected Stories* 07)

The Queen, now unrelentingly toughened against any soft emotions, is the same woman who had been vulnerable when her brother, the haughty Pharaoh, was alive. She has undergone an unspeakable metamorphosis:

> A woman clung to his stiffened arm. She was tall and as majestically handsome as he. A grab of linen as brilliantly golden as the sum, entwined her body closely. Closely, and bands of jet were around her throat and forehead. She was the fair and well-loved Nitocris; sister of the Pharaoh. (*Collected Stories* 02)

From Nitocris as a woman clinging to the stiffened arm of her brother to Nitocris the queen ruthlessly carrying out a macabre revenge is a metamorphosis that only a woman with an intense degree of motherhood is capable of. The horror of her revenge (and of the story as well) gets increased manifold when the reader comes to know that immediately after the successful execution of her plan, she puts an end to her own life by burning and suffocating herself in her boudoir.

It takes least effort to place the story in perspective with the author's childhood and adolescent years at St. Louis. In the empathetic and friendly private world of Rose and Tom, there was no room for the warring parents. The playmates outside were a bunch of teasing and tormenting victimizers. The same story, "The Vengeance of Nitocris", turns into a remarkable representation of the author's experiences at St. Louis—there are no royal personages except the Pharaoh and his sister; and outside the royal palace there is the ubiquitous presence of the fanatic, blood thirsty mobs of Thebans. The resemblance between the fanatic mobs of Thebans (in the story) and the tormenting children at St. Louis is too obvious to be explained. Likewise, there is a good degree of parallel between the two-member private world of the author (in his early days at St. Louis) and the presence of two royal personages in the story. The Story represents the earliest stage of Tennessee Williams's relationship with his sister. This was the stage when he consciously looked up to her as the ultimate playmate and friend, and unconsciously as a mother figure. As stated earlier, this brother-sister bond with sufficient ingredients of a mother-son relationship was a two-way phenomenon throughout the childhood, even early adolescence, of Tennessee Williams and Rose. The profundity of this relationship got revealed, and felt painfully by the author, when Rose's adolescence created a barrier between the brother and the sister. "Although she loved Tom, there were times when she became distant and aloof towards him, and there would be abrupt changes in her that he could not understand and that hurt him and made him resentful. Rose was suffering late menstrual periods, and at his age Tom was unable to comprehend the stress she was under emotionally" (Leverich 62). Another barrier between the brother and the sister was created by the beginning of a psychological disorder in Rose which, her psychiatrists later explained, was caused by her unconscious repression of physical urges. This tragedy of separation from his sister and the loss of their ebullient, isolated world as children would later be mourned by Tennessee Williams in "The Resemblance between a Violin Case and a Coffin", an autobiographical short story. The story explains that the separation and the dissolution of the childhood relationship were unilateral 'losses' for the author. The opening of the story is a touching account of the loneliness of the author in this tragedy of losses:

> With her advantage of more than two years and the earlier maturity of girls, my sister moved before me into that country of mysterious difference where children grow up. And although we naturally continued to live in the same house, she seemed to have gone on a journey while she remained in sight. The difference came about more abruptly than you would think possible, and it was vast, it was like the two sides of the sunflower river that ran through the town where we lived. (*Collected Stories* 270)

This was the tragic, unimaginable end of a relationship, a virtual world of childhood imagination and games together:

> I saw that it was all over, put away in a box like a doll no longer cared for, the magical intimacy of our childhood together, the soap bubble afternoons and the games with paper dolls cut out of dress catalogues and the breathless races here and there on our wheels. (*Collected Stories* 274)

We can remind ourselves that the one who perished, the one who was lost in "that country of mysterious differences", was the same sister whom the author had looked up to as a mother figure as aggressively and ferociously protective as Nitocris in "The Vengeance of Nitocris". Of course, the author unconsciously looked upon the bands of tormenting children in the various localities of St. Louis as the fanatic and bloodthirsty mobs who tore to pieces the injured Pharaoh. The beginning of Rose's steady and certain drift towards insanity started the process of Tom's metamorphosis into Tennessee Williams. Reminiscing about the opening of the process of the metamorphosis, the author writes in "The Resemblance between a Violin Case and a Coffin": "And it was then, about that time, that I began to find life unsatisfactory as an explanation of itself and was forced to adopt the method of the artist of not explaining but putting the blocks together in some other way that seems more significant to him. Which is rather a fancy way of saying I started writing" (*Collected Stories* 274).

There cannot be a more straightforward statement about the momentous and significantly formative influence upon his creative career of this sudden annihilation of the author's relationship with his sister. Written and published in his mid-teens, "The Vengeance of Nitocris", the story cited a while earlier, marks the first and the primary stage of the relationship, the stage of the isolated private world, of reciprocation and intensity. As the transition from the first to the second stage began, Tom (not yet grown into Tennessee Williams the writer) found himself a befuddled and confused being, unable to reconcile himself to the shift and change in his sister. As she drifted farther and farther towards Richard Miles, her co-practitioner and performer in musical concerts, the author began watching, almost fixatedly, his rival in the private world of Rose. Interestingly, what he watched was Richard Mile's physical attributes of manhood, attributes that made him an admirable male. Tennessee Williams was unconsciously aware that he was not destined to ever possess that admirable male physique. Though not so much related to the context of this study, it must be added here that his constant observation of Richard Miles was the beginning of what has been so much blown out of proportion about the author's homosexuality. Looking back upon the time through the haze of decades, Tennessee Williams wrote:

> When I recall what a little puritan I was in those days, there must have been a shocking ambivalence in my thoughts and sensations as I gazed down upon him through the crack of the door. How on earth did I explain to myself, at that time, the fascination of his physical being without at the same time, confessing to myself that I was a little monster of sensuality? (*Collected Stories* 277)

The confession (in "The Resemblance between a Violin Case and a Coffin") sheds ample light upon a confusion that ultimately resulted in his turning into a "Rebellions Puritan". It may have been a tormenting war between the opposite instincts lodged in the author's personality, but out of this war emerged such an unforgettable character as Brick Pollitt of *Cat on a Hot Tin Roof*. Though not directly so, Richard Miles became an important formative influence or, at least, an important catalyst towards the influence. If we take the liberty, for once, to disregard the view of Rose's psychiatrists, we can almost reach the conclusion that Richard Miles, in his life and premature death, was the undoing of Rose, and, consequently, of Tennessee Williams. Whether or not Richard died of pneumonia, as Williams wrote in his story, he did evidently die while still a teenager. Tom was too young to understand what that meant to Rose; nor could he understand what had come between him and his sister: "Now Tom was on his own. The sister who had so suddenly grown up, the one who was older and wiser, the one whom he could trust and look up to, had become someone else. It represented another loss" (Leverich 63).

The confusing and excruciatingly painful transition over, the author reached the second stage of his association with his sister. This was the stage of a one way association, lacking in reciprocation, in which Tennessee Williams was a hapless observer and sufferer of his sister's malady and tragedy. The stage got poignantly portrayed and explained in his magnum opus on Broadway—*The Glass Menagerie*. Carrying a good deal of autobiographical material, the play shows Tom helplessly watching his sister suffering her physical and psychological handicaps. Laura, the sister in the play, is what Rose had become after her "many disappointments in love" (Leverich 63). "As an actor inside the illusion and the narrator or playwright on the outside", Tom could only watch his sister in her obsession with her collection of glass menagerie (Scheye in Tharpe 208). Her particular obsession for the unicorn among her menagerie quite amply explains the character and the source of her psychological disorder. But the actor-narrator in the play, Tom, is still helpless because of his mother's "confused vitality clinging fanatically to another time and place" (*Menagerie* 228). The best he can do in this state of helplessness is a flight like his father, out and away of responsibilities he is in no position to carry out:

> Tom: I didn't go to the moon, I went much further—for time is the longest distance between two places. Not long after that I was fired for writing a poem on the lid of a shoe box. I left St. Louis. I descended the steps of this fire-escape

> for a last time and followed, from then on, in my father's footsteps, attempting to find in motion what was lost in space. I traveled around a great deal.... (*Menagerie* 313)

This utterance of Tom captures in microcosm the author's drift unto death. The drift in his life began as early as his teens; and the point of start of this drift was the loss of a friendly and motherly sister, not to death but to the living death of insanity. The 'fugitive' and the 'faded belle' hereafter became the permanent fixtures of typical Tennessee Williams writings.

Years later, far from the days of *The Glass Menagerie,* Tennessee Williams's association and relationship with Rose reached the third and the final stage, the stage where he found himself a sufferer alongside Rose in a claustrophobic situation common for both of them. This was the stage when Tennessee Williams had surrendered himself to the struggle among the many complexes and paradoxes in his personality. Fighting with himself, because of the irreconcilables in his personality, he was no less pathetic a case than his sister. This common suffering in the aforesaid claustrophobic situation has been afforded an effective representation in *Out Cry* and its revision as *The Two Character Play*. The play shows a brother and his sister, Felice and Clare, trapped in inescapable physical and psychological circumstances. Physically, they are holed up in the house belonging to their parents; psychologically, they are the victims of some malicious rumor about the death of their mother. Here is an utterance of Clare expressive and representative of their paranoid condition:

> ...My brother Felice and I are surrounded by so much suspicions and malice that we almost never, we hardly ever, dare to go out of the house. (*Out Cry* 35)

The play which the two characters are shown rehearsing never materializes and, as a result, their predicament becomes the play proper. As has been stated earlier, the play, along with its revision, defines and outlines the sensibilities of a writer who has suffered a lifetime of victimization and tragic circumstances.

The final stage of Tennessee Williams's association with, and feelings towards, his sister was an antithesis of the first.

The warm reciprocation, the friendship and the two-member private world ultimately got transformed, in the final stage, into a confinement where friendship was painfully absent and where the 'outcry' of one did not reach the other. For Rose, mentally arrested in her adolescence, the pains and frustrations of her brother had no meaning; and the brother was so much removed from her alien world of quiet insanity that he could never know what went in her mind. It must be mentioned in the context that the author wanted this miserable stage of his relationship with his sister noticed and properly understood. For this reason alone he placed a strong clue in the form of an epigraph, a quotation from *Song of Solomon* 4:12, before *The Two Character Play*—"A garden enclosed is my sister..." (*Two Character Play* 303).

The long discussion and analysis of Tennessee Williams' relationship with his sister is quite in proportion to the significance and vital importance of the relationship from the point of view of the formative influences on the author. The best possible illustration of the immensity of the formative influence of this relationship has been provided by Donald Spoto:

> From then on, the spirit of his sister haunted his life, her personality trapped in a childish permanence like a pinned butterfly. From his earliest one act plays in 1938 to the end of his life, the name and image of Rose and her beloved roses pursued him. (60)

"Then" in the above quote particularly refers to the frontal lobotomy performed upon Rose Williams. The operation was a terrible mistake and disaster. As suggested by Donald Spoto, the rose imagery (symbolizing his sister) can be seen proliferating in a number of Williams's plays. Some specific examples are: *The Rose Tattoo, The Unsatisfactory Supper, The Milk Train doesn't Stop Here Anymore, Camino Real, The Last of My Solid Gold Watches, Small Craft Warnings* and *The Two Character Play.*

A relationship and feeling of affinity that started quite early in Tennessee Williams's childhood and continued well into his youth was the one with Rosina Dakin, his maternal grandmother. Though it is difficult to exactly define the contours of this relationship, it is easy to gauge the direct bearing of the association upon the creative career of the author. With a father looking down upon the "sissy" business of writing, and with a mother trying to cope with an impossible husband and a psychologically derailed daughter, Tennessee Williams drew sufficient support and sustenance from his grandmother, lovingly called Grand by the author and his sister. On more than one occasion, Grand bailed him out of situations of crisis at the University of Missouri. These situations of crisis occurred when his father, dismayed that he had failed ROTC (a military training program), refused to pay the tuition. During this troubled period, Tennessee Williams could follow his inclination to write without much worry because "he knew that he could always depend on the Dakins, and that even with their meagre resources Grand would continue to send Edwina money for the children" (Leverich 125). The financial support from Grand contributed to the author's development as a creative writer in a crucial way. In one of his late stories, autobiographical "Grand" (published 1964), Tennessee Williams pays rich tributes to Grand by portraying her strong character in minuscule. The story is a faithful narration stemming from a sensitive observation remembered over all those years. The last section, in particular, speaks of a warm, tacit reciprocation that the author enjoyed in his relationship with Grand. Of exceptional importance is the event of the author's visit home at St. Louis in 1943 from California where he was doing a stint for a film studio:

> ...'Grand' was waiting up alone to receive me at whatever hour—I had not wired precisely when—I might appear at the family door for this last home coming of mine that she would take part in. As my grandmother drew the door open in response to my knock, I remember how she laughed like a shy girl, a girl caught sentimentalizing over something like a sweetheart's photograph, and cried out, in her young voice, "Oh, Tom, Oh, Tom!" And as I embraced her, I felt with terror almost nothing but the material of her dress and her own arms burring with fever through that cloth. (*Collected Stories* 386)

Emaciated to her bones, Grand had survived on the strength of her powerful will only "to take part" in this homecoming of her beloved Tom. Shortly afterwards she gave up and passed away. Tennessee Williams did not have enough toughness to see the passing away of someone so dearly loved:

> I only dared to look in. My mother was crouched over the figure of my grandmother on the bed, mercifully obscuring her from me. My grandfather was kneeling in prayer beside his armchair.... (*Collected Stories* 387)

Even at the moment of her death Grand has some money to give to Edwina, as she had done in her healthier days in the past. As she was breathing her last, she was desperately trying to tell Edwina about some money she had secretly saved for her. The poignant closure of the story sums up the brief biographical sketch of a woman of immense fortitude, who had almost been a Good Samaritan to Edwina (her daughter) and her children (the author and his sister):

> Then, a year or so ago, my mother happened to tell me that she had finally found out what my grandmother was trying to tell her as she died, but hadn't the strength to. "Your grandmother kept pointing at the bureau, and later I found out that she had her corset in there with several hundred dollars sewed up in it!" (*Collected Stories* 387)

The vital magnitude of Grand's influence on Tennessee Williams' life and creative career can be measured through a couple of touching entries in *Memoirs*:

> ...and I can recall no roses in all the years that I spent in St. Louis and its environs except the two living Roses in my life, my grandmother, Rose O. Dakin, and, of course, my sister, Rose Isabel. (17)

and

> ...whatever I have of gentleness in my nature, and I do have much in response to gentle treatment, comes from the heart of 'Grand', as does the ineluctable grace and purity of heart that belong to the other Rose in my life, my sister. (111)

Any attempt to explicate the entries, and the sincere sentiments therein, would mean a dishonor to the rich tribute that they carry. However, it would not be inconsistent with our purpose to state that the two statements cited above reveal the depth of the formative influence that the two living Roses—his sister and Grand—exerted upon Tennessee Williams the creative writer and Tennessee Williams the man.

Outside the family circle, Tennessee Williams's meeting and association with Hazel Kramer came at a time when he was failingly struggling to come to terms with a frustrating loneliness because of the hostility of the children outside home and a motherly-friendly sister receding into her incurable dementia inside. Of his own admission, Hazel "was the great extra-familial love of my life" (*Memoirs* 15). When the two met, and started going steady, the author was aged fourteen and Hazel twelve. It was natural in view of their adolescence that "they would put aside their playthings and become involved in such grown-up pursuits as dating and dancing and going to the movies together" (Leverich 72). What drew the author towards Hazel was her female physical attributes. Going by the account of it in *Memoirs,* his first encounter with her had been of the fictional and celluloid nature. As the two came closer and made friends with each other, Tennessee Williams began drawing a lot from her imaginativeness to temper and enrich his own creative imagination:

> Being imaginative children, we invented many games, but the chief diversion that I recall was illustrating stories that we made up. Hazel drew better than I and made up better stories. (*Memoirs* 15)

This association, though it could not prove a complete substitute, somewhat alleviated the loneliness that Tennessee Williams was made to suffer since his sister's distancing. Through the 'confessions', though slightly fictionalized, it is made possible to determine the exact dimensions of the relationship. However, the relationship couldn't last. The author's parents joined, for their different reasons, to abort his relationship with Hazel. While the prudish Edwina felt that Hazel was too 'common' for her son, Cornelius Williams prevailed upon Hazel's father (his junior at the workplace) to send her off to the University of Wisconsin in order to interrupt and finally end the association. Their association practically ended when the two went their separate ways to Wisconsin and Missouri. Tennessee Williams was still hopeful about a restoration of their relationship. But that was not fated to happen. The news of Hazel's marriage was quite a shock to him. His reaction to the news was an intensified activity of writing, alongside some cardiac problem:

> The onset of my cardiovascular condition..., in the spring of 1934, was triggered by two things. First, the quite unexpected marriage of Hazel to a young man named Terrence McCabe, whom she had been dating at the University of Wisconsin. I felt as though the sky had fallen on me, and my reaction was to start working every evening on short stories, overcoming fatigue with black coffee. (*Memoirs* 38)

At least three of Tennessee Williams's short stories can be linked to this shattering experience, as though verifying the truth of the above statement in *Memoirs*. All of the three—"The Important Thing", "The Field of Blue Children" and "The Accent of a Coming Foot"—"reflect something of this frustrated young love" and "have a youthful innocence" setting them apart from the other short stories of the author (Tischler 36).

Though the individual relationships studied above have played a remarkable role in the formation of his artistic psyche, Tennessee Williams the artist has been a composite of influences and impressions imbibed during his entire childhood, adolescence and early youth. This covers his Mississippi, St. Louis and Missouri years. A childhood in multiple Mississippi rectories, the harshness and snobbery of St. Louis along with its inhospitable tenements, and an experience of liberty converting into a frenetic creativity at Missouri—all of these have found their ways into his work in a fairly recognizable form.

One can note in the above discussion that Tennessee Williams, especially in his formative years, had a particular response system to counter disappointments, frustrations and experiences of hostility. Every time he confronted a disappointment or a hostile experience, he took recourse to his world of imagination and literary creativity. Patently escapist though it may seem, it was the particular response mechanism that saved the author from going his sister's way to an unmanageable, uncontrollable and incurable dementia. A scholar in Tennessee Williams studies, however, would always look upon those disappointments, frustrations and experiences of the author from a different point of view. The scholar would eventually find out that Tennessee Williams the artist emerges out of a series of disappointments working upon his hyper sensitive response system. In a conversation with Joanne Stang, Tennessee Williams said:

> I have always been more interested in creating a character that contains something crippled. I think nearly all of us have some kind of defect, anyway, and I suppose I have found it easier to identify with the character who verge upon hysteria, who were frightened of life, who were desperate to reach out to another person. (in Devlin 110)

The identification with crippled and hysterical characters, which he speaks of in the conversation, would not have been there if his sensibilities had not been specifically tuned by the harsh and discordant atmosphere he grew in. He never ever tried to adjust himself to the harshness and discordance of his circumstances. His refusal to, and failure of, adjustment has produced a series of neurotic artist characters in his writings. Bigsby observes:

> In one direction such a failure of adjustment may generate neurosis and psychosis; in another, art. And if his character are indeed pulled towards mental instability they also tend to be artists, literal and symbolic.... Blanche turns her life into an art work...Laura arranges her menagerie with an artist's touch. Val Xavier is a musician, Chance Wayne an actor. Sebastian, in *Suddenly Last Summer,* and Nonno, in *The Night of the Iguana*, are both poets. (Bigsby, *Modern American Drama* 33)

Quite obviously, the family relationships and the general ambience have been of immense significance in shaping the creative psyche of the budding author. However, the particular character of the author's writings has certainly been determined by various literary influences. The prominent among these have been Henerik Ibsen, Anton Chekhov, D.H. Lawrence and Hart Crane. Williams' introduction to the art of Ibsen happened at the University of Missouri at Columbia, where he came across a touring production of Ibsen's *Ghosts*. Tennessee Williams's response to the experience was almost prophetic: "It was so moving that I had to go and walk in the lobby during the last act. I'd stand in the (doorway) and look in, then I'd rush back to the lobby again. I suppose the play was one of the things that made me want to write for the theatre" (qtd. in Spoto 37-38). Taking the statement on it's merit, one can easily infer the extent of impression and influence the drama of Ibsen, and, by implication, other dramatists of his ilk, had on Tennessee Williams. From Ibsen, he learnt the fact that art could be used as a tool to "bridge the gap between flesh and spirit," and from Strindberg "the dramatic potential of a harsh family background" (Spoto 38-39). Around May 1935, Tennessee Williams got to familiarize himself with Anton Chekhov's writings at the libraries of Memphis. "From then on, Chekhov, like Ibsen and Strindberg", became his "spiritual mentor" (Spoto 45).

The most enduring influences upon the author have been those of D.H. Lawrence and Hart Crane. The amazingly wide range and pervasiveness of Lawrence's influence upon Williams have been exclusively explored by Norman J. Fedder in his book entitled *The Influence of D.H. Lawrence on Tennessee Williams*. Fedder analyses the resonance between the two writers in the spheres of poetry, fiction, One-Act and Full-length drama. Before it begins to evince itself in his drama, Lawrencean strain can be seen emerging in the pre-drama stories of Tennessee Williams. Fedder explains: "The grotesque and pathetic life depicted in these stories result from Lawrence's and Williams's common purpose: to demonstrate the negative consequences of sensual or spiritual fragmentation" (27). The major plays of Tennessee Williams, too, have obviously visible influence of D.H. Lawrence. The plays include *The Battle of Angels* (revised as *Orpheus Descending*), *The Glass Menagerie, Summer and Smoke, Camino Real* and *The Night of the Iguana. The Battle* finds corresponding notes from *Lady Chatterley's Lover*; *The Glass Menagerie* from *Sons and Lovers*; *Summer and Smoke* from *The Virgin and the Gypsy*; *Camino Real* from 'St. Mawr'; and *The Night of the Iguana* from *The Rainbow* and *Women in Love*. The Lawrencean influence on Williams is best represented in *I Rise in Flame, Cried the Phoenix,* a one-act play exclusively dedicated to Lawrence and his wife Frieda. The play carries the extent and depth of Williams's regard for and subscription to Lawrence's beliefs. In the Author's note, Williams writes:

> Lawrence felt the mystery and power of sex, as the primal life urge, and was the life-long adversary of those who wanted to keep the subject locked away in the cellars of prudery. Much of his work is chaotic and distorted by tangent obsessions, such as his insistence upon the woman's subservience to the male, but all in all his work is probably the greatest modern monument to the dark roots of creation. (*I Rise in Flame*, Author's Note 56)

The play is a compassionate presentation of Lawrence's last hours and a dramatization of the "tangent obsessions". The "tangent obsessions" are somewhat permanent fixtures in Williams's writings. To borrow Norman Fedder's observation, *I Rise in Flame, Cried the Phoenix* incorporates three main Lawrencean elements which recur throughout Williams's poetry and fiction—the flesh and spirit conflict, as we have indicated above, the antagonism towards bourgeois civilization, and the animal symbolism—and thus presents us with an early version of Williams's characteristic use of Lawrencean themes and symbols (54).

Like that of Lawrence, Hart Crane's influence, too, is prominently present in Tennessee Williams' writings. He acknowledges his indebtedness to Hart Crane in "Preface to My Poems":

> About this time (1935-36) I acquired my first copy of Hart Crane's collected poems and began to read with gradual comprehension. The poems included in this volume are a sort of spiritual witness of these years: at least they are the

> product of an unattached and nomadic existence of six or eight years' duration...I am inclined to value Crane a little above Eliot or anyone else because of his organic purity and sheer breath-taking power. (*Where I Live* 3 and 6)

An interesting aspect of Tennessee Williams's strong fascination for Hart Crane has been revealed by Paul Bigelow, who had had the opportunity to observe the author from close quarters. Williams developed so much of affinity towards Crane that he began to feel that his own life was a replication and re-enactment of Crane's. Bigelow confides that the frenetic and the relentless in Williams's writings was prompted by the growing feeling that "he must write more than Crane did" to save himself from growing "gradually demented" like Crane (qtd. in Leverich 461). There had been an intensity and an unfading conviction with which Tennessee Williams identified himself with Hart Crane. It was precisely this factor that prompted him to publish the one-act entitled *Steps must be Gentle* around 1980, barely three years before his death. The one-act is almost a 'ghost' play in the sense that it shows Hart Crane and his mother having a conversation after their death. Throughout this conversation Hart Crane (or his 'ghost') justifies his life with the strength of conviction:

> A number of us who rest here on the great bed of the sea, those of us who chose to rest here, paid dearly for their rest and deserve not to have it broken.... A dead man speaks this way.... *Recognition of a way of life imposed on me like a prison sentence. I had to give to the truth and you abhorred it, loathed it, that confession... I had to somehow subsist. In order to continue my work which I had to continue....* (*Steps must be Gentle* 318 and 322)

The communication that seems to be taking place (and does take place) between Crane and his mother is due to this situation only—throughout his life the unfortunate poet tried to justify himself to his mother but she only "abhorred it, loathed it". The close of the play shows Grace, Crane's mother, finally coming to know the mystery of her dead son: "Traveler, stranger, son—my friend" (327). Gilbert Debusscher finds the play important for two reasons. First, it sheds "new light not only on Williams's familiarity with the facts of Crane's biography, but also on the pervasive influence of Crane, both as man and poet, on Williams's writing" and, second, it contains "the seeds of what was to develop into *Suddenly Last Summer* (1958)" (466 and 468). Whether or not Debusscher suggests it, if Crane in *Steps must be Gentle* were to be resurrected, he would make an apt model for Sebastian Venable in *Suddenly Last Summer.* The depth and range of the literary influences upon Tennessee Williams are deep and wide. Lyle Leverich, his painstaking biographer, has this to say about those influences:

> As for literary progenitors, D.H. Lawrence professed one of Williams's basic tenets.... Chekhov's writing was a beau ideal.... One can find the trace elements of a number of writers, including Strindberg, Lorca, O'Neill, Ibsen, Melville, Pirandello, and even the more modern Harold Pinter, whom Williams both admired and envied. But in the end, however, the most pervasive influence in his life and career was that of the poet Hart Crane, to the same degree that Shelley influenced Crane.... (591-92)

It can convincingly be said on the basis of the evidence shored up in the preceding paragraphs that Tennessee Williams learnt very early in his life the art of transcribing the cruel humiliation, the bitterness and the confusion he suffered all along. Apart from his early childhood at Clarksdale, which forms a kind of background in contrast, all that gets transcribed in his writings is a litany of bleak and shattering experiences suffered by a person sensitive almost to the extent of neurosis. At the productive point of this transcription we have a long series of writings starting with the narrative of a psychopathically vengeful sister in "The Vengeance of Nitocris" and coming to an end with the claustrophobic cries of a brother and his sister in *Out Cry* (a late play).

2

The "World of Light and Shadow": An Art Steeped in Paradoxes

> A World of light and shadow is what we live in, and—it's confusing.
>
> (*Orpheus Descending*)

In the Introduction of her immensely informative book on Tennessee Williams, Felicia Hardison Londre writes:

> "I am Blanche DuBois," Tennessee Williams has said on more than one occasion. He refers, of course, to the sensitive and neurotic, yet iron-willed heroine of *A Streetcar Named Desire,* a character who has clearly entered the realm of American mythology. (21)

The statement points to the crucial factor of insurmountable gloom and confusion surrounding William's characters, in fiction as well as in drama. The source of the intensity and complexity of this gloom and confusion can be gathered from the author's own statement in the course of an interview with C. Robert Jennings:

> I can identify completely with Blanche—we are both hysterics—Alma and even with Stanley, though I did have trouble with some of the butch characters. If you understand schizophrenics, I am not really a dual creature. (in Devlin 226-27)

From Tom Wingfield to Blanche DuBois, to Brick Pollitt, to Orpheus, to Val, to Sebastian, to Chance Wayne, to Felice and so on—throughout the creative world to Tennessee Williams there are these major or minor portraitures of the author's self.

Along with the self-portraiture come the gloom, the hysteria, the schizophrenia, and the complexities of the personal, religious and sensual experiences suffered by the author. The cases of self-portraiture mentioned above are from the author's world of drama. But a look at his (short) fiction characters reveals a much greater faithfulness and a strikingly low degree of transformation from the self to the portraitures. It is an easy inference, therefore, that a truer picture of the nature and magnitude of Tennessee Williams's experiences, sufferings, surroundings, fantasies and visions can only emerge when his drama and fiction are treated as resources of relative and complementary importance. In his Introduction to *Collected Stories*, Gore Vidal makes it all very compact—the author's self, his being, going into the making of many of the classic 'fugitives' in his writings:

> He puts himself, sick and vicious as he is, on the stage in the drag; and then he travesties all good, normal, family-worshipping women and their supportive mature men.... He could inhabit any gender; his sympathies, however, were almost always with those defeated by the squares or by time, once the sweet bird of youth is flown—or by death, which has never been much in the way of completion. (xxiv)

By way of atmosphere, a vitally important element in Tennessee Williams's writings is a religiosity which takes on highly personalized and fantastical forms. As is the case with most of the elements, this, too, has a point of beginning in an intense personal experience of the author during his visit to Europe with a small Episcopal congregation in the leadership of his grandfather. The particular experience came to him, almost in the manner of a divine visitation, in a cathedral in Cologne. Reminiscing the experience, Tennessee Williams writes in his *Memoirs*:

> Let me say that I am not predisposed to believe in miracles or in superstition. But what happened was a miracle and one of a religious nature and I assure you that I am not bucking for sainthood when I tell you about it. It was as if an impalpable hand were placed upon my head, and at the instant of that touch, the phobia was lifted away as

> lightly as a snowflake though it had weighed on my head like a skull-breaking block of iron. At seventeen, I had no doubt at all that the hand of our Lord Jesus had touched my head with mercy and had exorcised from it the phobia that was driving me mad. (21)

The phobia which "the hand of our Lord Jesus" exorcised had tormented the author for quite some time. It had been the phobia about "the process of thought" being "a terrifyingly complex mystery of human life". It had begun as a dreadful idea and had grown to the proportions and magnitude of a shattering phobic experience. To believe the author's experience recorded in *Memoirs,* he would have gone "quite mad from it", if he had not been saved by the Savior at the moment of the climax of the experience (20). Having been familiar with the nature of Tennessee Williams's creative imagination and his intensely personalized abnormal experiences, there is no reason to disbelieve the account of the phobia and the redemption from it. Populating the expanse of Tennessee Williams' creative world, there are many characters suffering psychological conditions not dissimilar to the "phobia" suffered by their author. Quite frequent are the characters high-strung on their passionate religious visions and visitations, often of an indigenous nature. Two streaks of abnormality enter into a combination in most of these characters. Those suffering from phobic or crazed psychological state have a strange religiosity; and the ones with passionate and personal religiosity have an inevitable streak of abnormality. The combination, almost assuming the status of a frenzied fanaticism, produces a substantial number of characters in the fiction and drama of Tennessee Williams. This incorporative and broad class of characters includes the complete range of Signi Falk's categorization of Williams's personae (dramatic or fictional) into 'Southern Gentlewoman,' 'Southern Wenches', 'Desperate Heroes', 'Deteriorating Artists', and the ones making 'unabashed confessions' (07).

An interestingly representative example of obsessive passion in the fiction of Tennessee Williams is the case of Jacob Brodzky in "Something by Tolstoi". His passion is his love for Lila; and it has a psychic touch about it. The intensity of it carries him through two obstacles to marriage—the usually unbridgeable chasm between a Jew and a Gentile, and his own mortifying shyness. These obstacles apart, Jacob Brodzky even takes in his stride "a complete antithesis of temperaments": he, "timid and spiritual and contemplative"; and she, "something of a hoyden—full of animal spirits, life and enthusiasm" (*Collected Stories* 18). Quite understandably, a passion so intense and a love so overwhelming are not only fraught with the danger of tragedy but also fated to end in a devastating catastrophe. There are enough forebodings about an impending disaster in the description of Jacob Brodzky's love for Lila: "His love for her was the core of his life. There is a great danger to such a love. When the love is lost, the life is lost. It crumbles to pieces" (19). His life does crumble to pieces when his wife, "full of animal spirits", leaves him to join the life of boisterous glamour with a touring vaudeville company. As has been said, passionate souls have strange powers of clairvoyance; and Jacob Brodzky can foresee her return even before her departure. But separating the departure and return is a long stretch of fifteen years. During this period of one and a half decade, Jacob takes to reading "as another man might have taken to drink or to drugs". His effort to escape from reality in this manner succeeds "with a dreadful effectiveness" (*Collected Stories* 21). When Lila returns after all those years, she finds him irretrievably lost in the imaginary and unreal world of his readings. Befuddled by an indefinite amount of indiscriminate reading for fifteen years, he has lost almost every touch with reality, with his own past and present, and even with the nature of his existence. He does not recognize Lila; nor when she narrates their own story of youthful love, their marriage and their separation all those years ago. The excruciatingly poignant and tragic moment in the story occurs at the point of the climactic culmination, when Lila waits for Jacob's reaction to her narration of their past in a story form:

> She was searching his face desperately, but there was nothing in it but bewilderment. He said at last: "There is something familiar about the story. I think I have read it somewhere. It seems to me that it is something by Tolstoi." (*Collected Stories* 25)

What Tennessee Williams would intend through the story is not just the evocation of the tragic. He quite succeeds in evoking a horrible, hair-raising sense of loss and terror. The terror brews, works up and grips the reader, who would almost find himself a first-hand witness to the tragic climax.

Published in 1930-31, the story discussed above, "Something by Tolstoi", belongs to an early period in Tennessee Williams's creative career. But the kind of horror it evokes is not an isolated example; the horror proliferates and assumes multiple shapes and shades as the author progresses further into his creative world. A story entitled "Sand" published some five years later in 1936, sufficiently represents the proliferation. The story shows two elderly characters, husband and wife, separately suffering their correlated predicaments. The husband has lost a good part of his body to a paralytic stroke and the wife is constantly worried about his life. The opening of the story builds up an apprehension that grows uncontrollably with the progress of the story:

> The old woman is awake listening to the sound of his breathing. Night after night it is the same. She cannot sleep for listening to that hoarse, painful rasp. Whenever the sound is interrupted she lies tense, waiting, while the excruciating moments gather upon her own nearly motionless chest like weights of iron. Then slowly or quite suddenly the sound of it recommences. He has not stopped breathing. He has awakened for a few minutes only and then gone back to sleep. "Thank God!" she breathes "Thank God!" (*Collected Stories* 49)

Her non-stop apprehension, a constant and alert vigilance, gets much more painful and poignant for her as she reminisces about her youthful days with him. It is a horrible and painful movement back and forth for her, between the past and the present. She always finds an immeasurable and inexpressible apprehension hoisted against the memory:

> The glittering sun is lost. It is dark.... She can hear him breathing. Still breathing. The hoarse dragging sound goes wearily on. A tired, heavy thing crawling painfully

> forward...when will it stop? She shudders. No, it must not. Never. (*Collected Stories* 52)

Though the story focuses on the fear and apprehension of the wife, Rose, the husband Emiel is the greater sufferer of the two. He suffers his physical incapability, his dependence on Rose, the memory of the past and the consciousness of the fact that he is the cause of his wife's painfully constant apprehension. His thinking is eating into him as fiercely as his wife's fear about his life.

It is worth noting here that Tennessee Williams makes *sand* a paradoxically dual symbol in the story. Inside the past of the time frame of the story, sand has the sense of youthful sensuality attached to it. Usually, beach sand would have everything lively to suggest, as it briefly has and does in the story too. In the memory of Rose, the seashore sand is laden with a youthful sensuality—she remembers the bright grains of the sand trickling over her bare legs and arms. But in hers and her husband's present state, sand would effectively symbolize life (or something as precious) unstoppably sliding and slipping through fingers. From the quintessentially romantic to the dreadfully inescapable—the qualitative symbolic value of sand undergoes this stunning and chilling and yet acceptable transformation. The tragic predicament of the two sufferers and the atmosphere in the story earn an otherwise impossible starkness out of this dual symbolism of sand.

As noted earlier, the story comes from the early, the pre-*Menagerie* period in the author's career. In many ways, the story represents the case of a combination of deep-rooted phobias and quietly intense passions, including fervent religiosity, in Tennessee Williams's writings. This theory of the combination of phobias and religiosity in the characters in his writings applies with equal validity to his early, middle and late writings. For illustration we take up the outstanding example of *Vieux Carré*, a play produced in late 1970s. The play comes from the time in the author's life when he had made a "vertiginous plunge into the drink and drugs which came close to annihilating his personality" (Bigsby, *Modern American Drama* 67). It comes from the time in the history of American theatre when, to quote

Bigsby again, the "dramatic attention, meanwhile, had switched elsewhere—to the hyper realism, the demotic prose, the forceful metaphors of David Mamet and the lyrical, oblique myths of Sam Shepard" (67). *Vieux Carré* is a play with an assemblage of persons tragically imprisoned in their respective circumstances. Each one of them tries to reach out to someone else and fails. The failure is not because of any unwillingness to respond; it is there because the individual circumstances and cynicisms create a situation of cell-like enclosures that forbid interaction. The characters thus trapped irredeemably are Mrs. Wire (the rooming house owner), Jane, Nightingale (a consumptive painter), Tye, Sky and the writer as the narrator as well as a participant in the action. Of their separate tragedies, the one that acquires center stage is Nightingale's. He is under the double blight of two incurable diseases—one physical and the other psychological. His alternatively directed physical passion has spiraled out of control, and his tuberculosis has reached the final stage. Either as an inveterate lover of life or as a person mortally afraid of death, Nightingale relentlessly refuses acknowledging the two ailments. It is a pitched battle inside his psyche, between his unconscious awareness of the ailments and a conscious refusal of their presence. He regularly coughs up blood, but vehemently clings to the illusion that his pillow is being spoilt by bedbugs. As he shares his troubled thoughts with the Writer, he exposes his scarred psyche:

> Nightingale: ...(He coughs) Oh Christ. You know my mattress is full of bedbugs. Last night I smashed one at least the size of my thumbnail, it left a big blood spot on the pillow. (He coughs and gasps for breath).... (A note of uncertainty and fear enters his voice) (48)

His psychological bent of an alternative desire is equally tormenting to him; and he relentlessly tries to camouflage it behind the excuse of a desire for companionship, which he finds as "necessary as bread, as blood in the body". When he finds a responsive note in the writer—"Yes, loneliness is an affliction" —he readily offers himself, only to be rejected when the true intent of his offer is revealed (20). The following excerpt from their conversation in Scene Five shows that a growing bitterness, born of rejection, has become a torment for him:

> Writer: I'm afraid I'm tried, I need to sleep and.... I don't want to catch your cold.
>
> Nightingale: And I don't want to catch yours, which is a cold in the heart, that's a hell of a lot more fatal to a boy with literary pretensions.... You've gone mad, you've gone out of your mind here, you little one-eyed bitch! (He coughs again and staggers out of the light) (50-51)

Nightingale, suffering from the banality of consumption and alternative desire, has a passionate religiosity that is stronger than that of an average priest. A series of utterances by him in Scene Ten of Part two express a religiosity that is uncorrupted by any human intervention or mediation. This extreme religiosity is not ill at ease with his sensual preferences. Under threat of eviction from his tenement cubicle because of his contagious consumption, he is offered medical help by the writer. But the manner of his refusal is more than disarming: "My faith is in Christ—not doctors" (90). In the character of Nightingale, there is this weird combination of passionate carnality and absolute faith in the basics of Christianity. From a skeptical point of view, Nightingale would still appear a case of transformation from carnality to spirituality, from the faith in his body to the faith in God. Either a case of combination or of transformation, Nightingale presents a strange proximity between two blatantly discordant streaks. This combination of the two discordant elements accentuates the sense of fear that keeps skulking under the surface of his seeming poise. When his fear of death joins the general fear of eviction suffered by the other boarders, the result is an ominous concoction and an inescapable atmosphere of fear.

Nightingale is a character that falls in the class of what Jaqueline O'Connor calls "boarders on borders" in the world of Tennessee Williams ("Boarders on Borders" 101). Moreover, he is one of the characters who bring to us certain well defined aspects of their author's being and experiences. Characters like him are the permanent fixtures in the author's works along with "the lower class boarding or rooming houses that serve as the apt encapsulation of his characters' vagabond lives" (O'Connor 101). Quite interestingly, the tragedies of his transient characters are played out in high relief against the atmosphere of a rooming or boarding house. Alternatively, we can have a hotel room or a dark, stuffy apartment instead of a boarding house. The consonance between the transient lives of the transient characters and the transience suggested by boarding house or hotel room is far too obvious to be explained. A good number of Tennessee Williams' plays exhaustively exploit this consonance. Four of the one-acts in *The Theatre of Tennessee Williams,* Vol. VI use a transient space as the arena for the enactment of action. In *The Lady of Larkspur Lotion,* Mrs. Moore's fear of eviction is played out through her false complaint about cockroaches in her chamber in the rooming house. The "hotel room in a Mississippi Delta Town" in *The Last of My Solid Gold Watches* has been the witness to Mr. Charlie Colton's steady physical deterioration over the past forty years—once he moved "with a tidal ease and power" but now he "puffs and rumbles" (93). The tragic companionship between the Little Man and a cat, Nitchevo, begins and grows in a small rooming house room in *The Strangest Kind of Romance*. For the Man and the Woman in *Talk to Me Like the Rain,* "the furnished room west of Eighth Avenue in midtown Manhattan" is no more and no less than the trap called life (265). The Woman's fantasy of escape, of an interminable freedom is poignantly projected against this closeted situation:

> Woman: ...then I will know—looking in the mirror—the first time has come for me to walk out once more on the esplanade with the strong wind beating on me, the white clean wind that blows from the edge of the world, from even further than that, from the cool outer edges of space...(she sits down again unsteadily by the window)— Then I'll go out and walk on the esplanade. I'll walk alone and be blown thinner and thinner. (272)

Another collection of one-acts by Tennessee Williams, *Dragon country,* has eight plays—all grounded in situations of transience. Though each of the eight has its own particular significance, at least four stand out because of their atmospheric specifications and related characteristics. As if representing all in the collection, the first, *In the Bar of Tokyo Hotel,* presents the entire action in a hotel bar. Each of the five characters appears in the bar for short or long durations. The first part of the play is constituted out of two confrontations of the female protagonist in the play, Miriam, with the Barman and her husband, Mark, who is failingly struggling to keep his mental faculties together. The first confrontation, to be precise, is between Miriam's vitality and the Barman's impassivity. As suggested, it becomes, ultimately, a confrontation between the un-channelized and disorientated 'vitality' of Miriam and the inner serenity of the Barman:

> Miriam: "Inner resources of serenity". Some professor mentioned them to me once. Hog wash, wash a hog in it, don't turn it on me. "Inner resources of serenity" is a polite way of describing a lack of vital energy. There may be exceptions. (05)

Miriam, a tourist from America, is spiritually untrained, and, therefore, is restive and uncontrollable with her unused energy to an extent that she would "absorb a pagoda in a minute" (08). The Barman on the other hand is quite a representation of the oriental principles of Buddhism. His place and nature of work cannot distract him from his duty or spiritual religiosity. In spite of the nature of his work, he is prompt in pointing out to Miriam that her absorption of a pagoda in a minute would not be a reverent absorption. Of course, the very powerfully potential symbol of Buddhism in 'pagoda' is up against the crazed and uncontrollable vitality of Miriam. It is an interesting situation because of the irony involved here: Miriam doesn't know that pagoda is a symbol of the same faith (Buddhism) that trains a person to deal imperturbably with the world and his own vital energy. Throughout the confrontation between the Barman and Miriam, an atmosphere of Oriental spirituality is available as a solution to the passion of Miriam.

The second confrontation in the play involves Miriam and her husband, Mark. The confrontation between the two emerges from their diverse attitudes. While Miriam is crazily in pursuit of physical gratification, Mark, a painter, is still struggling to produce a masterpiece. He has been a successful artist with a somewhat successful career behind him; but his insatiable hunger to create a masterpiece of his own design has driven him out of a normal frame of mind. The extent of his maddening search for that design for an elusive masterpiece takes him "crawling naked over a huge nailed down canvas", because he thinks that an "intimacy" and "one-ness" has to exist between the painter and his art (17). Mark's manner of attaining "one-ness" with his art is shocking, but not seriously surprising in view of similar portraits of crazy artists in several other works by Tennessee Williams. He is the farthest extension of the demented psyche of the Writer in *The Lady of Larkspur Lotion* or Nightingale in *Vieux Carré*. What really surprises one about Mark is the manner of his eviction from the play. While Nightingale, like many other insane characters in Tennessee Williams, is sent off to an asylum, Mark dies on stage putting an end to the efforts of Miriam to send him back to America in the care of his agent, Leonard.

The Buddhist reading in the play is not just incidental or a case of extended interpretation. In fact, Buddhist insight is throughout presented as a solution to the emotional and psychological sufferings of Mark and Miriam. If the play "expresses Williams's own artistic turmoil" through Mark, it also shows him "searching for absolutes in Buddha or Tao" (Londre 160). Allean Hale observes a definite Oriental religious principle in the mismatched pair of Miriam and Mark: "I believe that Miriam, far from being a life force as has been suggested, is the oriental death principle, the Yin: the earthly, negative, female, cold and dark element. Mark is the Yang: Heavenly, positive, active, male, light" (210). Though unconsciously, Miriam suggests the Yin-Yang principle twice, during her flirtation with Barman and during her conversation with Mark. In the first instance she just drops a mild hint—"convex demanding concave" (*In the Bar* 13). But in the second she heavily underlines the principle:

> Miriam: Are we two people, Mark, as are we—
>
> Mark: (With the force of dread): Stop there! (she lifts her hands to her face, but the words continue through it)

> Miriam: Two sides of!
>
> Mark: Stop!
>
> Miriam: One! An artist inhabiting the body of a compulsive....
>
> Mark: Bitch!
>
> Miriam: Call me that, but remember that you're denouncing a side of yourself, denied by you! (30)

Apart from the particular Oriental principle illustrated above, the play also expresses a general, unrestricted religious principle. Interestingly, the pronouncement of this general religious principle comes from Miriam, who indulges in flirtation with Barman and shows a shocking degree of apathy towards Mark. However, the sincerity of her final enlightenment cannot be doubted as it comes after the death of Mark right in front of her in the bar. She defines her religiosity and enlightenment in terms of "the circle of light" that is "productive" and "the protection of our existence" (51). She aims at an explanation of her spirituality a little later:

> Miriam: If I should say that the circle of light is the approving look of God it would be romantic which I refuse to be...of the man who has made a crossing that neither of us but each of us (53).

To allay any skepticism about the heavy co-presence of spirituality and carnality in the play, it would be opportune to add that Tennessee Williams was suffering an inner turmoil at the time of the writing of the play. The turmoil ultimately led him to convert from his inherited Episcopalian faith to Roman Catholicism in 1969.

A vital aspect of the religiosity and faith in Tennessee Williams is the shift from skepticism to a forceful acknowledgement and declaration of a broad, all-encompassing faith in religion and God. The skepticism, though, should be looked upon as a stage somewhere in the transition between a youthful assertion of individual capability to a submission of sorts later that is characteristic of old age. At the one end of this transition is the short fiction of the author and, at the other, his late plays. This theory of transition from skepticism to all-encompassing faith can be illustrated by an elaboration upon "One Arm", an early short story, and *Small Craft Warnings*, a late play. Though not strictly so, "One Arm" would still be called an early story because it almost belongs to the pre-*Menagerie* period. Moreover, the story belongs to that period in the author's career when he was using fiction as some kind of preparation for drama. The protagonist in the story is Oliver Winemiller who gets lodged in a death cell in prison on charges of murder. It has been a steep descent for him. There had been a time in his life when he was a boxer in the navy and had become an outstanding contender for the navy championship. The life, then, had been good fun and no thinking. Having lost one arm, "he was abruptly cut off from his development as an athlete and a young man wholly adequate to the physical world he grew into" (*Collected Stories* 176). Before getting into the death cell, he had lived a life of vagrancy and had fallen into the trap of a racket of obscene filmmakers. Disgusted, he unknowingly killed the broker in the racket, got nabbed, tried, and condemned to death. The latter half of the story shows the interaction of the condemned youth with young Lutheran minister trying to bring the "consolation of faith" to him (183). If we blink at the heavy suggestiveness behind the young minister's conflicting eagerness for this mission, the interaction would begin to appear a long series of monologues heading in two different directions:

> "Are you prepared," he whispered.
>
> "I'm not prepared for the hot seat, if that's what you mean. But the seat is prepared for me, so what's the difference?"
>
> "I'm talking about Eternity," said the minister. "This world of ours, this transitory existence, is just a threshold of something immense beyond".
>
> "Bull", said Oliver.
>
> "You don't believe me?"
>
> "Why should I?"
>
> "Because you are face to face with the last adventure!"
>
> (*Collected Stories* 185-86)

The conversation, better described as twin monologues, rambles on with Oliver intent upon the physical senses and the young minister, in spite of himself, trying to bring a spiritual message to him. The episode in the cell becomes an interesting instance of insight into the mechanism of the psyche of Oliver and the minister. While Oliver is unrepentantly straightforward about his desire, the minister is still fighting his own desire upon barbital tablets. Ultimately, the story makes a negative comment upon the kind of religiosity espoused by the Lutheran minister.

The amount of religious skepticism in the story is directed towards the psychologically dangerous manifestation of religious faith. This is the kind of faith that Rita Colanzi terms "bad faith" by reference to *Being and Nothingness*, a classic of Existentialism by Sartre. It is a faith which the practitioner of it adopts as "a religious posture" in his desperate attempt to stave off meaninglessness (Colanzi 457). If we continue in the domain of psychology a little longer, we would begin to notice Tennessee Williams's alter ego equally reflected in the Lutheran minister and Oliver—the one representing his troubled puritan side, and the other the rebellious. The judgment of the author regarding the divergent faiths of the minister and Oliver is least camouflaged in the story. In spite of all his training in the seminary, the minister crumbles under the force of irresistible sensuality turning himself into an example of "bad faith". Conversely, Oliver, a vagrant who has lived a life of sensual gratification, is a person with near saintly detachment. Tennessee Williams makes a loud call for a posthumously pagan apotheosis of Oliver. The message and the judgment are unmistakable:

> The body, unclaimed after death, was turned over to a medical college to be used in a classroom laboratory. The men who performed the dissection were somewhat abashed by the body under their knives. It seemed intended for some more august purpose, to stand in a gallery of antique sculpture touched only by light through stillness and contemplation, for it had the nobility of some broken Apollo that no one was likely to carve so purely again. (*Collected Stories* 188)

The story, thus, creates a heavily religious atmosphere by taking up the issue of faith and by arguing it out through Oliver and the minister.

As we enter the zone of *Small Craft Warnings* in the late career of Tennessee Williams, we find him in his stage of theological convictions. So dominant is the Christian message in the play, and yet so neglected, that Philip C. Kolin finds it urgent to specifically emphasize this aspect of *Small Craft Warning*:

> Unfortunately, Williams's highly symbolic Christian beliefs have not been given attention in *Small Craft Warnings,* where they translate into something far more elevated than the bar mumblings of a decadent writer. Except for a brief reference by John Mac Nicholas to the sacrament of confession in *Small craft,* critics have avoided the productive intervention of Christian ideas, ideologically and structurally, in the script. (*Undiscovered Country* 111)

Tennessee Williams had been so much passionate about the Christian message in the play that he personally entered its script and action to play the important role of Doc in June 1972 at New Theatre, New York. Emerging from *Confessional*, an evocative One-Acter, *Small Craft Warnings* has less substance by way of plot and subject matter. The location of the play is a bar meaningfully situated on a beachfront that is suggestive of a spiritual conflict because of its amphibian position between water and ground. The spiritual suggestiveness is further enhanced by the "effect of fog rolling in from the ocean" (225). The location of the bar on the beach-front is quite in line with many of Tennessee Williams's later plays which "similarly use a coastal setting to allegorize spiritual conflicts—*Night of the Iguana, Gnädiges Fräulein, Milk Train, Something Cloudy, Something Clear*" (Kolin, *Undiscovered Country* 112). The characters in the play are virtually unrelated to one another—they are "a group of regular patrons who are nearly all so well known to each other that it is like a community club..." (*Small Craft* 225). The vital absence of a relationship among them is accentuated by a sequence later in the play where each one of them is put under a spotlight to show their seclusion, and is made to speak out their confessions most probably to the audience. The interaction among them is so much based on needs that it can never achieve the generative power to grow into a relationship. Bill and Leona, Steve and Violet, Quentin and Bobby—each of the three failed associations has been based on the requirements of space, or of company, or of flesh. The worst of the three is the one between Quentin and Bobby, because it is "infected with all that sadness and sickness in the heart of a gay boy" (254). Analyzing the psyche of the "infected", Quentin says that the disorder originates out of the loss of "the capacity for being surprised" (260). The loss either indicates or grows into the loss of sensibility. The lost or dead sensibility converts these homosexual encounters, "infected" as they are, into "the jabbing of a hypodermic needle to which they're addicted but which is more and more empty of real interest and surprise" (260). Away and apart from his diagnosis of the psychology of the infected, Quentin appears in the play as an agnostic who is frustrated because his questions to God have not been answered:

> ...I've asked all the questions, shouted them at deaf heaven, till I was hoarse in the voice box and blue in the face, and gotten no answer, not the whisper of one, nothing at all, you see, but the sun coming up each morning and going down that night.... (*Small Craft* 261)

Since he can't visualize God, he can only think of Him as "a carved rock by the desert, a...monumental symbol of worn out passion and bewilderment in you, a stupid stone paralyzed sphinx that knows no answers..." (261).

Projected against the agnosticism of Quentin is the faith of Doc, who is embittered too; but his bitterness is directed against the sacrilege that man has committed to defile the "holy miracles" by surrounding them with "expedients that seem to take away the dignity of them." He feels that birth, the holier of the two miracles, passes through such instruments of sacrilege as "rubber gloves, boiled water, forceps, surgical shears"; and, death passes through "the wheeze of an Oxygen tank, the jab of a hypodermic needle to put out the panic light in the dying out eyes, tubes in the arms and the kidneys, absorbent cotton inserted in the rectum to hold back the bowels discharged when the...the being stops" (249). Beyond and behind this "irreverent paraphernalia" attending upon birth and death, there is God arguably in heaven but certainly in a coal mine:

> Doc: ...*I've always figured that God is a black man with no light* on his face. He moves in the dark like a black man, a Negro miner in the pit of a lightless coal mine, obscured completely by the...irrelevancies and irreverencies of public worship...standing to sing, kneeling to pray, sitting to hear the banalities of a preacher.... (*Small Craft* 250)

For Doc, faith has been corrupted by "irrelevancies and irreverencies" of people. However, he holds his faith so strongly in his heart that it is possible for him to visualize a second Redemption. He has seen "a clear bright star in the sky", like the one that had shone over Bethlehem to indicate the Birth of Jesus the Christ. "A new Messiah", he feels, is about to be born "tonight" (250).

Leona in the play is a character who has lost something as precious and as beautiful as Heaven. For an image of God she would constantly return to her young brother, Haley, now dead but apotheosized in her memory. When alive, he could create such a vision of beauty by his Choir music at the church that the people cried..."and the preacher was still choked up when he delivered sermon"—his head was so "touched with heavenly light" (247). Leona finds the principle of beauty essentially bound up with and leading to a vision of God. For an "Appreciation of the beauty of God in the sky", it is necessary that everyone has at least "one beautiful thing! In the course of a life time" (246 and 248). Her role in the play is a reminder of the principle of chastisement. Throughout, she keeps reprimanding Bill and Violet, and even frets to drive out these parasitical pests.

There is Quentin, an agnostic still asking his questions; there is Doc calling for a stop to the sacrilege against the holy miracle of life; there is Leona illustrating the principle of beauty. But the one who puts the basics of Christianity to practice is Monk, the bar owner. If his bar be understood to mean earth, or life on earth, there would be found ample suggestions in the play to equate him with a saint or, at least, a priest. The most significant indicator to the parallel is his residence upstairs that is very frequently mentioned but never shown. A dim view of the staircase leading to the living quarters above is likened by Doc in a bizarre metaphor to "the uterine passage to life" (276). A fuller explication of this shocking metaphor would lead to a parallel between Monk's unseen residence and God's unseen Heaven. The parallel here is by no means superimposed; rather, it is heavily underscored at the close of the play where the homeless Violet is permitted to stay there as a recognition of and reward for her "ultimate supplication that would break the heart of a stone" (286). There is much more to be understood about Monk than the parallelism between his upstairs residence and Heaven. He is a compassionate 'confessor' to his customers, and he has the benignity to desire an end to their problems. Evening after evening he would love to come down the stairs from his abode for their sake:

> Monk: ...these things, these people, take the place of a family in my life. I love to come down those steps from my room to open the place for the evening, and when I've closed for the night, I love climbing back up those steps with my can of Ballantine's ale, and the stories, the jokes, the confidences and confessions I've heard that night. (*Small Craft* 265)

The sublime moment of Christian humility arrives when Monk personally removes from Violet's feet the slippers that are "Dirty, worn out...sour smelling with sweat from being worn too long" (286). Philip C. Kolin observes in Monk's act a commendable initiation of Mary Magdalene's devout gesture of love in washing Christ's feet. In precise words, Kolin explains the striking parallels between Monk's acts and the Christ-like:

> Two of Christ's injunctions to Peter also help to gloss Monk's behavior. ("If I do not wash your feet you can have nothing in common with me" John 3:18). Alluding to the possibility of a bond between Violet and Monk only if she heeds his request to wash.... The water that Monk supplies—plus his commentary on Violet's slippers—further allegorize him as a disciple, a man of faith in the sordid, secular world, ready to give in the service

> of another, one of Christianity's, and Williams's highest goals. (*Undiscovered Country* 122)

As has been observed in the instances cited above from both the fiction and the drama of the author, a religious undercurrent in the form of struggles for or related to faith can be found throughout Tennessee Williams's major works (Leverich 591). The religious undercurrent extends to the author's minor works too, especially in cases where the minor ones have been a preparation for the major. From early Williams to late is a movement that has two corresponding sides to it. The first relates to the personal life of the author in his journey from a growing child in a string of Episcopal rectories to his conversion to Roman Catholicism in 1969. The second relates to his creative life and designates his progress from the skepticism of Oliver in "One Arm" to the fanatic faith of Doc in *Small Craft Warnings*. The skepticism or near atheism of Oliver is, however, not a rejection of faith or God. In fact, the story is one of the first attacks of Tennessee Williams upon the inhibitions of "puritanism and its persecution of the artist, and, incidentally, upon his own religious upbringing"; and, at the same time, the play presents Williams's personal model of faith through Doc in *Small Craft*, a model that manages "to depict the heroism of a freethinker" (Leverich 113).

For all those generations of scholars that remained focused upon finding the author in his works, the revelation of his intense faith (very much like Doc's) may still come as a surprise. Tennessee Williams finds it natural and necessary for an author "to put his persona into his work"; otherwise, it would only be "a manufactured, a synthetic thing" ("Too Personal" 157-58). In support of the argument, it would be appropriate to reproduce some lines from a manuscript found not long ago and first published in the 2003 issue of *The Tennessee Williams Annual Review*:

> Dear Father in Heaven
>
> Help me to receive with interest and courtesy all advice, whether solicited by myself or offered to me gratuitously, to read and consider all notes no matter who makes them....

> And let me know the honesty and the good faith and true affection of my friends and collaborators, all whom I work as with, and let me believe continually as I can in all good things in people". ("A Playwright's Prayer" 1 and 3)

Entitled "A Playwright's Prayer", the work shows Tennessee Williams in his ultimate, Christian humility and compassionate consideration. Never intended for publication, the work proves the catholic faith of the author and also provides a background to the religious undercurrent flowing through his works.

If an unmistakable but personalized religiosity runs garbed through Tennessee Williams's works, a dominant southernness envelops his entire creative repertoire. In his plays, he incorporates "a comprehensive symbol of the South" in the form of "usually Victorian Gothic" houses (Watson 175-76). As a short story writer, he can safely be placed "in the southern Gothic tradition, along with Flannery O'Connor, Eudora Welty, Carson McCullers, Truman Capote, and others" (Vannatta xi). Both in his fiction and his drama, Tennessee Williams loves to engage himself in the paradox of the South that manifests itself in more ways than one. Whatever has been memorable in Williams has essentially been grounded and reared in the South. A successful engagement and employment of the opposites has enabled him to produce many memorable works with memorable characters. The desire and an irrevocable inclination to grapple with opposites can be noticed even in so early a work as "Isolated", reproduced by Philip C. Kolin in the premier issue of *The Tennessee Williams Annual Review*. The piece carries the distinction of being the "first extant published short story" by Tennessee Williams ("Isolated" 33). The story was first published in one of the November 1924 issues of *The Junior Life*, the bi-weekly newspaper of Ben Blewett Junior High School in St. Louis. Though Lyle Leverich dismisses this 251 word short story as "one of the class exercises in the development of paragraphs from topical sentences", there is a noticeably vital 'southern' element in it (65). As noted earlier, the story produces one of the first evidences of the author's lifelong involvement with paradoxes and opposites. Narrated in the first person, the short story shows the narrator swimming to the fictional White Fan Island, trying fishing in the "sparkling water" of the river, taking two hours of sleep, being surrounded by "a torrent of brown eddies", and finally being rescued by "one of these searching parties" ("Isolated" 35-36). The story presents water as an idyllic symbol ("sparkling water"), and also as a source of horror ("a torrent of brown eddies"). The confrontation between the two images of water grows and assumes portentous proportions in some of the later writings of Williams. One of the best examples of the presentation of water in a paradoxical manner is "Vengeance of Nitocris", a memorable and accomplished story showing Nitocris converting the life giving water of Nile into an instrument of a blood chilling massacre. Another set of engaging opposites that the story employs is the set of the two forms of a single character. The two forms of Nitocris's character, her transformation from the one to the other, has a capacity to create as much Gothic terror as the deluge of water submerging the subterranean chamber full to capacity with feasting people. From a woman hanging onto his brother's arm, from a mere pleading sister to a Queen planning and successfully carrying out a vengeful massacre is a transformation that adds a substantial dimension to what has been termed the 'Southern Gothic' of the story.

The flood that takes so many lives in the subterranean chamber in "The Vengeance of Nictocris", has been artificially created. But the flood that keeps threatening with "insistent murmur" in *Kingdom of Earth* is natural, and finally proves a tool of heavenly justice to set right the wrongs heaped upon man by man (*Kingdom of Earth* 125). The play involves three characters—Chicken, Lot and Myrtle. Chicken is a physically capable man, sturdy and fit for things agrarian. Quite understandably, he has no fear of floods; rather, he likes floods because they "make the land richer" (183). However, he is at the receiving end of the unjust regulations of the law of inheritance. Without a legal set up with his half-brother, Lot, he cannot claim anything legally. He has to suffer this disadvantage for no fault of his own. The advantage is enjoyed by the frail and consumptive Lot, who marries Myrtle in order to undo the "set up" with Chicken. The shenanigans of Lot, however, fail when he is consumed by the rising flood and Myrtle joins the earthly and earthy Chicken. Distant to begin with and close and imminent at the end, the floodwaters stand guard in the background throughout. The poetic justice of sorts that is effected by floodwaters is unbiased. The consumptive, frail, dying Lot is granted a final release in the form of death; Myrtle is granted release from her marriage with Lot; and Chicken gets to own the ranch he deserves to own.

One of the (Southern) paradoxes consistently present in Tennessee Williams's creative world is "the effect of the past on the present, especially that of the southern past" (Prenshaw in Tharpe 10-11). Blanche Dubois of *Streetcar Named Desire* is the worst victim, throughout Williams's canon, of the tension that generates out of a failed balance between the past and the present. She carries with her the southern past of the comfortable aristocracy of plantation ranches. When she arrives at the non-descript residence of her sister Stella, she is already broke trying to sell off her past for a comfortably acceptable present. Her tragedy emerges out of her refusal to let go of the past. Belle Reve, the rich plantation ranch, is lost; but Blanche still loves to cling to the lost aristocracy. She is a perfect foil to her sister who has smoothly transferred herself physically and psychologically from Belle Reve to the ghetto-like colony. To get to the cause of Blanche's tragedy, it would be appropriate to look at the following piece of conversation from her last and unfortunate romance with Mitch:

> Mitch: ...I'm talking to Miss—
>
> Blanche: Du Bois
>
> Blanche: It's a French name. It means woods and Blanche means white, so the two together mean white woods. Like an orchard in spring! You can remember it by that.
>
> Mitch: You're French?
>
> Blanche: We are French by extraction. Our first American ancestors were French Huguenots.
>
> Mitch: You are Stella's sister, are you not? (*Streetcar* 150)

The glaring incongruity between her present identity as Stella's sister and the elaborate lineage drawn out by Blanche is the cause (or one of the causes) of her tragedy. There is yet another strand of Blanche's past that clings to her to spoil her present. This strand is brought to notice by Stella. It pertains to her marriage to "a boy who wrote poetry". Blanche "worshipped the ground he walked on! Adored him and thought him almost too fine to be human!" But then she found out "that he was" a degenerate (189-90). Her drift has a beginning in her passage from ignorance to knowledge about Allen, the man "she thought too fine to be human". The misery emanating out of this passage from ignorance in the past to knowledge in the present is better illustrated in the short story "The Vine". Curiously, the story delineates the psyche of a macho man after the discovery of his sterility. Following the discovery, Donald not only loses his male pride but also begins to feel the need to depend on and cling, vine like, to his wife Rachel. With the shattering awareness of his sterility, his past begins to work adversely upon his present. His past, in which he took every physical attribute as a sign of superior male vigor, is now a cancerous memory for him. The story shows him disconcerted to the brink of madness during the brief absence of Rachel—so much dependent has he been on her since the discovery of his inability to procreate.

Decadent 'Southern Belle' is an important fixture in Tennessee Williams's creative world. The Southern Belle moves by her tragedy and, simultaneously, points out "the desiccation of the old tradition" (Prenshaw in Tharpe 12). Beginning with the likes of Irene ("In Memory of an Aristocrat"), Myra ("The Field of Blue children"), Tina ("The Dark Room") and Mrs. Stone ("The Roman spring of Mrs. Stone") in fiction, the Southern Belle continues to figure in a more refined manifestation in the drama of the author. The immortal examples of Southern Belle in drama include Laura and Amanda (*The Glass Menagerie*), Sandra (*The Battle of Angels*), Alma (*Summer and Smoke*) and Blanche DuBois *(A Streetcar Named Desire)*. It is quite possible to stretch the class to include Fraulein (*Gnädiges Fräulein*) as the culmination of the Southern Belle tragedy. On the way to that culmination are the cases of Hannah Jelkes (*The Night of the Iguana*) and Alexandra (*Sweet Bird of Youth*). Each one of these belles is a moth-like creature, carrying a memory of a personal and general past upon her fragile shoulders. Her predicament emerges out of her irresistible move towards "lightning": "Nowadays is indeed lit by lightning, a plague has stricken the moths, and Blanche has been 'put away'" (*Memoirs* 125). Whether the prototypes like Irene ('In Memory of an Aristocrat') and Willie (*This Property is Condemned*), or the most representative ones like Blanche and Alma, these Southern Belles are doomed to suffer because they have to inescapably stay between the two grating blocks of irreconcilables—"calm grace and raw hatred. Polished manners and violence. An intense individualism and intense group pressures towards conformity. A reverence to the point of idolatry of self-determining action and a caste and class structure presupposing an aristocratic hierarchy" (Holman 01).

Being one of the prototypes of the class of Southern Belle, it would be warranted here to take a close look at Irene and know the defining dimensions and contours of the Southern predicament of these Southern "moths". One can bear in mind, however, that Irene's case substantially overlaps into the domain of the artist figures in Tennessee Williams. Irene is "a very loveable person" and "the good kind of Bohemian". Her "raw and terrific" paintings carry "a tremendous wallop"; and they hit a person "right smack between the eyes with the force and precision that only comes from the fury of a first rate talent" (*Collected Stories* 82, 85). Her present as a bohemian artist has an overwhelmingly molding influence on her past. When the narrator (evidently the author) brings her home from a small bar where he finds her unconscious, he learns all about that sordid past through her drunken talk. (Though she never willingly tries to distance herself from her past in the manner or Blanche):

> She talked all night. Lay there too exhausted to move except when she had to vomit, but kept on talking and talking. The whole of her former life passed before me in brilliant parade. I saw the mean-souled bosses and the gallant strike workers, I saw the brutal policemen, I saw the shrewd self-interested union organizers and the relief workers who kept their hearts in their notebook. I saw

> stray, beautiful glimpses of fire and passion and tenderness. (*Collected Stories* 86)

Drawing upon C. Hugh Holman's analysis of the southern dichotomy between two sets of polarized elements, it can also be said of Irene that she represents the struggle between "intense individualism and intense group pressures towards conformity" (01). Her art is glaringly nonconformist—"Pictures of pregnant women in soiled cotton dresses and bums sleeping in doorways. Screaming strike-workers, hideous scabs and bosses..." Not unexpected, her paintings are rejected by "society crowd making a gracious bow to respectable art" (*Collected Stories* 85, 88). Evidently, the conformist "society crowd" doesn't have the moral courage or the ingenuity of thought or the respect for artistic imagination to at least entertain Irene's rather shocking portrayal of hideous social reality.

At a discreet distance from these "moth" like Southern Belles are the practical Southern women—women that have somewhat transgressed the limits imposed upon them by south. The Southern women constitute a type that is "not blighted by the outmoded proprieties of a Victorian culture or by the bridling restrictions of a Southern Puritanism" (Falk 76). Leading the type are the most uninhibited of them, Serafina and her daughter (*The Rose Tattoo*) followed by Maggie (*Cat in a Hot Tin Roof*), Baby Doll Meighan (*27 Wagons Full of Cotton*), and, debatably, even Stella Du Bios (*A Street car Named Desire*). It can safely be concluded that these women represent the cavalier side of the South (the Puritan side being represented by the moths). Each of them is unscrupulous about her physical passion and its gratification. Though not in an immoral way, the most striking instance is that of Stella in *Streetcar.* Looking deeper into the talk of Blanche and drawing inferences out of that talk, the sensibilities of Stella must have been either blunt or subservient to passion to make her leave 'Belle Reve'. In marrying Stanley Kowalski, she must have been unmindful of the deaths back home. Her sister and her opposite in the play, Blanche, has this legitimate complaint against her:

> I, I, I took the blows on my face and my body! All of those deaths! The long parade to the graveyard! Father,

> mother! Margaret, that dreadful way.... And funerals are pretty compared to deaths.... Death is expensive, Miss Stella! Why, the Grim reaper has put up his tent on our doorstep!... I talk, Belle Reve was his headquarters! (126-27)

As the play closes, one wonders whether it is for the sake of her coming baby or her passion that Stella overlooks a rather sadistic treatment meted out to Blanche by Stanley Kowalski. In spite of many exhaustive studies, all concentrated upon Blanche, it remains a pathetic puzzle. The puzzle grows more pathetic and intriguing in the last scene where Stanley, along with the doctor and the matron from mental asylum, acts as a poacher hustling and hounding Blanche. To call Stanley a poacher is no exaggeration. In all likelihood, Tennessee Williams intends the analogy while describing Blanche's last desperate attempt to escape the Doctor and matron by going back into the house:

> Stanley: Did you forget something?
>
> Blanche: (Shrilly) Yes! Yes, I forgot something! (She rushes past him into the bedroom. Lucid reflections appear on the walls in odd, sinuous shapes. The 'Varsouviana' is filtered into weird distortions, *accompanied by the cries and noises of the jungle*. Blanche seizes the back of a chair as if to defend herself. (222)

The analogy suggested by the expression "noises of the jungle" is confirmed by the description of the final surrender of Blanche:

> ...the Matron catches hold of Blanche's arm and prevents her flight. Blanche turns wildly and scratches at the matron. The heavy woman pinions her arms. Blanche cries out hoarsely and slips to her knees. (224)

Throughout this tragic poaching of her sister, Stella looks on helplessly and just manages to utter a bye of sorts.

Serafina in *The Rose Tattoo* is much possessed by her passion and, somewhat consequently, almost makes herself a comic character. An Italian peasant, Serafina espouses and embodies a credo that is diametrically opposed to the Puritan strand of the South. The most powerful aspect of her rejection of Puritanism is her "embodiment of a credo, the affirmation of passion as the root feeling of a complete existence" (Clurman 22). She doesn't find her physical desire a distraction from her passionate religiosity. In fact, she is so deeply religious that she even thinks she can hold communication with Mother Madonna. She has a very gaudily decorated "small shrine against the wall between the rooms of her house consisting of a prie-dieu and a little statue of the Madonna in a starry blue robe and gold crown. Before this burns, always, a vigil light in its ruby glass cup" (*Rose Tattoo*, Production Notes 17). An indication of her seemingly crazy religiosity is apparent in the way she tries to communicate with the holy statue in order to seek her (Madonna's) approval of Alvaro as her lover after suffering a short 'celibacy' as a widow:

> Serafina: ...Madonna Santa! My husband's body with the head of a clown! (She crosses to Madonna) O Lady! (She makes an imploring gesture) Speak to me!—What are you saying?—Please, Lady, I can't hear you.
>
> Is it a sign? Is it a sign of something? What does it mean? Oh, speak to me, Lady! (73)

As is evident in Serafina's utterance, she has carried her passion to such heights that she begins to see in Alvaro an incarnation of her dead husband's body with the head of a clown. Though in a slightly comic vein, Tennessee Williams has a broad statement to make through Serafina—the only conceivable way to lead a physically and psychologically healthy life is to have and combine physical and spiritual passions. Not consciously though, Serafina has learnt this art of living. Her passionate spirituality is entirely indigenous and free from the need of priestly endorsement; and her physical passion is unscrupulous: "To me the big bed was beautiful like religion. Now I lie on it with dreams, with memories only" (64). Her scathing ridicule of her puritan neighbor has a sharp edge: "At thirty years old they got no use for the letto matrimonial, no. The big bed goes to the basement! They got little beds from sears Roebuck and sleep on their bellies!" (64).

Two more of this sorority of southern women having abandoned Puritanism are Maggie (*Cat on a Hot Tin Roof*) and

Baby Doll Meighan (*27 Wagons*). Both have their counterparts or originals in the short story versions—respectively in "Three Players of a Summer Game" and "27 Wagons Full of Cotton". Maggie is a worldly woman with a fierce drive; and she makes a strange validation of her physical desire to Brick by going to bed with Skipper, Brick's friend and mate. In her confession to Brick about Skipper she says that she had indulged in the act "to dream it was you". Far from feeling guilty and penitent, she calls it (the act) "one of those beautiful things they tell about in the Greek legends" (*Cat* 26). However, this pagan justification of adultery is incongruous with her overall character. She is a practical woman with a material attitude towards the plantations owned by Big Daddy. One of her major concerns is to have an issue in order to be able to claim the plantations. Maggie has her foil in Flora Meighan of *27 Wagons*. Flora Meighan of the one-act gets a more onomatopoeic name in the film version of the play, *Baby Doll*. Contrasted with her motivation and drive is the plumpness and dullness of Baby Doll (Flora). The wronged Vaccaro in *27 Wagons* tries to get even with Jake Meighan by cuckolding him, though it is no recompense for a money-minded businessman like him. Baby Doll's response to the overtures of Vaccaro is neither eager nor suggestive of rejection. For a woman like her, everything comes easy—she cannot have qualms about anything, not even about what Vaccaro has done to her. She is not gentle like Stella, nor highly imaginative like Serafina, nor fiercely motivated like Margaret. Yet she has something distinctly Southern about her, which brings into noticeable relief her passive surrender to Vaccaro. Her repeated comparison with a lump of cotton by Vaccaro, though suggestive in a different way, has a significance vis-à-vis the Southern atmosphere evoked in the opening Production Notes. Her masochistic surrender to Vaccaro's advances is a streak that discordantly rises against the Southern atmosphere in the background.

The portrayal of these women characters in contrast to the "moths", the Southern Belles, brings to light an aspect of Tennessee Williams as a "desperate moralist" who is "committed to the Romantic dictum inherent in his neo-Lawrencean point of view, that the natural equals the good..." (Ganz in Stanton 136).

The encounter between women from the two categories is the closest in *The Glass Menagerie* (apart from *A Streetcar Named Desire*), where Laura is at the receiving end of the manipulations of her mother, Amanda, who carries with her the memories of a rich and comfortable plantation South. However, the encounter can be seen getting closer than the closest in Alma of *Summer and Smoke*. In her case, the two categories descend into a single character, as is suggested by her parentage—she is the daughter of "a desiccated religion and of the sort of dementia that causes retreat into childhood" (Adler in Tharpe 35). Simplified to its basics, the puzzle would yield this result—she is the soul of the South lodged in a body that would not accommodate it. Again, reduced to the bare basic, the role of John Buchanan in the play is that of a catalyst. He is there to constantly remind Alma of her body. The sharp and pungent 'anatomy lecture' that he delivers to Alma (with the anatomy chart for illustration) creates an amazing effect on her (*Summer and Smoke* 221). When she next meets John two brief scenes later, she tells him rather candidly that "the girl who said 'no'...doesn't exist anymore" and that "she died last summer—suffocated in smoke from something on fire inside her" (224). Alma ends up a tragic character at the close of the play, losing both John and her long cherished Puritanism. Her tragedy in summed up in the following utterance of hers:

> The tables have turned, yes the tables have turned with a vengeance! You've come around to my old way of thinking and I to yours like two people exchanging a call on each other at the same time, and each finding the other one gone out, the door locked against him and no one to answer the bell! (247)

The persona of Alma becomes an exemplary embodiment of South, because her being is constituted out of the complex union of the antithetical opposites. The 'South' in Tennessee Williams is not an independent element; it is intricately connected with the "Gothic situations and settings" that "reveal the darkest side of life" (Hart 441). Though a fiercely contested term, the 'Gothic' persists somewhere near the core of the author's works. It enters into a relationship with the 'South' where it closes in on the irreconcilable, paradoxical opposites that the author has dealt with throughout his creative world. The relationship can be briefly illustrated by reference to Maggie Kilgour's view that the Gothic carries the symptoms of a nostalgia because it "looks backwards to a kinder, simpler paradise lost of harmonious relations that existed before the nasty modern world of irreconcilable opposition and conflict" (15). The most fearsome of this "irreconcilable opposition and conflict" takes place in the cases of individuals. Alma's is an example cited above. However, two of the most representative examples of the conflict are Fräulein in *Gnädiges Fräulein* and Felice and Clare in *Out Cry.* The first is a classic instance of Fraulein's failed struggle against herself, and the second delineates a failing struggle against claustrophobia. The struggle and conflict against oneself, or against claustrophobia, may assume varied shades and shapes. In "The Mysteries of Joy Rio" (short story), for instance, Pablo Gonzales briefly contests and then surrenders to his alternative desire of flesh. The story has a strong element of the weird towards the end where Pablo Gonzales is eased out of life by his dead master and mentor, Emiel Kroger, from whom he had caught the pleasure or contagion of the alternative desire. The story weaves a claustrophobic situation by first describing the small watch-repairs shop of Gonzales and then the dark, mysterious and unused gallery of the theatre (Joy Rio). The repairs man, Gonzales, is a compulsive visitor from the shop to the gallery, from the first enclosure to the second. To take David Punter's word for it, both claustrophobia and cases of psychoanalysis (like that of Gonzales) are essential elements of the Gothic. "The prevalence of claustrophobia" and the "foreclosure of escape from institution or destitution", according to Punter, are "all recognizably Gothic" (1-2). Throughout the creative world of Tennessee Williams, there is always present a character who lends himself or herself to psychoanalysis. There are many varieties of abnormal psyche portrayed in his works alongside the systems creating repeated trauma. Whichever angle one looks at his works from—the point of view of characters or issues or atmosphere—the 'South' coupled with the 'Gothic' persists. The paradoxes, the situations of transience, the complex union of religiosity and passion, the phobias, the shades of old age and the related shades of madness—all contribute towards the shaping of an atmosphere which is typical of Tennessee Williams writings. Borrowing the observations of Annette J. Saddik to conclude, all along his creative writing career "Tennessee Williams presented himself as a paragon of contradictions, both a Puritan and a Cavalier, an artistic revolutionary who insisted that his place was always on the margins of Bohemia" (*Theatre of Excess* 11).

3

"Noise into Music": Non-conformism as Creative Substance

> What is the heart but a sort of—instrument!—that translates noise into music.
>
> (*Camino Real*)

There was something portentous in the unexpected shifting of *Battle of Angels* to Boston from "a projected out-of-town opening in New Haven, Connecticut, on December 27, 1940". The shifting happened in spite of the support of John Gassner, "who never lost faith in the play", and the fact that Miriam Hopkins was playing the lead character of Myra (Leverich 386-87). Even Gassner, a revered drama critic, and Ms. Hopkins, a celebrated Broadway artist, would not have been able to read the catastrophe in the shifting. At Boston, the play turned out "a colossal failure" (Hirsch 18). Following the rejection of the play by Bostonians came the outrage of the Newspaper reviewers and their brutally acerbic attack on the play for whatever they supposed it propagated. Back in New York, the failure of the play in Boston was viewed from a different perspective, represented by the observation of Audrey Wood, Tennessee Williams's theatre agent. The perspective was that Boston was the worst choice for a commercial production of a Tennessee Williams play. Absolutely convinced about the quality of *Battle of Angels*, Tennessee Williams blamed the choice of Boston for its inauguration. Quoting the author, John Lahr calls the play "Williams's first full scale attempt" to '*fuse lyricism with realism*' (16). Right from the beginning, the play thus becomes an exercise in nonconformist paradoxes for its author. The paradoxes, in fact, would be found inherent in the play if we take note of what Tennessee Williams says he used as the creative material for it—"the country of childhood" with "the violent symbols of my adolescence" projected onto it (qtd. in Lahr 16). Systems and constructs, of which social structure is one, are usually not compatible with adolescent energies or imaginative and independent logic. Independent imagination and logic compounded with youthful energies of the mind and the body, therefore, create quite a potentially non-conformist material. Made of and from this material, though sometimes very subtle, the art of Tennessee Williams thus produces messages and suggestions that are either largely independent of any systems or broadly non-conformist.

The then Bostonians may have felt outraged at what they thought was an intolerable amount of blasphemy loaded in *Battle of Angles*; but the author had declared through the play his manifesto of the themes, structures, symbols, myths, issues and patterns that he was to deal with in a long career of nearly two successful decades. The declaration, and the desire to stick to it in the face of hardest criticism was implicit in the author's introduction to the first published version of *Battle of Angels,* carried by a small magazine named *Pharos.* By the time he was reaching close to the end of the successful part of his career, he had earned himself the reputation (though somewhat dubious) of a playwright whom the theatre goers paid to get their nightmares. However, Tennessee Williams had announced his creed, or of his works to come, much before *Battle of Angels*—way back in 1928 with the publication of "The Vengeance of Nitocris", his first professionally published short story. Right behind the Gothic narrative of the story can be seen the author's alternating stand between the iconoclastic and the heathen. This alternation, in its various forms, has characterized the author's works and has been his strength as well as weakness. In its candidly shocking form, as in *Battle of Angels,* the iconoclasm earns him the wrath of the theatregoers; but in its sensibly convoluted form, it earns him the Pulitzer prizes for *The Streetcar Named Desire* in 1948 and for *Cat on a Hot Tin Roof* in 1955. It must be borne in mind, though, that the elite circle of drama critics had accorded a general reception even to the notoriously failed major inauguration of Williams the dramatist at Boston on 30 December 1940.

The iconoclasm of "The Vengeance of Nitocris" is direct, candid and prophetic. The pharaoh in the story is frustrated and angered because the bridge across the Nile, which had taken five years in construction, has been swept away by floods. Gone berserk with frustration, he avenges himself upon temple priests and the god of gods, Osiris:

> Raging with anger, he had flogged the priests from the temple. He had barred the temple doors and with his own breath had blown out the sacred candles. He had defiled the hallowed alters with the carcasses of beasts. Even, it was said in low, shocked whispers, in a mock ceremony of worship he had burned the Carrion of a hyena, most abhorrent of all beasts to Osiris. (*Collected Stories* 02)

The Pharaoh pays for this willful sacrilege by death—he dies by falling and rolling down the steps of his palace. The sacrilege in the story is as much willful on the part of the Pharaoh as on the author's, for we understand that the Pharaoh is almost a half conscious self-portrayal of Tennessee Williams. Neither of the two is repentant for the sacrilege. The unrepentant attitude gets heavily projected in the haughty yet bold demeanor of the Pharaoh in the face of the death sentence pronounced upon him by the high priests of the ancient Egyptian religion. It can even be argued that the accidental death of the Pharaoh saved him any punishment by human hands and tools, though the accident would be looked upon by the believing as "a sign from the god!" (*Collected Stories* 03). The iconoclasm of the story takes shape in its explicit and implicit attacks on idolatrous fixations. The Pharaoh in the story has a passionate temper that would not be accommodated in the framework of the faith, because the only variety of passion that earns sanction here is religious frenzy. Unlike the case of "The Vengeance of Nitocris", *Battle of Angels* presents the brewing revolt within a broad religious framework. The revolt, non-conformist in nature, is directed against everything that is puritanical or stagnant. The restrictions imposed by the taboo infested customs and religions evoke a response that is symptomatic of a revolt. The complaint of Val is an articulation against the restrictions that tend to stamp out the very spirit of existence:

> Val: How do you get to know people? I used to think you did it by touching them with your hands. But later I found out that only made you more of a stranger than ever... Don't you see how it is? We're all of us locked up tight inside our own bodies. Sentenced you might say—to solitary confinement inside our own skins. (*Battle of Angels 50*)

The complaint comes from Val, a tramp wearing snake jacket, whose full name immediately evokes religious connotations and connections. Valentine Xavier, his full name simultaneously reminiscent of a famous saint and Christ, enters a dry goods store owned by Myra Torrance and her husband, Jabe, whom she married "in a sort of self-destroying, legal prostitution" (Tischler 75). Jabe is now dying a slow cancer induced death. Val Xavier is the target of attention and the possible source of love for Myra, Sandra and Vee (who would portray Christ with the features of Val). At the close of the play, there is police in the store to arrest Val on made up charges. He wishes to escape, but is hampered by Myra and Sandra, both wanting to accompany him. Jabe arrives from his room above, shoots Myra and blames it on Val who is caught up and lynched. The dry goods store flares up in flames. Even this highly elliptic outline of the play suggests an overbearing presence of iconoclastic symbolism in it. Myra in the play is the "robust representative of life and procreation" thwarted by "Jabe as the epic antagonist" (Tischler 76-77).

The non-conformism of *Battle of Angels* begins with the relationships that develop after Valentine Xavier enters the play with the obvious connotations of his name. He is spotted, simultaneously, by three women as a possible source of happiness through love. There are elements of revolt, of non-conformism, in all the three relationships being sought here. Myra is already married to Jabe, though in a loveless and barren union; Sandra is a dipsomaniac on Val's trail; and Vee (the Sheriff's wife) is a woman possessed by religious visions. The first of the three is suggestive of the dismantling of a marriage, backed and solemnized by Church, which has given Jabe his authority over Myra in spite of his physical and spiritual incapability. Of his two appearances in the play, the first is as a patient doomed to die of cancer and the second as "a living symbol of death" with his "clumping fatality of the traditional spook" (111). During his long absence between the two appearances, he keeps on thumping his cane in his room right above the dry goods store where the socially unacceptable relationship between Myra and Val is struggling to develop. His cane thumping above is symbolic of a social code system trying to assert itself in the face of its rejection by Myra. That Myra's relationship with Val is sacred like the memory of Christ is suggested by her passionate preparations for Christmas. Moreover, the relationship is suggested to have been blessed by Nature, if not by the society, as it leads to the most precious gift of life by natural procreation. "I knew that I wouldn't be barren when we went together the first time", Myra exults on getting to know of her pregnancy, "I felt it already, stirring up inside me, beginning to live! The first little fig on the tree they said wouldn't bear. What a mistake they made!" (107).

Sandra's seeking to unite with Val is equally iconoclastic from the point of view of religious morality. Sandra in the play is an allegorical figure representing Cassandra, the Trojan princess—prophetess whose prescience is cursed with disbelief. The suggested union of the Christian with the heathen—of Valentine Xavier with Cassandra—has every potential to jolt the purist camps. Even outside the symbolism of their names, their union has a potent threat directed at the establishments of the society. The threat is articulated by Sandra in one of her dipsomaniac visions:

> Sandra: ...you know what I feel when I look at you, Val? Always the weight of your body bearing me down...you think I ought to be ashamed to say that? Well, I'm not. I think passion is something to be proud of...whoever has too much of passion, we are going to be burned like witches because we know too much.... The atmosphere is

> pregnant with disaster!... A battle in heaven. A battle of Angels above us! And thunder! And storm! (98-100)

Vee Talbott relates to Val quite in the manner of her Church art. Her apostolic religious visions are the product of a frenzy which quite possibly has a source in her passion. She has the knack of converting her passion to vision through fasting. In one such vision, chastened by fasting, she claims to have seen Jesus:

> Vee: I've waited and prayed so long. Now it's finally come.... The vision. I seen him early this morning. I painted the picture...of Jesus! ...I been tormented...Evil thoughts. Those men in the lock up, they write nasty words on the walls. At night I can see them. They keep coming up in my mind. (*Battle of Angels* 89)

As her words suggest, and as has been observed, Vee's visions have two facets—they are angelic and religious, but they have a source somewhere in her repressed passion. The most revolutionary instance of iconoclasm in the play occurs when Vee displays a canvas which, she claims, has a portrait of Jesus as He appeared to her in her vision. The canvas would shock any devout Christian because it carries the portrait of Val as Jesus. By any calculation, the portrait of Val presented as that of Jesus is material enough to be interpreted as an instance of blasphemy. Tennessee Williams may have wrought this situation in the play to underline and impress upon the audience his own views about an illiberal and fastidious faith. What may have heightened the tension for the first audience of the play is the presentation of fire as a symbol of consecration and purification. All that is dead, ossified, corrupted or decayed is consigned to fire in a striking resemblance with some rites and rituals of Oriental faiths. Following the consecration by fire, there can be heard "the sound of chanting from a Negro church" and the store looks like a "pillaged temple with the late afternoon sunlight thrown obliquely through the high Gothic windows" (*Battle of Angels,* Epilogue 119).

The ideology and morality of the play remained dearest to Tennessee Williams throughout. He had been so much convinced about the validity of the stated or discovered messages in his early writings that he continued to propagate the same ideology and the same morality right up to his late works. However, whatever is glaringly iconoclastic in his very early works grows into a mellow non-conformism in the subsequent and the later. The most pronounced form of his non-conformism is a tramp like individual's refusal to fall in with the established norms. Refusing to accept the norms—social, political, intellectual and even sexual—this tramp like individual subjects himself/herself to the hopeless choices of either suffering at the hands of the society or a painful isolation. In both the genres of his writings, this individual appears with unfailing regularity. The short fiction of the author carries such unforgettable portraitures of this individual as the Pharaoh in "Vengeance of Nitocris", the unnamed trash picker in "A Lady's Beaded Bag", Jacob Brodzky in "Something by Tolstoi", Big Black in "Big Black: A Mississippi Idyll", Bud in "The Accent of a Coming Foot", Homer in "The Field of Blue Children", Irene in "In Memory of an Aristocrat", Pablo Gonzales in "The Mysteries of the Joy Rio", Lucio in "The Malediction", Oliver in "One Arm", Alma in "The Yellow Bird", the poet in "The Poet", Billy and Cora in "Two on a Party", Brick Pollitt in "Three Players of a Summer Game", Gewinner Pearce in "The Knightly Quest", Miss Rosemary in "Completed", and Mrs. Stone in the author's novel *The Roman Spring of Mrs. Stone*. Apart from the proper ones listed here, the fiction of Tennessee Williams also has quite a few peripheral cases of the perennial tramp. In the drama of author, the most obvious examples of the portraiture of the susceptible non-conformist tramp are (as referred in the preceding chapter too) Valentine Xavier in *Battle of Angles* (and *Orpheus Descending*), Tom in *The Glass Menagerie,* Alma in *Summer and Smoke* (and *The Eccentricities of a Nightingale*), Serafina in *The Rose Tattoo,* Kilroy in *Camino Real*, Brick Pollitt in *Cat on a Hot Tin Roof,* Blanche in *A Streetcar Named Desire,* Sebastian in *Suddenly Last Summer,* Chance Wayne in *Sweet Bird of Youth,* and Fräulein in *The Gnädiges Fräulein.*

"A Lady's Beaded Bag" an early short story of Tennessee Williams, brings in the perspective of the socio-economic angle of the non-conformism of the author. The manner and method adopted to highlight the angle is that of tragic irony. The trash-picker in the story comes upon a lady's beaded bag in a milliner's box, carelessly relegated to the dust bin by the maid of a rich lady. The beaded bag, with its contents intact, is "one of those things for which he (the trash-picker) had been searching for fifteen years" (*Collected Stories* 14). The search, which the scavenger has so religiously pursued, had been motivated by the desire to bring "the fulfillment of his beggar-dreams" (13). The story culminates in a situation of tragic irony after the trash-picker, out of some vague fear, returns the bag to its owner. Out of the same beaded bag, the lady pays several hundred dollars as the price of "an evening wrap of diaphanous white material", and then rejects the "wrap" with a "grimace of disgust" saying that she must have been out of her mind to "dream of wearing anything so perfectly ridiculous" (16). The gaping chasm between the trash-picker's shattered "beggar-dreams" and the Lady's rejected diaphanous evening wrapper is a sad commentary on the two economic poles in the society. The one pole is represented by the trash-picker scavenging the streets of rich localities, and the other by the careless wastefulness of the insouciant rich lady. The story makes a poignantly effective statement against this unfair polarization without indulging in any loud mouthed sloganeering. Again, there is some clear meaning suggested through the nameless existence of the trash-picker. His namelessness makes him a member of the faceless crowd in a modern industrial city sharply divided between two economic poles.

Not so often though, Tennessee Williams does raise a curse-like slogan against the perpetrators of this unfair economic divide. One of the very few instances occurs in "The Malediction", a short story that becomes the source of a poignant one-act entitled *The Strangest Kind of Romance*. The story is a narrative about a person's frustrating search for love and livelihood. He doesn't find either. Lucio, the susceptible vagabond in the story, somehow avails accommodation at a rooming house. For love, he has none except a cat named Nitchevo left by the previous occupant of the room. He also avails a menial job at a factory on the recommendation of the landlady, but gets laid off when the demand for the produce of the factory meets a decline. Then comes the malediction, the curse, from a beggarly old man who, in all probability, has suffered in his younger days the same frustrations as those of Lucio:

> Don't be afraid of these stinking sons-of-bitches. They grow like weeds and like stinkweeds are cut down. They run away from their conscience and can't be still a minute —Watch for the sun!—It comes up out of their graveyard every morning!... They want to be scabbed all over, they want no skin but the crust of their greediness on them! Okay, okay, let them have it! But let them have *more* and *more*! Maggots as well as lice! Yeah, pile the friggin' dirt of their friggin' graveyard on them, shovel them under *deep* —till I can't *smell* 'em. (*Collected Stories* 155, 158)

What the old man shouts is more than the proletariat sloganeering; it is a curse from the one who claims to be "God Almighty" (*Collected Stories* 155). The tramp in the story, Lucio, could not have summoned up this vehement articulation of protest and abortive anger. He can only communicate with the unresponsive cat, because his beast-like existence has only conditioned him so.

Slightly but vitally different is the case of Big Black in "Big Black: A Mississippi Idyll", a story probing the psyche of a black laborer working for "The White boss, a giant of an Irishman, wet and fiery red as if he had just been dipped into a tub of blood" (*Collected Stories* 26). Without making an issue out of it, Tennessee Williams has wrought an exposure of the divide between the 'haves' and 'have-nots' of the society. The white boss in the story can bend the law to wriggle out of its reach. His economic strength and racial identity as a white man has equipped him with the capacity to do so. The laborers working for him know "that he had once burst a Negro's head open for calling him a name, and that he had gotten away with it" (*Collected Stories* 26). Big Black in the story doesn't have a name to give him a specific identity—he is just a member of that numerical Negro strength which has been striving for the benefit of the white boss and his clan. But this Negro, unnamed except for his physical bulk, has a protest and resentment rooted deep in his heart. Occasionally, he releases the accumulated mass of the protest in "a savage, booming cry—Yow-ow. Yow-ow-w-w" (27). His protest is best articulated in this savage cry. Any socio-political jargon would only take the powerfully uncouth effect out of it. The cry, the narrator tells, is "elemental, epical" and is "like a prayer and like a challenge flung at life" (31). The nameless Negro, like the nameless trash-picker and the insignificant Lucio, is still an individual, a unique being, deserving of respect due to him. By his subtly poignant and effective portrayals of this kind, Tennessee Williams seems to be concurring with Hermann Hesse's view of "everyman" as "more than just himself", representing "the unique, the very special and always significant and remarkable point at which the world's phenomena intersect only once in this way and never again" in "every man, as long as he lives and fulfills the will of nature" (qtd. in Sahu 87). Since the society would not accept this romantically philosophical view about the dignity of a vulnerable individual, he would routinely be placed at the receiving end of the socio-politico-economic brutality. The vulnerable, susceptible and yet non-conformist individual in Tennessee Williams is "nobly disciplined" as a member of Ortega Y Gasset's "selective minority" making "great demands on themselves" and engages himself in some kind of feeble confrontation against "the mass" that "sets no value on itself—good or ill..." (qtd. in Sahu 86). Some of the classic instances of this confrontation occur in the best drama of Tennessee Williams, in *The Glass Menagerie, Cat on a Hot Tin Roof, A Streetcar Named Desire* and *Sweet Bird of Youth*.

The Glass Menagerie is as much a tragedy of Tom as of Rose. Tom, who is "an itinerant dreamer like his creator, is trapped not only in a monotonous warehouse job but also by responsibilities to his mother and sister" (Falk 47). Tom is trapped inside two insurmountable social constructs. At the warehouse, an agency of the society's economic structure, he is an unwilling menial worker caught in the hierarchy-ridden system. At home, he has a nagging mother and a neurotic sister. The construct of the family burdens him with responsibilities in the absence of his father. He has to earn for his people and has also to find a marital match for his sister. His mother, Amanda, in some ways represents the puritan arm of the construct of religion. She believes that Christian adults should be concerned exclusively with things of the mind and spirit and give up words like instinct for monkeys and pigs:

> Amanda: Man is by instinct! Don't quote instinct to me! Instincts is something people have got away from! It belongs to animals! Christian adults don't want it!
>
> Tom: What do Christian adults want, then, mother?
>
> Amanda: Superior things! Things of the mind and the spirit! Only animals have to satisfy instinct! Surely your aims are somewhat higher than theirs! Than monkeys—pigs—. (*Menagerie* 260)

Quite Obviously, Tom is trapped in the 'triple prisons' of social, economic and religious constructs. Moreover, he is the character in the play suffering an amphibious existence between the realistic and the non-realistic. He informs the audience in his introductory monologue that "the most realistic character in the play", "an emissary from the world of reality"...is Jim O' Conner (235). Tom employs his own, ingenious devices to flout the norms of the constructs he is trapped in. At workplace, a typical domain of business activity, he would indulge in writing poetic compositions on shoe boxes to such an extent that he would be nicknamed Shakespeare by his nearest colleague. Since imaginative literature is least compatible with business involving buying and selling, Tom's poetic creativity at the warehouse would amount to a subtle revolt. At home, his revolt is two pronged—he would insist on reading D.H. Lawrence and would speak of his love for adventure. Tom refuses domestication by first bringing in D.H. Lawrence, to the utter discomfiture of his mother, and then by talking of adventure and instinct. The following piece of conversation between him and Amanda illustrates his non-conformism, of which he is convinced:

> Tom: I like a lot of adventure.
>
> Amanda: Most young men find adventure in their careers.
>
> Tom: Then most young men are not employed in a warehouse.

> Amanda: The world is full of young men employed in warehouses and offices and factories.
>
> Tom: Do all of them find adventure in their careers?
>
> Amanda: They do or do without it! Not everybody has a craze for adventure.
>
> Tom: Man is by instinct a lover, a hunter, a fighter, and none of those instincts are given much play at the warehouse. (*Menagerie* 260)

What Tennessee Williams does through this argumentative conversation is the "questioning of domestic values" and the articulation of "a negative view of domesticity as incarceration..." (Gross in Kolin, *Undiscovered Country* 128). Tom defies "domesticity" and surmounts "incarceration" by going "the longest distance between two places", by descending the steps of "this fire escape for a last time" and "attempting to find in motion what was lost in space..." (*Menagerie* 313).

In *Cat on a Hot Tin Roof,* Brick Pollitt's refusal to fall in line with the norms of the constructs of family and sexuality is conspicuously obvious as compared to Tom's feeble though subtle revolt in *The Glass Menagerie.* However, unlike Tom, Brick has a sympathetic and responsive being in Big Daddy. Curiously enough, Big Daddy becomes not only his confidante but also a co-crusader of sorts, who, "with his son Brick, relentlessly pursues the truth, despite the mendacity and deception that hide it" (Griffin 143). Brick's manner of revolt is not subtle, but it is quietly defiant. When Margaret demands his love, he tells her to "take a lover"; when Margaret reveals to him her one instance of the indiscretion of adultery, he holds his head "unnaturally still"; when Margaret expresses her discomfort about the relationship between him and Skipper, he says that "not love with Maggie" but "friendship with Skipper was that one great true thing" (*Cat on a Hot Tin Roof* 15, 26-27). A man telling his wife to take a lover, a man keeping cool at his wife's adultery, or a man saying that he respects his homosexual relationship—all these can quite easily be seen as instances of the non-conformism of a serious nature. Brick's revolt has, after all, a diagnosis—"disgust" (*Cat* 56). In their conversation spread over most of the second Act, Brick and Big Daddy manage to discover the source of the former's "disgust" and latter's "frustration":

> Big Daddy: Lying, have they been lying? About the report from the clinic? Did they, did they—find something?—Cancer. May be?
>
> Brick: Mendacity is a system that we live in. Liquor is one way out and death's the other.... I'm sorry, Big Daddy?... being almost not alive makes me truthful—I don't know but anyway—we've been friends.... And being friends is telling each other the truth.... (*Cat* 69)

Now, having learnt the truth about each other, each of them has a mate in the other. There is a vital suggestion in their mutual sympathy, consideration and even candidness. Both are fighting—Brick against mendacity, and Big Daddy against cancer. By a slight application of somewhat mathematical substitution, it can be proved that mendacity is cancerous, and is as much dangerous and incurable. It doesn't require stating that both have to succumb—Brick to "mendacity" and Big Daddy to "cancer". At the Curtain, Brick can be seen surrendering to Margaret.

A Streetcar Named Desire is a unique case of the interaction, though brief, of the two extremes of conformism and non-conformism, represented respectively by Stella and Blanche. Interestingly, however, the drama in *Streetcar* emerges out of a conflict between Stanley and Blanche with Stella nearly in the background as a mere onlooker. As Blanche enters the play, she has dubious antecedents and a character that would be disproportionate with 'Elysian Field', the locality in the poor quarters of New Orleans where Stella lives with her husband. 'Elysian Fields', in its ordinary sense is a 'place or state of perfect happiness', and Blanche's arrival creates a disturbance that only grows in magnitude until she is almost evicted at the tragic close of the play. Blanche, in all probability, has turned an unconscious non-conformist after the death of her homosexual husband. Purportedly in need of help, she looks a woman with disruptive tendencies at least from Stanley's point of view. The disruption she causes is not contained in anything violent, but in her very incongruous appearance: "She is daintily dressed in a white suit with fluffy bodice, necklace and ear-rings of pearl, white gloves and hat, looking as cocktail party in the garden district" (*Streetcar* 117).

Though her appearance suggests that she should be a delicate creature, she is exceptionally headstrong and resolute in trying to coax Stella into a discord or confrontation with Stanley. While doing so she is at the best of her argumentative skill:

> Blanche: I have to plan for us both, to get us both-out!
>
> Stella: You take it for granted that I am in something that I want to get out of.
>
> Blanche: I take it for granted that you still have sufficient memory of Belle Reve to find this place and these poker players impossible to live with. (*Streetcar* 161-62)

In spite of a noticeable degree of sibling feeling between the two, this attempt of Blanche to incite Stella grows into an interesting encounter between the one who has joined a system with complete dedication and the other who wishes to disrupt it. The encounter doesn't last long. Stella's 'pragmatic' wisdom and dedication to her marriage is strong enough to withstand Blanche's effort. Instead of prolonging the argumentation, Stella brings it to an end by giving it a turn unexpected and stunning for Blanche. She bluntly and forthrightly tells Blanche that the sheer physicality of her relationship with Stanley is so precious to her that it renders every other consideration immaterial. To protect his household from a possible disruption, Stanley comes out in the worst form of animalistic ferocity. The manner in which he protects his relationship with Stella is downright brutal and unsparing. His first and persistent instinct is to crush Blanche, who suggests a "moth". As "the defender of the hearth and home", Stanley acts against this "hysterical intruder" with his "animal vigor, realism and solid connection to the living present" (Boxill 80).

Blanche cannot stand up to the requirements of this pitched battle which results from Stanley's commitment to his motive of having her out and away. Blanche loses, tragically surrendering herself to "the kindness of strangers" (*Streetcar* 225). Her loss, however, is not due to the single reason of Stanley's aggression. There are two accompanying factors: Stella's attitude and her own somewhat self-annihilating tendency. Stella, perhaps, knows intuitively that sexual union is a sure way to defeat separateness. She does not mince words in telling Blanche that what happens between her and Stanley "as a man and a woman in the dark" leaves everything else "seem—unimportant" (162). Blanche contributes to her own tragedy by entertaining desires that quite resemble death wish. She finds the sky so "pretty" that she feels she "ought to go there on a rocket that never comes down" (141). Again, towards the end of the play, she expresses a desire to spend "the rest of her (my) time" and "die on the sea" (220). The more popular viewpoint about Blanche passes her off as a victim suffering with Stanley as the predator. But there have been quite a few critical interjections showing her in the light in which she has just been studied. A representative instance is that of Roger Boxill, quoted nearly a paragraph ago, calling her a "hysterical intruder".

The non-conformist in Tennessee Williams demands nothing more than the sympathy of those who have seen him. The demand and the need is very clearly and representatively enunciated by Chance Wayne at the close of *Sweet Bird of Youth*: "I don't ask for your pity, but just for your understanding—not even that—no. Just for your recognition of me in you, and the enemy, time, in us all" (111). The appeal comes from the one who has lost his battle against a socio political system with its relentless perpetrators. Desperately eager to get his love in Heavenly, he finds himself up against Boss Finley, one of those relentless perpetrators of the unfair socio political system. Instead of his love, he gets threats of castration and a gang of Boss's henchmen on his trail. Princess Kosmonopolis, a retired Hollywood star under a disguised name, to whom Chance clings, proves another perpetrator of the system. In spite of all his persuasions and even attempts at blackmail, he fails to secure anything for himself at Hollywood. Having lost his struggle against the system, Chance is already castrated psychologically; and his physical castration is imminent after the curtain. Of all the non-conformists of Tennessee Williams, Chance Wayne has arguably the worst fate to suffer.

The definite stream of non-conformism in Tennessee Williams, particularly in his later works, has an antecedent in his own experiences. The stream is noticeable in his early stories and it grows to prominent proportions after his visit to Mississippi in late 1955 for Elia Kazan's filming of the screenplay *Baby Doll*. The screenplay, which in fact is the screen version of *27 Wagons*, pointedly criticizes the prejudice against foreigners, especially Italians; and, Williams's criticism of this prejudice in the play is reflective of his "interest in this nationality during the years" (Watson 184). The protest against the inane constructs is first put up by the individual non-conformists of his early writings including stories. This protest later reaches a lonely revolt in *Gnädiges Fräulein*, where Fräulein in seen determinedly and singly engaged in a courageous and defiant struggle against the Cocaloony birds that have a definite symbolic significance and an allegorical meaning. On the basis of the evidence shored up here, it can safely be contended that the thematic strand of non-conformism, socio-political and religious, runs throughout the works of Williams.

Steadily moving through the creative repertoire of Tennessee Williams, a definite religious pattern can be seen emerging and getting settled as an inseparable part of the author's creativity. Though deeply religious in his own way, he brings in "the absence of God or a savior" as a "major theological issue" in his writings (Presley 33). From the Godlessness of the short stories, to the agnosticism of his first Broadway success (*The Glass Menagerie*); from *Menagerie* to the vociferous call for faith in God's systems in *The Small Craft Warnings;* and from there to the final assertion of faith in *The Red Devil Battery Sign*—there can be seen a steady growth of Tennessee Williams's religiosity through all these phases and stages. The Godless world of the short stories is the farthest removed from religious thinking. Generally, the doing-and-suffering individual is in some kind of pre-religion state in the stories. That doing-and-suffering individual in the stories of Williams is usually far enough from the pale of practiced religion; and, therefore, usually follows instincts. Far from any religious principles and free to follow one's instincts, Williams's individual is free to exercise his free will (like Adam in Eden) and, thereby, to raise or damn himself. The theory of 'free will' that has been cited to explain Williams's individuals in stories is "that of St. Augustine, which is that of the Church as a whole" (Lewis 66). The application of the theory explains, quite logically, the perversion-prone psyche of the individual in Williams's stories. He prefers to go the other way rather than choosing to arguably cultivate and equally arguably civilize himself by bridling and harnessing his instincts.

One of the stories, "The Mysteries of Joy Rio", moves deep into the dark recesses of the psyche of the protagonist to such an extent that it nearly assumes the character of a weird ghost story. There is an interesting parallel to note here—the narrative enters the dark recesses of Pablo Gonzales's psyche much in the same manner in which Pablo enters the dark recesses of the upper, unlit galleries of the third rate movie theatre (Joy Rio). Pablo Gonzales, whose shady existence the story describes, contracts his homoeroticism from his employer and mentor, Emiel Kroger. In the course of time, his eroticism becomes his sole passion and pursuit to alleviate his loneliness. He proves a successor to Emiel Kroger in every possible meaning and connotation of the word. Not only does he inherit Kroger's worldly belongings, but also his shady passion. Through his deathbed confessions, Kroger had succeeded in transmitting to Pablo everything he had in his being:

> Much of the final months of the life of Emiel Kroger, increasingly dimmed by morphia, were devoted to these whispered confessions to his adored apprentice and it was as if he had breathed the guilty soul of his past into the ears and brain and blood of the youth who listened. (*Collected Stories* 102)

The site for the practice of this tabooed eroticism could be no better than the dark upper-galleries of an old opera house converted into a cheap theatre catering to a particular taste. Something weird occurs when Pablo has spent a lifetime of the practice of this less familiar kind of sexuality, which, in the course of time, he finds "almost as unreal and basically unsatisfactory as an embrace in a dream" (*Collected Stories* 104). He catches the same malignant disease that Emiel Kroger had died of; and, when it is time for him to die, it is the ghost of Emiel Kroger that quietly leads him out of life. The world of Pablo and Emiel has been so dark, so shadily infected, that God's grace would never reach it. The mentor and his apprentice have never been touched by anything religious, not even a normal sense of guilt and penitence. They have, in the quintessential Christian sense, chosen to 'fall' by indulging in things proscribed by the accepted and adopted norms. Restraint is one of the means by which a person can cultivate himself and rise; and restraint is what Emiel Kroger and his apprentice have cast away to 'fall'.

"One Arm" written about three years after "The Mysteries of Joy Rio", shows a crippled man willfully rejecting and refusing the "Consolation of Faith" (*Collected Stories* 183). The case is unusual because it involves a man condemned to the electric chair. The death sentence against Oliver, the one-armed protagonist, is the result of a somewhat biased trial intended to shield a racquet of influential people involved in the making of pornographic films. As a convict, Oliver has some sympathizers who feel that he is "the archetype of the Savior Upon The Cross who had taken upon himself the sins" of his exploiters (*Collected Stories* 179). The unusual thing about his rejection of 'faith' is that it is done in the face of death. Such expressions as "eternity", "transitory existence" and "threshold to something Immense beyond" is cant, "bull" to him (*Collected Stories* 186). Oliver, in refusing the "Consolation of Faith", has chosen to fall out of the reach of the redemption from the Original Sin and from the possibility of priestly benediction. His refusal is a voluntary, self-imposed excommunication and a rejection of God's grace.

"The Kingdom of Earth", a short story published in 1954 (which carries the plot and characters for a play later with the same title), provides a solution to the problem of spirituality for an individual. This can well be a solution for the reader looking for spirituality or its elements in Tennessee Williams's short fiction:

> Talking about salvation I think there's a great deal of truth in the statement that either you are saved or you aren't and the best thing to do is find out which and stick to it. What counts most is personal satisfaction, at least with most people, and God knows you'll never get that by straining and struggling for something which you are just not cut out for. (*Collected Stories* 368)

This is how the narrator and the main character in the story settle the issue of spirituality and faith for himself. The narrator and the character, Chicken, know quite well what he is "cut out for", and decide not to strain for salvation. The narrative takes up, indirectly, the issue of injustice suffered by people born outside legal marriage. There are two apparent things in whatever Chicken does, says or thinks: a quiet acceptance of his lot and, ironically, a straightforward rejection of things spiritual. He feels that he would never face any spiritual problem because he has "no gates of the soul got to close on the body and keep the body out" (*Collected Stories* 373). He lives, therefore, on his physical instincts till he has "everything in [my] life straightened out" (378). Having seen to it that his consumptive brother dies uncared for, he marries his widow whom he has already been steady with. His conscience is so clear and straight about it: "I don't ever worry about them spiritual gates the preacher said to shut. Not having no gates can save you a lot of trouble" (378). His rejection of acknowledged faith may have two interpretations: having been rejected by society, he does not find it obligatory to espouse a system of faith devised by it; or he retaliates for having been treated as a sub-human being.

The absence of religious faith or its rejection, so apparent in the short stories of Tennessee Williams, is not so overtly available in the plays. On the contrary, the early plays almost begin to express the need of benediction, of cultivation through socio-religious codes. It has already been illustrated that Val Xavier in *Battle of Angels* provides an unprecedented unification of the principles and messages espoused and held forth by St. Valentine and Jesus Christ. Again, it has also been illustrated earlier that the play was rejected by its first audience at Boston because their understanding and vision could not measure up to the width and breadth of Tennessee Williams's highly visionary, incorporative and non-puritanical concept of Christianity. As pointed out earlier, one of the most unequivocal statements about the need to rise above the world of animal instincts is made by Amanda in *The Glass Menagerie* when she tells Tom to leave instinct for monkeys and pigs. If *Battle of Angels* designates the romantically heightened and broadened view of Christianity, *The Glass Menagerie* displays the puritan.

Summer and Smoke, a major presentation after *Battle of Angels* (1940) and *The Glass Menagerie* (1945), significantly brings together the worlds of instinct and spirituality. This definitive statement can be logically averred on the basis of the evidence and arguments visibly lodged in the play. From an objective point of view, *Summer and Smoke* seems to be underlining the impossibility and improbability of any compromise between the two. At the start of the play, John Buchanan and Alma are stationed at the opposite ideological and emotional extremes from each other—John as a man obsessed with an 'anatomical' perception of things, and Alma, as her name suggests, with the spiritual. Unknowingly driven by their love for each other, the two start unconsciously drifting towards each other's extreme obsessions. They cross each other, midway, each failing to recognize the other. Each one of them ends up at the extreme previously represented by the other. The tragedy resulting from the impossibility of conciliation between the two extremes is stated thus by Alma:

> You've come around to my old way of thinking and I to yours.... I came here to tell you that being a gentleman doesn't seem so important to me anymore, but you're telling me I've got to remain a lady. (She laughs, rather violently). (*Summer and Smoke* 247)

Then comes the finale of Tennessee Williams's personal religiosity and spirituality in *Small Craft Warnings* in 1972. This final settlement of Williams's religiosity is significantly revolutionary in view of his conversion to Roman Catholicism nearly three years before, on 10 January 1969. Doc in the play, almost a spokesperson for the author or his alter ego, turns a near heretic by announcing that he is "going to deliver a new

Messiah". Further, Doc says that "God is a black man with no light on his face" (250). The mission of the "new Messiah" can be read in what Doc says about birth and death as "holy miracles". The mission would be to liberate human life from all the unnaturalness that surrounds it to bring man close to nature so as to enable him to look upon instincts as the creation of God. The 'new Messiah' would dismantle the obscurity created by the "irrelevancies and irreverencies of public worship" (*Small Craft* 250).

Doc in *Small Craft Warnings* is as much an alter ego of Tennessee Williams as Sebastian and Shannon, respectively in *Suddenly Last Summer* and *The Night of the Iguana.* Sebastian finds his God in the strange spectacle of the carrion being eaten by birds of prey "diving down on the hatched sea turtles, turning them over to expose their soft undersides, tearing the undersides open and rending and eating their flesh" (*Suddenly Last Summer* 356). He intently watches this spectacle to get "a clear image of Him"; and keeps on watching till it is too dark to see, and then returns and says, "I have seen Him!" (357). Sebastian's God, therefore, operates somewhere in the Darwinian system where the big and the capable instinctively swoop down upon the hapless. Shannon's God in *The Night of the Iguana,* on the contrary, is a "senile delinquent," an "angry, petulant old man", "a bad-tempered childish old, old, sick, peevish man"..., the sort of old man in a nursing home who is "putting together a jigsaw puzzle and can't put it together and gets furious at it and kicks over the table". For Shannon, God, the "senile delinquent", has been "blaming the world and brutally punishing all He created for His own faults in construction" (303-04). Ever since he has been defrocked for a disgraceful act, Shannon has been touring "God's World", "collecting evidence" of his "personal idea of God" (304).

The images of God held forth by Doc, Sebastian and Shannon have the capacity to shock the believing out of their wits. More so, because the three (Doc, Sebastian and Shannon) are the creations of Tennessee Williams who tried to prove his credentials as a faithful Christian by converting to Roman Catholicism. However, the faith of Williams can be rationalized by locating it midway between the visionary procreative religion in *Battle of Angels* and the cruel in *Suddenly Last Summer* and *The Night of the Iguana.* The rationalization becomes almost imperative in view of his admissions about the two distinctly discordant strands in his own personality. In "Facts About Me", an essay included in *New Selected Essays: Where I Live*, edited by John S. Bak, Williams writes, "Roughly, there was a combination of Puritan and cavalier strains in my blood which may be accountable for the conflicting impulses I often represent in the people I write about" (65). The idea of envisaging and setting up a new religion is nearly mooted by Williams through Doc raving about the imminent possibility of the arrival of a "new Messiah". This is radically blasphemous from the conventional standpoint and is not much inconsistent with Bertrand Russell's view that religion is "not only intellectually but morally...pernicious," and that ethical codes are "not conducive to human happiness" (Russell 22).

A man torn between "conflicting impulses" of his own admission, Tennessee Williams creates characters that are impulsive and radical but try to stamp out that radical and impulsive streak in their personality. This acutely tense psychological strife forms the background of the various masochistic measures adopted by some of his characters in fiction and drama. The masochistic measures can even be looked upon as 'acts of penance'. The most outstanding example of masochistic penance in Williams's fiction can be seen in the case of Anthony Burns in "Desire and the Black Masseur". Tormented by some vague sense of guilt, he shuffles "from one kind of protection to another". He feels "more secure at the movies... where the darkness absorbed him gently" (*Collected Stories* 205). Accidentally, he comes upon "the principle of atonement" to assuage his sense of guilt. He finds his "atonement" in being sadistically massaged by a Negro at 'Turkish Baths and Massage'. An understanding develops between the two, the Negro and Anthony Burns, about the requirements of each other. While one is in "search of atonement", the other hates "white skinned bodies because they abused his pride" (209). The story culminates in an unexpectedly gruesome juxtaposition of cannibalism and priestly exhortations to "suffer, suffer, suffer!" (210). The juxtaposition becomes the occasion for some cruel humor:

> The preacher was not fully conscious of what he wanted, nor were the listeners, groaning and writhing before him. All of them were involved in a massive atonement.... The congregation could not remain in the building but tumbled out on the street in a crazed procession with the clothes torn open. The sins of the world are all forgiven, they shouted. (210-11)

Alongside this priestly exhortation is placed the actual cannibalistic act, which, at the same time, can be seen as the farthest possible precipitation of masochistic atonement:

> All during this celebration of human atonement, the Negro masseur was completing his purpose with Burns.... "You know what you have to do now?", the victim asked him. The black giant nodded. He picked up the body, which barely held together, and placed it gently on a clean-swept table. The giant began to devour the body of Burns. It took him twenty four hours to eat the splintered bones clean. (211)

Apart from this overtly horrific and gruesome instance of the masochism of Anthony Burns, there are quite a few in the short fiction of the author which border onto the territory of this psychic tendency. The Pharaoh in "The Vengeance of Nitocris", Jacob Brodzky in "Something by Tolstoi", Bud in "The Accent of a Coming Foot", Mrs. Meighan in "27 Wagons", Tina in "The Dark Room" and the narrator character in "The Angel in the Alcove" are some of the obvious examples of borderline masochism. The Pharaoh indulges in a willful desecration of the altar of goddess Osiris to invite the wrath of the Thebans; Jacob Brodzky immerses himself punishingly in reading to lose his relationship with the real world; Bud's shyness is self-deprecatory; Mrs. Meighan likes the sensuality of the sting of Vaccaro's whip; Tina shuts herself up in a dark room for having lost a lover; and the narrator character unconsciously likes the tragic travails around him in the rooming house. All these characters from the stories of Williams have, consciously or unconsciously, come upon a masochistically inclined 'principle of atonement' in their own different ways.

This tendency to injure or torture oneself is noticeably visible in the drama of the author too; the only difference being that the masochistically puritanical characters here are obvious examples in comparison to the peripheral ones in fiction. The representative cases are those of Val Xavier in *Battle of Angels* (and later in *Orpheus Descending*), Tom in *The Glass Menagerie,* Brick Pollitt in *Cat on a Hot Tin Roof* and Chance Wayne in *Sweet Bird of Youth.* The extreme example of this puritanical tendency is Eloi in *Auto-Da-Fé,* a one-act. Eloi is psychologically tormented by the awareness of his needs of the flesh going the unusual way. For quite some time, he remains vaguely conscious of some uncomfortable streak in his being. And then comes the shocking and devastating revelation when he happens to look upon a particularly 'perverse' photograph. That very moment he feels his face "scalded with acid", his hands blown up with "something exploded" (*Auto-Da-Fé* 144). He feels that he would "pluck out" his eyes "before they would look at that picture" (149). The purgation, the atonement, he employs is unimaginably horrible. He locks himself up in the cottage leaving his mother out and sets it on fire, consigning himself to the 'purification' him death by fire.

Among the other characters that choose the way to self-destruction, the most prominent is Val Xavier. He, a "virile artist, enters the Hell of the small southern town on the note of a Choctaw cry" and ends up "in a situation...far grimmer" (Nelson 169). Tom in *The Glass Menagerie* first engages himself in the self-destructive act of writing poetry at the cost of work at the warehouse, and then chooses to put himself in the suicidal situation of a fugitive. Brick Pollitt's suicidal instincts are absolutely conspicuous. His excessive drinking and voluntary celibacy are the instruments with which he punishes himself. Chance Wayne in *Sweet Bird of Youth* is irresistibly drawn to the place of his doom, St. Cloud, in spite of the threats of castration. The threats and the persuasion employed by Princess Kosmonopolis fail and, at the Curtain, he can be seen being surrounded by Boss Finley's henchmen. What would follow is predictable enough—castration rendering him incapable of a life through procreation. The representative male characters in Tennessee Williams find the world and their surroundings a puzzle beyond their emotional, intellectual and physical capacities. Routinely, therefore, they can be seen putting themselves into a fugitive-like unstable state. Being on the move, ironically, towards their own destruction, is their manner of coping with or escaping this puzzle. However, there is an interesting parallel to be noticed in the world of the female characters—they prefer to put themselves in various situations of an unstable mind. These two modes of response to the inhospitable atmosphere are the means by which Tennessee Williams manages a successful display of their fragmented, tortured psychologies. These symptoms of "the dislocated mind"—tendencies towards flight and confinement—help the author to depict these characters against a haunting environment, which is itself a "condition of their alienation and unhappiness" (Davis in Tharpe 192). The exact sense of what Joseph K. Davis states, in the specific context of *The Glass Menagerie*, is that the "dislocated mind" becomes the common "landscape" in the background to highlight the individual tragedy of Laura Wingfield. It can be observed and explained, however, that Davis's theory of "dislocated mind" can be successfully applied to all the representative cases of women characters in Tennessee Williams, in drama or in fiction.

"The Vengeance of Nitocris", again, offers an illustrative example of a mind that has been irreversibly dislocated by an irrepressible urge to seek revenge. As the Queen Nitocris broods upon her brutal method of revenge, she becomes quite oblivious of it's magnitude and destructiveness. In her psychic pursuit of it, she drives herself to an untimely death through suicide. The inordinately ambitious, young Mrs. Brodzky, in "Something by Tolstoi" chases her ambition almost dementedly. She ends up, eventually, destroying her idyllic marriage with Jacob. Irene's artistic passion and vision in "In Memory of an Aristocrat" falls outside the territory of the normal. She has an exceptional artistic perspective that opens to her the raw and terrific face of the surroundings. What she paints, therefore, is such phenomena as "pregnant women in soiled cotton dresses and bums sleeping in doorways, screaming strike workers, hideous scabs and bosses" (*Collected Stories* 85). She is "a furious girl... possessed of demon" and, therefore, has a decidedly destructive fate reserved for her (85). The scene she makes at the picture gallery is consistent with her demented or abnormal artistic makeup of the mind: "Like human tornado, she swept around the four walls, plucking the nice pictures down and tossing them onto the floor, hurling them at her pursuers or at the tea-table. The glittering percolator went over, the cut-glass bowl full of pale green sherbet followed right after it" (*Collected Stories* 91). Miss Kimball in "Oriflamme" has a reason to "become a little disoriented" because her hope has "died in a basement" of the city she lives in, her faith has "died in one of its smug churches" and her love has "not survived a journey across it". She becomes, consequently, a manic roamer driven by "that anarchy of the heart" which characterizes dementia more than anything else (*Collected Stories* 128-33).

In some of his late stories, Tennessee Williams focuses on the varieties of the manic condition of old maids, widows or lovely women unable to cope with the process of aging. These are the women who seem to have commanded a good degree of physical charm in their younger days. As they age, they, naturally, have to let go of their only prized possession. Elphinstone in "Happy August the Tenth", written in 1970, is one such woman. She feels that "middle age was not approaching on stealthy little cat feet this summer but was bursting upon her" (*Collected Stories* 465). She is a professional woman living in a shared apartment with another of her sort, Horne. The difference between the two exists only at the surface—while Elphinstone is more or less self-employed, Horne is an office worker. Every passing day is a grave reminder to them of their advancing years. The fear of this, or the efforts to escape it, has come to be expressed in a strange manner of morning greetings. At the start of the story, Horne greets Elphinstone "Happy August, the Tenth". After a whole day spent to decipher the sense and meaning of this strange greeting, Elphinstone finally recognizes the horrifying importance of it and, then, returns her greetings with a clear trace of exhaustion: "Elphinstone whispered Happy August,the Eleventh to Horne's kneecap in a tone of condolence" (476). A story written two-years later in 1972, "The Inventory at Fontana Bella", is a humorous and vivid description of the senile behavior of a rich old woman almost on the verge of death. She has lived alone ever since her fifth and last husband had died fifty years ago. There is a good amount of raucous and somewhat obscene humor in the description of her dreams in which she seems to be engaging in some physical interaction, probably intercourse, with Sebastiano, her last husband. Whenever she sends a cry of nostalgia (remembering Sebastiano) or presses the electric buttons by her bedside to summon her train of servants, attendants and other employees, there always is an air of a rather secret expectation—her death. This expectation gets inadvertently and involuntarily enunciated by her physician once when he enters her bed chamber, hoping that Isabella has "finally been stricken by a cardiac seizure". On seeing her bolt upright in front of her mirror, he blurts out, "Cristo, no, this creature is immortal" (*Collected Stories* 477). The crazed, demented old lady dies on board a hired boat while crossing a lake to Fontana Bella, making her excessively large train of employees heaving a sigh of relief: "A miracle has happened, the lady is dead" (483). Another story written in the same year, 1972, first shows a geriatric old woman keeping a tight grip on her granddaughter, Miss Coynte. Her age and related problems are no hindrance to her voyeuristic desire to discuss the scandals in the city. After her death, the story almost takes a somewhat picaresque turn. The remainder of the story, thus, becomes the description of Miss Coynte's passionate pursuit of her fetish. At the close of the story, Miss Coynte is an old spinster trying to recall and write about "the incalculable number of black lovers who had crossed the river with her from Tiger Town" (*Collected Stories* 501).

The geriatric female cases pointed out here develop almost into a category which is closest to the class of the Amazons thought of by Toni Wolff, a close associate of Carl Jung. This class, Wolff feels, "is characterized by the emphasis placed upon the individual's own personality and it's development within the limits of the objective cultural values of our time, quite independent of other persons and of instinctive or other psychic factors" (Wolff 10). It is possible to incorporate the non-geriatric females in Williams's short fiction, discussed a little earlier, into the class of Wolff's Amazons by relaxing the definitive boundaries. The certain candidates absolutely for this category in Tennessee Williams's drama are: Myra in *Battle of Angels* (and *Orpheus Descending*) and Princess Kosmonopolis in *Sweet Bird of Youth*. Mrs. Stone in the author's novella *The Roman Spring of Mrs. Stone* is also a strong candidate joining the category.

It can be emphatically pointed out here that the geriatric and non-geriatric female characters in the fiction of the author have been found to be carrying and suffering from the streaks of the landscapes of "dislocated mind", as has been explained and illustrated earlier by reference to the theory of Joseph K. Davis. Wolff's theory of the 'Amazons' and Davis's theory of "dislocated mind" do not seem to be anomalous with each other. However, it is important to understand that Wolff's categorization of the feminine psyche as Mother, Hetaira, Amazon and Medium sometimes falls short of applications to certain cases in Tennessee Williams. The glaring instances eluding and escaping an application of Wolff's categorization are Tina in "The Dark Room," Myra in "The Field of Blue Children", Rosa in *The Rose Tattoo* and Laura in *The Glass Menagerie*. They do not fit in any of the four categories envisaged by Wolff. The cases of these elusive characters, therefore, can best be illustrated and understood through reference to and application of Davis's theory of the "dislocated mind".

Talking about the Amazonian tendency, or that particular variety of psychological misdirection (or dislocation), the two women that readily come up for reference are Myra in *Battle of Angels* and Princess Kosmonopolis in *Sweet Bird of Youth*. The Amazonian streak has always been there in the mental framework of Myra of *Battle of Angels*, right onward from her childhood dreams of something tremendous to happen. The abnormal streak, in her girlhood, had made her dance all night, come home drunk at daybreak and tiptoe barefoot up the back stairs. Her perception of the elements in nature, too, had an abnormal color. The one thing that troubled her even that early was the manifestations of barrenness: "We had a fig tree in the back of our yard that never bore any fruit. We thought that it never would. I'd always pitied it so because they said it was barren. But it surprised us one spring. I was the one that discovered the first little fig. Oh, my God, I was so excited" (*Battle of Angels* 107). Grown up, Myra is equally excited about the life she carries in her womb. Almost as a replication of the history of the fig tree of her childhood, this pregnancy of hers has come very late, almost as a miracle. In her obsessive and lyrical state of mind, she is justified in treating her unborn child as a "Miracle" because it is the result of her relationship with Val Xavier (with due emphasis on the connotations of his name). Moreover, this "Miracle" has happened to her after a barren marriage with Jabe who, with his consumptive disease, resembles an image of death. In being drawn to Val Xavier, and in having an intimate relationship develop, Myra does something that would not be accommodated in the socio-religious ethos of the time. Her willing emotional and physical dedication to him can have more than a single interpretation. Her act involves a defiance of the socio-religious code, prompted and precipitated by her Amazonian streak or her obsession. Her desire to align herself with Val has a near suicidal inclination. The situation calls either for solution or for purgation. Purgation by fire is what follows.

Princess Kosmonopolis in *Sweet Bird of Youth* is a case with a wide variance from that of Myra who relates to Val Xavier in spite of the intermittently constant knocking of her husband above. The relationship of Princess Kosmonopolis has a sublimation that awards it a transcendental status. Aggression, in every manifestation of life is her abnormal, manic streak. A physical inferior to Chance Wayne, she marches a victory over him in a pitched battle. It is an impressive victory in view of her near complete dependence (physical) upon him. She puts on her boldest and unfazed face to counter Chance Wayne's attempt at blackmail. Having had a career at Hollywood, she knows, at least, the basics of a psychological warfare. Chance Wayne, at his best, is no better than a 'stud' for her. She points out the puerility of his attempt at blackmail when he tries to mouth such words as "narcotics department" of the FBI

> Princess: You are trembling and sweating... You see this part doesn't suit you, you just don't play it well, Chance... I hate to think of what kind of desperation has made you try to intimidate me, ME? ALEXANDRA DEL LAGO?... Put this away. And you leaky formation pen...when monster meets monster, one monster has to give way, AND IT WILL NEVER BE ME. I'm an older hand at it... (*Sweet Bird* 40-41).

Not only does she defeat him at his own game, employing the tricks of the same game, she also abandons him shamelessly on finding that he has embroiled himself in a suicidal struggle with Boss Finley.

Tennessee Williams writes in the Production Notes to *The Glass Menagerie* that it is a memory play that "can be presented with unusual freedom from convention". Writing further in the Notes, he includes specific instructions about the use of a particular "screen device", "the music", and "the light". The screen device, he states, "is to give accent to certain values in each scene", the music is to provide "emotional emphasis to suitable passages", and the lighting has to be "in keeping with the atmosphere of memory" (229 and 231). A scrutiny of this elaborate piece reveals a paradigmatic status and form awarded to memory and all its concomitants. Outside the 'Notes', in the play that follows memory can be seen functioning almost as a myth providing a structural basis to the play. Outside *The Glass Menagerie,* in the other successful plays and in his stories, memory interacts and intermingles with myths of various making. A logical conclusion, therefore, would be to call memory in Tennessee Williams either a mythical pattern or a device supportive to the pattern. Whether a pattern in itself or a supportive device, memory functions as myth in the plays and stories of the author. It functions as a recurring structural pattern, more exclusively in the plays of the author. An idyllic, demonic, or otherwise mythicized memory of a past event in the life of the protagonist is recounted in the course of each play, usually delivered in monologue by the protagonist himself or herself as part of the exposition at the play's beginning (Thompson 1). Drawing upon Northrop Frye's differentiation between 'idyllic' and 'demonic' memory, Thompson explains the functioning of the two in the context of Tennessee Williams's writings. The two kinds of memory represent two polar situations. The former, 'idyllic', is the protagonist's psychological quest to recapture a "romanticized past"; the latter, on the contrary, is his attempt to "escape or transcend a corrupt past" (Thompson 1-2). In either case, however, memory is mythicized to any possible degree.

An idyllic, mythicized memory provides a sustainable, structural framework in the short story "Sand". The story showcases a somewhat typical case of two elderly characters, a man and a woman, living a dual existence. Their present agony is both created and enhanced by the myth-like memory of their young days. Emiel, the paralyzed old man in the story, "sits brooding a great deal. He lies on the couch by the radio and hears nothing. The music is wasted. The comedians, the amateurs, the news. Reporters, and the symphony orchestras are all wasted on his ears" (*Collected Stories* 49). His existence is inseparably hitched to a time nearly fifty years ago, like his wife's. Both have their own, though related, reasons to remain connected with that far flung but well defined past very nostalgically. Except for the memory of that well defined past, Emiel is emotionally and psychologically dead; Rose, on the other hand, would draw upon the same well defined past:

> He sinks back onto the couch and she tucks the Indian blanket around him. It is the red and black Navajo blanket that they bought nearly fifty years ago on their honeymoon trip to the West Coast. She remembers how frightened she was, or pretended to be, of the grim looking Indians gathered around the station platform, how she squealed with delight over the turquoise bracelet and then with terror when the gesticulating grunting squaws formed a greedy circle around her, pushing things into her face. (*Collected Stories* 50)

In this situation, the red and black Navajo blanket is more than a relic from that past. It becomes a structural element serving as a vital and concretizing agent for the past hovering over the present. While so treating the blanket as a structural element, it would be necessary to look upon 'sand' as a symbol steeped with structural significance. The 'sand' of the West Coast seashore is now an active part of her mind that draws it's solace as well as tragedy by placing the past in perspective with the present. Routinely and involuntarily the memory of sand "sliding from his palm and trickling over her bare legs and arms" comes to her mind whenever she tries to go to sleep. The memory has become "timeless", and now (as it did then) "it forms a perfect arc through space" (50-51).

"The Vine", a story about a childless couple, involves a memory that is demonic as opposed to the idyllic in the case of 'Sand' where the elderly couple feverishly draws sustenance from a memory about something nearly fifty years past. In the case of "The Vine", the couple would like to get rid of something that haunts them. The revelation of Donald's infertility all of a sudden, alters the nature of their relationship. Donald's macho pride is suddenly transformed into a childlike dependence and insecurity. The structure of the story, therefore, has two distinct flanks on either side of the event of the revelation of Donald's infertility. The trauma and tragedy of Donald and his wife, Rachel, stem from their impracticable attempt to keep the present shut off. The memory of their happiness together is an unbearable torture now. The turning point between the present and the demonic past is represented poignantly enough by Tennessee Williams:

> But their relations had been altered by the discovery. They laughed to think what trouble they had taken all those years to avoid something that could not have happened. But the joke was on Donald, really, and it was hard to accept for that reason. For a while, the psychic trauma was so acute that he found it difficult to make love to Rachel. But Rachel understood it better than he. She won him tenderly back and gradually the humiliation faded from his mind and the things became almost the same as they had been before. (*Collected Stories* 138)

The terms idyllic and demonic vis-à-vis memory earn their significance by reference to the contrast they create. What needs to be noted is the fact that in either case, idyllic or demonic, memory creates an equally potent structural contrast. The difference, however, is that in the one case the person wilfully clings to it and in the other he desperately tries to escape it. It has already been seen that in "Sand" the elderly couple lives in the past, or its memory; but in "The Vine", the youthful couple tries to run away from it.

Memory-as-myth depends so much upon a system of compatible symbols. It scarcely needs any illustration that in the examples of the two stories treated above, 'sand' and 'vine' function as symbols in tandem with their respective mythicized memories. Though used quite admirably in fiction, this structural pattern reaches its bloom and fullest development in the situations of drama. The most readily available example is *The Glass Menagerie,* subtitled a 'memory play' by the author. "Consisting of seven memory scenes framed by the present time monologues of Tom Wingfield, the narrator of the play, and also a character in it, the play focuses on Tom's remembered experience of the single momentous event in the drab life of his mother Amanda and his sister Laura: the arrival of a gentleman caller, Jim O'Connor" (Thompson 13). Amanda's memory of that afternoon in Blue Mountain when she received seventeen gentlemen callers becomes the mythicized past. In the course of the play, the past, or the memory, is re-enacted and thus, gets shorn of it's myth like status. The re-enactment begins in second scene with Laura's entry meaningfully preceded by the lighted screen with the legend in these words: "Laura, Haven't you Ever Liked some Boy?" (*Menagerie* 241). As the play progresses, a gentleman caller is actually received by Laura. The arrival of Jim O'Connor is the re-enactment of Amanda's memory that now attains to the level of myth. It is to be pointed out here that the value of a myth is routinely preserved through it's periodic re-enactment in the form of a ritual. At the same time, a particular ritual tends to take away something from the original magnificence of the myth over a period of time. Thus, in the case of the *The Glass Menagerie,* it is a significant fall from seventeen to one, and from serious callers intent upon marriage to a caller already engaged to marry. Alongside the myth, degraded through re-enactment, is the symbol of the menagerie that is Laura's single occupation or obsession. It is more than obvious that the menagerie symbolizes the shattered dreams of Laura and Amanda, and even of Tom.

Contrasted with the idyllic memory of Amanda in *The Glass Menagerie* is the demonic one of *A Streetcar Named Desire*. Blanche's struggle and consequent tragedy originate out of her desperate efforts to escape the memory of her marriage with a "beautiful and talented young man" who turned out to be a "degenerate" (*Streetcar* 190). Since hers is a demonic memory, which she is trying to escape, the corresponding symbol is a 'light shade'. While the general purpose of the shade is to put off the glare of light, the particular purpose, unconsciously for Blanche, is to escape her unconscious sense of guilt. The shade may also signify her efforts to keep up a failed romance. The significance of the failed romance and the inescapable memory is represented through the violence involved in the tearing off of the shade by Stanley. It is helpful to put together two of Blanche's utterances to fully appreciate the symbolic value of the lampshade. First, she tells Mitch that she "can't stand a naked bulb any more than...a rude remark or a vulgar actor" (*Streetcar* 150). And then, three scenes later, she blurts out her unconscious fear of the glaring light:

> Blanche: When I was sixteen, I made the discovery—love. All at once and much, much too completely. I was like you suddenly turned a blinding light on something that had always been half in shadow... But I was unlucky. Deluded. (182)

Another piece of heavy symbolic value in the play is the repeated cry of the Mexican woman selling 'Flores'. Whenever the flower vase of Blanche, her dream world or fictitious world, receives a jolt, the cry rises in the background. The cry of "Flores para los muertos. Flores. Flores." reaches it's highest pitch and climax in Scene Nine when Blanche discovers that her developing relationship with Mitch has been cruelly dismantled by Stanley (206). As has already been pointed out in the context of *The*

Glass Menagerie, the structural pattern of the mythification of the past (or its memory) and its ritualistic re-enactment is repeated in *A Streetcar Named Desire*. The mythicized memory of Blanche's romantic marriage with Allan is ritualistically re-enacted through the short lived romance of Blanche and Mitch, thwarted just short of marriage. Again, the mythicized memory of Blanche suffers substantial degradation through the ritual of the re-enactment.

The structural pattern of memory first presented as myth and then demythicized, as observed in the four instances studied above (two stories and two plays), continues through the drama of Tennessee Williams produced in the prime of his career in 1950s and 60s. However, the pattern becomes somewhat convoluted and complicated in the case of such late works as *The Night of the Iguana* and those following it. The demonic memory mythicized in *The Night of the Iguana* is that of Shannon's misdemeanor leading to his defrocking. The misdemeanor involves his physical relationship with a girl inside the church premises. How he tries to escape the demonic memory of the unfortunate incident is explained by his self-hypnotizing to be able to recall the event in words. Once he has talked about the incident, he is also able to recall his tirade against an obsolete religion with "theologies, the whole mythology of them...based on the concept of God as a senile delinquent" (*Iguana* 303). The demonic, frightening memory, which is being sought to be blacked out, is nearly re-enacted through the development of "the vibrations" between Shannon and Hannah (*Iguana* 322).

The foregoing discussion of memory, it's mythification and demythification, capitalizes substantially on two terms: idyllic and demonic (to refer to the nature of memory) as specified by Northrop Frye. While applying the terms to the nature of memory in Tennessee Williams's drama, Judith J. Thompson pointedly refers to such celebrated works of Frye as *The Secular Scripture: A Study of the Structure of Romance and Anatomy of Criticism: Four Essays* (Thompson 205).

A structural hallmark of Tennessee Williams's short stories is their sparseness of characters. Many of his memorable stories have plots with no room for a third character. "Sand", "The

Vine", "Desire and the Black Masseur" and "Something by Tolstoi" are a few of the obvious examples. Another important feature of his stories, from the point of view of structure, is the extension and reinforcement of a person's experiences by another who is usually much younger. The pattern or device appears very close to the system of the ritualistic re-enactment of memory observed in the stories and plays studied in the preceding paragraphs. In the "Mysteries of Joy Rio", for instance, the life of Pablo Gonzales is an extension of his patron Emiel Kroger's lifelong pursuit of homoeroticism. In "Miss Coynte of Green", the plan gets a further extension over a third generation. First, Miss Coynte lives a life of profligacy drawing upon the example of her grandmother. Then, in the later part of the story, she gloats over the profligate ways of her daughter born outside marriage. Decidedly, her happiness is the result of her unconscious sense of satisfaction to see her own existence receiving an extended duration through her daughter. Olga Kedrova in "The Mattress by the Tomato Patch" relives her various experiences with different lovers by renting out the rooms of her house to pairs of lovers for short periods. Her lenient and somewhat indulgent attitude towards the small damages made by these pairs is a strong indicator to the fact that she unconsciously observes a replication of her memory in these short-term affairs.

The structural system dependent upon the minimum number of characters becomes particularly noticeable in some of Tennessee Williams's one-acts and late plays. The notable examples are *I Rise in Flame Cried the Phoenix* (two characters); *The Last of My Solid Gold Watches* (three characters); *Auto-Da-Fé* (two characters); *This Property is Condemned* (two characters); *Talk to Me Like the Rain* (two characters); *Something Unspoken* (two characters); and *The Two Character Play* (two characters). In all of these one-acts, memory functions as a key structural element in the form of a myth. Almost without exception, all these have a mythicized past or memory providing a structural base for the characters to act upon.

A singular achievement of Tennessee Williams with regard of his use of a proper myth and it's recreation in the context of our time has been *Orpheus Descending*. The part of the Orpheus myth that becomes relevant in the play is the one relating to his adventure into Hades in search of his beloved Eurydice, separated from him by the bite of a poisonous viper. He manages to entice the rulers at Hades by his music and also manages a conditional release of Eurydice. The condition is that he would not look back till he is safely out of Hades. Unfortunately, he looks back a little too early—before Eurydice is out of the shades of Hades. The consequence is that he loses his beloved irretrievably. An incarnation of mythical Orpheus, and an alter ego of the author, is Val Xavier in *Orpheus Descending* (and also in *The Battle of Angels*). His arrival at Torrance Mercantile Store brings to mind (in the modern and, therefore, corrupted form) the descent of Orpheus into Hades with his lyre:

> ...Val enters the store. He is a young man, about 30, who has a kind of wild beauty about him... His remarkable garment is a snakeskin Jacket, mottled white, black and gray. He carries a guitar which is covered with inscriptions. (*Orpheus Descending* 302)

The relationship he develops with Lady Torrance is obviously reminiscent of Orpheus's love for Eurydice. He breathes life into Lady Torrance by generating love in her, and also by lifting the bane of barrenness upon her. He nearly rescues her out of the 'store', but fails at the last moment. Throughout the play Jabe lurks in the background as ominously as the dark powers of Hades. But, as it happens in the Orpheus myth, the Lady flies defiance at Jabe, a little too early:

> I've won, I've won, Mr. Death, I'm going to bear! (Then suddenly she falters, catches her breath in a shocked gasp and awkwardly retreats to the stairs. Then turns screaming and runs down then, her cries dying out as she arrives at the floor level. She retreats haltingly as a blind person, a hand stretched out to Val, as slow, clumping footsteps and hoarse breathing are heard on the stairs. She moans.) Oh, God! Oh God! (*Orpheus* 371-72)

Her 'hand stretched out to Val' would naturally evoke Eurydice's hand stretched out to Orpheus, who has just crossed over to the world out of Hades. The 'slow, clumping footsteps' and 'hoarse breathing' of Jabe, 'Mr. Death', again evoke the malicious powers of Hades.

As explained above, Tennessee Williams exploits the Orpheus myth to its maximum potential in *Orpheus Descending*. The echoes of the myth, however, are loud enough to transcend the scheme of a single play. The myth finds place in the scheme of things in both the short stories and the plays of the author. It gets a legitimate scope of application, though limited, wherever an itinerant and alienated character puts up a struggle against his hostile surroundings. The applicability and relevance of the myth generates out of two events in the Orpheus legend—his eventual failure to win his beloved back from Hades, and his ultimate dismemberment by the half crazed Maenads. The highly individualistic protagonists of Tennessee Williams, right from the Pharaoh in his early fiction to Gnädiges Fräulein in his late drama, suffer a wide variety of physical and psychological 'dismemberment' at the hands of their implacable circumstances and surroundings.

The onus in the preceding discussion has been on the specialized thematic structural elements in Tennessee Williams's writing. He has so arranged his material and so structured his writings as to bring into focus the inanity of several of our taboo infested systems. The foregoing discussion illustrates that many of his early works—like "The Vengeance of Nitocris" and *The Battle of Angels*—are, metaphorically speaking, literal conflagrations accordingly patterned and structured. They seem to suggest, like T.S. Eliot's "The Waste Land", that all that is decayed be consigned to water or fire to make way for the birth of new systems. It shouldn't be a mere coincidence that the story and the play destroy the inane socio-religious systems by consigning them to water and fire, respectively. The caretakers and perpetrators of tabooed religion in the story die by drowning in the deluge from the river Nile, a symbol of holiness, piety and preservation. The fire at the close of *The Battle of Angels* is a potential suggestion that the rotten and cruel socio-religious systems be turned to ashes. In Tennessee Williams, all those alienated characters ultimately overpowered by their surroundings are minor prophets in the structure being envisaged by their author. It is all bleak, yet there is a wild hope that this illustrious line of prophets will culminate in the birth of a 'new messiah'. It is the wild hope that gets a vociferous proclamation in the hallelujah by Doc in *Small Craft Warnings*.

4

Prelude to the "Great Outpouring": Stories into Plays

> For a long time, now, the poet had felt that his stories so far had been little more than preliminary exercises to some really great outpouring.
>
> (*The Poet*)

Tennessee Williams writes in his *Memoirs*:

> I had Saturday afternoons off from my job at Continental... I would go to the mercantile Library...and read voraciously there... And I would go home in a "service car"—to concentrate upon the week's short story. Of course all of Sunday was devoted to the story's completion. (37)

The period to which this piece of memory belongs is 1931-34, the author's bleak days as a menial employee at the International Shoe company. Obviously, the period is nearly six years before the first presentation of *Battle of the Angels* to the Boston people; and is nearly eleven years before the author scripted his first major Broadway success through *The Glass Menagerie*. Put together in a logical sequence, these facts produce a natural conclusion: that Tennessee Williams was consciously or unconsciously preparing himself, through his short stories, for the more demanding and classical genre of drama. Taking Williams's own word for it, his graduation from fiction to drama had been as natural as growing up from childhood into adolescence. He talks of this graduation through an interesting metaphor: "My conversion to theatre arrived as mysteriously as those impulses that enter the flesh at puberty. Suddenly, I found that I had stage inside me:

actors appeared out of nowhere; shaggy, undisciplined murmurs trooped out of the shadowy wings and took the stage over" ("The History of a Play", in Bak 15). Williams's drama, thus, has an evolutionary 'genetic' relationship with his fiction. The relevance and significance of the author's short fiction in relation to his drama can be indirectly brought into focus by quoting Thomas P. Adler's observation about his poetry:

> Perhaps because he wrote verse even before he turned to short fiction and drama (his poems, in fact, began to appear in little magazines as early as 1933, prior to his first plays being given amateur productions), Tennessee Williams often used poetry—his own and that of others—as *intertext* in his works for the stage. (in Roudané 114)

If his poetry serves as the intertext in his drama, his short fiction can be demonstrated as making the pre-text for it. The fact of this inter-relationship of Williams's fiction with his drama is borne out by the substantial correspondence between the author's creative expressions in the two genres. In many cases the correspondence is direct; and, it is indirect in some others. Many of his short stories have directly and ostensibly been overhauled into one-acts first and full length plays later. In order to create the right context for the following discussion, it would be worthwhile to enlist the short stories that have directly gone into the plays of the author. In the chronological sequence: "27 Wagons Full of Cotton" goes into the making of a play with the same title; "Portrait of a Girl in Glass" becomes *The Glass Menagerie;* "The Angel in the Alcove" undergoes a double transformation—*The Lady of Larkspur Lotion,* a one-act, and *Vieux Carré,* a full length play; "The Malediction" becomes *The Strangest Kind of Romance;* "The Yellow Bird" has two parallels—*Summer and Smoke* and *The Eccentricities of a Nightingale;* "The Night of the Iguana" serves as the basis for a play with the same title; "Three Players of a Summer Game" provides the major part of the plot and the core characters for *Cat on a Hot Tin Roof;* "Man Bring This Up Road" is metamorphosed into *The Milk Train Doesn't Stop Here Anymore;* and "The Kingdom of Earth" offers the draft for a play with the same title. This long sequence of the texts almost functioning as stories-as-drafts leading to plays, which lead to revised plays on some occasions, demand a close study of the many shades of inter-relationships growing in the process of the transformation. For any such study to be viable and worthwhile, it is necessary to individually take each instance of the transformations for a detailed analysis rather than taking all of them as a jumble of 'provisional studies' and resultant plays to make some general observations. The ensuing discussion, therefore, is concerned with the evaluation of these individual stories and the emanating plays. Such a study of the short stories and the corresponding plays offers ample insight into Williams's major themes of the conflicting worlds of flesh and spirit, time and mortality, and much more including the paradoxes and non-conformism discussed in earlier chapters.

First published in a journal and now a part of Williams's *Collected Stories*, the story "Twenty Seven Wagons Full of Cotton" opens on an uncomfortably hot September afternoon somewhere in the tropical region of Arkansas. The brief description of the landscape and the sounds emanating from the ginnery across the coppery fields of Johnson grass evoke an atmosphere of lethargy. This languid afternoon scene is peopled by two characters—Mrs. Jake Meighan and her guest from the nearby Syndicate plantation. The guest is here on business, waiting for his twenty-seven wagon loads of cotton to be ginned at Mr. Jake's ginnery. This pretty big piece of business has come Jake's way as a result of a fire destroying the ginnery of the plantation. After providing these primary and necessary bits of information about the situation, the story turns to the two individuals and their interaction. Hereafter, the story enters the description of the syndicate man's advances and Mrs. Meighan's languid and half-hearted resistance. The narration assumes a comic vein by repeatedly bringing into focus the physically disproportionate character of the two:

> "Aw, I know you big women!"
>
> "What makes you rub it in so much about me bein' big? You think I don't know it? Jake says that I'm the biggest woman in this part of the state!"

> "I never seen one bigger", said the syndicate man.
>
> "You're a shrimp, that's what you are. You're no bigger than a flea". The man laughed.
>
> "You're no bigger than an elephant. And even elephants have fleas". (*Collected Stories* 45)

The story ends with a clear suggestion that the big, dull woman has surrendered to the agile, little man's sexual advances. Quite obviously, the story has a very slender plot with nothing substantial about it. As it closes, the story turns out as a comic tale of the seduction of a big woman by a man "hardly more than half her size" in listlessly dull surroundings (45). Judging from the technical perspective, however, the story can be seen carrying a couple of remarkable qualities. First, there is a linguistic mode which underlines and highlights the indolence of the ambience, which serves as one of the two catalysts in the detestable yet comic process of seduction. The other catalyst is the cotton lint afloat in the atmosphere. A noteworthy quality of the story is the optimum explication of the dramatic element of conversation which livens up the otherwise stagnant plot. The story has a carnal character and a corresponding turn of phraseology and linguistic structure. It has an instinctive simplicity and demonstrates the overwhelming and, sometimes, destructive nature of passion. The catalytic functions of a hot afternoon indolence (in Arkansas), cotton and a tinge of sadomasochism in the story can be illustrated through a piece:

> Feeling a bit faint, she brushed the fuzz of cotton lint from her moist cheeks and leaned back in the swing which she kept lazily in motion with the lopsided heals of her white Kid slippers.... A swarm of flies was buzzing around her. The little man from the syndicate plantation kept brushing them off with his riding crop. Sometimes he struck her bare legs so smartly that it left a small red mark. (44)

As the plot of the story travels to a one-act play with the title unchanged (except the use of numerals to represent 'Twenty Seven'), it gathers dimensions and substance. Of the three scenes in the play, the middle one is a development and adaptation out of the story; the first and the last are extensions on either side of it. As in the story, the middle scene is the dramatization of the happenings on a particularly hot afternoon somewhere "near Blue Mountain, Mississippi" (*27 Wagons* 03). The first scene, an extension on one side, brings in the fire and the destruction of the plantation ginnery. The third and the last scene, which is an extension on the other side, adds a logical conclusion to the plot. The dubious and the surreptitious activity of the first scene gets an explanation in the middle and a conclusion in the last. At the opening of the play, Mrs. Meighan is seen surprised over her husband's sudden disappearance for a while. Before he returns from his undisclosed business, the Syndicate Plantation is already on fire. What passes between Jake Meighan and his wife in the rest of the scene, half discloses the cause of the destructive fire at the Plantation. There is a meaningful desperation on the part of Jake to keep the purpose of his brief disappearance a secret:

> Jake: I didn't go off!
>
> Flora: You certainly did go off...
>
> Jake: If you got sense you keep your big mouth shut!... (standing in front of her and gripping her neck with both hands) Look here! Listen to what I tell you!
>
> Flora: Jake!... Lem'me go!
>
> Jake: I ain't been off the Po'ch!...Not since supper! Understand that, now. (*27 Wagons* 06)

Flora Meighan, however, is not the kind of woman who would keep the secret long. In the middle scene, Silva Vaccaro, the superintendent of the Syndicate Plantation extorts a divulgence from Flora through his shrewdness and veiled threat of beating. It is not so much the shrewdness of Vaccaro as the stupidity of Flora that leads to the divulgence. Straightaway, Vaccaro decides that "it's no use crying over a burnt down gin" and that he would employ "the principle of tit for tat" (22). At the start of the third and concluding scene, late that evening, Flora Meighan is seen at the front porch with her appearance "ravaged". She is not properly dressed and there are "dark streaks on the bare shoulders", and a "dark trickle, now congealed, descends from one corner of her mouth"—Silva Vaccaro, obviously, has put to use the principle in combination with "the good neighbor policy". (17 and 33)

As stated earlier, the plot grows in dimensions and substance as it undergoes transformation from the fictional to the dramatic. The growth in dimensions and magnitude is entirely dependent upon the extension of the story line which is manifest in the first and the last scenes of the play. The more significant aspect of the transformation, however, is the growth in the substance of the plot. The flimsy tale of a sordid seduction in the process becomes a play with a strong socio-economic thematic focus. Why would Jake Meighan indulge in arson to destroy the Syndicate Plantation's Cotton gin? The question hangs in abeyance till it is logically and rationally addressed in his statement in Scene three of the play:

> Flora: I think it was a mistake.
>
> Jake: What was a mistake?
>
> Flora: Fo' you t' fool with the Syndicate Plantation...
>
> Jake: I don't know about that. We wuh kind of up against it, Honey. Th' Syndicate buyin' up all th' lan' aroun' here an' turnin' the Ole croppers off it without their wages-mighty near busted ev'ry mercantile store in the Two River country ! an then they build their own gin to gin their own cotton. I looked for a while like I was stuck up high and dry. (27 *Wagons* 35)

Jake's statement is a revelation of the socio-economic stand point in a direct way. The arrival of Syndicate Plantation, a symbol of industrialized agriculture, has jeopardized the survival of small farmers ("ole croppers"). This explains that the burning up of the cotton gin is the result of an act of arson, which has been carried out by Jake along with some others like him. The other thematic focus earned by the plot in it's reincarnated form in drama is the issue of a conspiracy of sorts. At the receiving end of this socio-economic and regional-cultural conspiracy are the Syndicate Plantation and it's Italian owners settled in New

Orleans. The theory of conspiracy regarding the fire assumes a formidable shape in a spoken rumination of Silva Vaccaro in Scene Two:

> Vaccaro: ... You feel what a lot an uncertain thing there are. Gins burn down. The volunteer fire department doesn't have decent equipment. Nothing is any protection... (lighting a cigarette): I shouldn't think you all would have been excited about the fire. (27 *Wagons* 18-19)

With the addition of these thematic strands, the drama plot gets purged of the ironical 'humor', which has been the significant characteristic of the plot in it's fiction form in the story. The play, instead, has a sour and bitter tone of satire in whatever Vaccaro says. His sensual swish of whip gets converted into the vengeful hiss of his speech. His sadism in the story is entirely transferred to Jake, and is displayed at length in the first scene. The palpability awarded to the locale at the opening of the play immediately engages our attention. Mrs. Meighan gets a name, Flora; and Jake Meighan becomes a 'present' character. The colloquialism in the play is quite in correspondence with the social, economic and regional ramifications. The fire destroying the cotton gin of the Syndicate Plantation remains accidental in the story; but in the play it is manifestly the result of a kind of racist sabotage. Every element deleted or added in the process of transformation helps to qualify a ruminative story into a substantial one-act play that is much closer to life than it's antecedent.

Tennessee Williams's first grand success on Broadway *The Glass Menagerie,* is the dramatization of "The Portrait of a Girl in Glass", a short story written some two years before the play. In it's independent capacity, it has the makings of a fine story apart from being the pretext to the play it provides for. The narrator in the story, Tom, who is "a poet" with a job in a warehouse", calls himself "an anomalous character slated for radical change or disaster" (*Collected Stories* 110). The "radical change or disaster" only gets disclosed towards the end of the story. The atmosphere that opens the story is portentous. The blackness evoked matches and corresponds with the catastrophe at the end. The alley between the apartment buildings, with the windows of Laura's room opening on it, turns into an image of imminent violence:

> We called this areaway Death Valley for a reason that seems worth telling. There were a great many alley cats in the neighborhood and one particularly vicious white chow who stalked them continually. In the open or on the fire escapes they could usually elude him but now and again he cleverly continued to run some younger among them into the cul-de-sac of this narrow areaway. (*Collected Stories* 111)

This unending violence, this non-stop hunting of the hapless by the strong, looms large upon the apartment inhabited by Tom, his sister and their mother. The constant shadow of violence upon the apartment resembles the effect of a curse or blight and, it appears, drives the inhabitants towards an inescapable doom. The three have already been deserted by the father, and the son is about to bound out. Laura's future is predictable in the light of her hypersensitive nature that verges onto a serious psychological disorder. The mother is hardly any better having suffered a steep descent from her happy and prosperous premarital past. The story is singularly the tragedy of Laura who can be called a fugitive in spite of her choice of her room as the ultimate refuge. She is neurotically and pathologically scared of positive motion, backward or forward: "She made no positive motion toward the world but stood at the edge of the water, so to speak, with feet that anticipated too much cold to move. She'd never have budged an inch, I'm pretty sure, if my mother who was a relatively aggressive sort of woman had not shoved her roughly forward" (110). Laura's tragedy could be of her own making from the reader's point of view. But her brother, the narrator, would have us look upon her case from a different perspective:

> I don't believe that my sister was actually foolish. I think the petals of her mind had simply closed through fear, and it's no telling how much they had closed upon in the way of secret wisdom. She never talked very much, not even to me, but once in a while she did pop out with something that took you by surprise. (112)

On close analysis, she appears a girl who has lost contact with time. Hers is a one dimensional world beginning with her glass menagerie and coming to an end with the "two pieces of fiction which she had received as Christmas or birthday presents" (113). She has developed a strong emotional attachment with one of the characters of the two novels. Her attachment with the character, Freckles by name, has grown to such a high-strung degree that she has nearly transported herself to that fictional world. There is an occasion when she briefly comes out of her static world to interact with Jim, a colleague of her brother at the warehouse. There is reason enough to believe that she has been persuaded to stir out of her shell, though temporarily, by the fact that Jim has freckles:

> "Oh – You have freckles!" Jim grinned. "Sure that's what my folks call me – Freckles!" "Freckles?" Laura repeated. She looked toward me as if for confirmation of some too wonderful hope. (*Collected Stories* 117)

Her terribly short lived hope intensifies her tragedy which has been the logical consequence of abnormal vulnerability. Though Laura is at the epicenter of the tragedy in the story, she is one of the two persons suffering from a pathological degree of shyness and vulnerability. The other person, obviously, is her brother Tom. The narrative begins with him and, also, ends with his wistful retrospections. What has saved Tom from going Laura's way is his maturing after being fired from the job. However, his tragedy is continual. Since Laura lives in a static world and doesn't have an existence away from the fictional lover of hers, she suffers in a situation with closed or limited dimensions. It may even be contended that she doesn't suffer at all, because suffering cannot, logically, exist in the decay free world of Laura's imagination. Tom, conversely, lives in a world that has traction with time and, therefore, is affected by the changes wrought by it (time). Suffering is the result of a change from the favorable to the unfavorable, from the conducive to the non-conducive, which can only happen in a non-static world fraught with the possibility of change. Suffering, therefore, is Tom's ultimate lot. The concluding lines of the story delineate Tom's tragedy, continual and unrelenting:

> But once in a while, usually in a strange town before I have found companions, the shell of deliberate hardness is broken through... I hear the tired old music my unknown father left in the place he abandoned... I see the faint and sorrowful radiance of the glass, hundreds of little transparent pieces...my sister's face appears among them—the night is hers!. (119)

The end of the story is the culmination of the constant retrospection. This is the point where the narrative first enters the present. The retrospection in the narrative brings in a sense of nostalgia and tragedy; the final arrival at the time present, on the other hand, creates an imminence and drama.

The Glass Menagerie, the amplification of "The Portrait of a Girl in Glass" into drama, makes the best of the retrospection with which the story ends. Williams designates *The Glass Menagerie,* a "memory play" with "unusual freedom from convention" (*Menagerie* 229). The resulting drama, therefore, consists "of seven memory scenes framed by the present time monologues of Tom Wingfield" (Thompson 13). What is observed in the play is much more than a simple truck between the past and the present. As Mary Ann Corrigan points out, "within the memory sequences, the further past" is evoked to act upon the present. The "further past" evoked in the play is Amanda's memory "about the countless gentlemen who called on her in her youth" (Corrigan 156). The significance of Amanda's memory (about the gentlemen callers) is that it is repeatedly evoked to decide and determine the standard for Laura. Besides, Amanda's past puts a misplaced emphasis on her presexual, virginal past. Implicit in Amanda's memory of her past are the demonic images of "separation, loneliness, humiliation, pain, and the threat of more pain" consequent upon the abandonment by the last gentleman caller, her husband (Frye, *Secular Scripture* 53). The past, thus, emerges as a vital structural component in the play. The character of 'the past' undergoes a transformation too as it moves from the fictional to the dramatic. In the story version of the plot, this structural element grows and progresses constantly up to a particular point of time when Laura permanently shuts the door on the present. "People in love," she says, "take everything for granted" (*Collected Stories* 119). The past in the story, thus, is encased and encapsulated into a static and inactive unit. But the drama version of the plot treats the past differently. The result being that it becomes a volatile and haunting entity instead of an inactive and encapsulated unit. That the past would keep on asserting itself, that it would keep on popping up in a sort of minor volcanic eruptions, is suggested by the very description of the dramatis personae at the start of the play:

> Amanda Wingfield (the mother): A little woman of great but confused vitality clinging frantically to another time and place...she is not paranoiac, but her life is paranoia...
>
> Laura Wingfield (her daughter): Amanda, having failed to establish contact with reality, continues to live vitally in her illusions, but Laura's situation is even graver...
>
> Tom Wingfield (her son, and the narrator of the play): A poet with a job in a warehouse. His nature is not remorseless, but to escape from a trap he has to act without pity. (*Menagerie* 228)

The specifications of the characters highlighted in the description serve to bring in the past as an important and live entity. The expectations of Amanda from her son and daughter have been established as a paradigmatic pattern by drawing upon the past. Following the expectations, there is a travesty of fulfillment culminating in the final loss. A paradigm made up of time past, the travesty of fulfillment and the ultimate catastrophe—this is the substratum that bears the weight of the elaborate structure of the play. The seven memory sequences (scenes) draw their sustenance from this elaborate structure which eventually enters the present through Tom's reminiscence at the close of the play.

Throughout this seven scene drama, there is an ever growing tension between the supposed ideal and the real. Laura's inability to draw gentlemen callers to the ghettoish residence is the reality in contrast to the supposed ideal presented by her mother several years ago in her 'Southern', palatial residence; Tom's easy and instinctual liking for Lawrencean fiction and for easy time out at movies is the reality haunted by the supposed ideal of "Celotex interior", "fluorescent tubes" and such puritanical slogan-like exhortations as "rise and shine! rise and shine!" (*Menagerie* 251-52). Again, the supposed ideal of "Christian adults" doing the "superior things! Things of the mind and the spirit" has jarring antagonism with the reality of Tom's liking for adventure (260). The high point of the constant tension between the inevitably deficient reality and the paradigmatic ideal is arrived at in the last scenes of the play. The situation is that of the sameness of the names of the caller on the one hand and a high school mate of Laura on the other. Jim O'Connor is the name that calls up for Laura, the uncomfortable memory of her first love. The subtle yet substantial maladjustment between the time past and the present reality is suggested by Laura's inability to dump the unhappy memory of a failed love:

> Laura: There was a Jim O'Connor we both knew in high school—(Then, with effort) If that is the one that Tom is bringing to dinner—you'll have to excuse me, I won't come to the table.
>
> Amanda: What sort of nonsense is this? [...] were you in love with that boy?
>
> Laura: I don't know, Mother. All I know is I couldn't sit at the table if it was him. (277-78)

The catastrophe, however, comes in the last scene, when Laura and Jim discover that they had been together at high school. What follows the discovery is instant spark of affection between the two. The catastrophe begins to take shape—the two have two different attitudes to the affection that has come up. For Laura, it is a miraculous revival of a failed romance; but for Jim, the situation is that of a brother drawing his sister out of a pathological shyness. "I wish that you were my sister. I'd teach you to have some confidence in yourself", he tells Laura (304). Judged from this angle, the 'de-horning' of the unicorn immediately before this statement may have a heavy symbolic significance which is too obvious for explanation. The broken unicorn becomes "A—souvenir" for Laura to present to Jim. She has lost him a second time, and forever. It is important to note here that Jim in the play version of the plot has a greater connectivity with reality than his counterpart in the story version. In the play, Jim presents a temporary renovation of the past; whereas in the story, he is an incarnation of a one-armed, orphaned youth. The change or the adaptation in the play version is an inductive improvement from the technical and structural standpoints. A particular piece of music, by name 'the glass menagerie', and the motifs or 'legends' suggested to be projected on the backdrop of the stage, aid the memory based structure of the play. In the theatre version of the play, these 'legends' keep up a relationship with the past, and also intensify the antagonism between the reality and the ideal. Referring to them in the 'Production Notes' for the play, Tennessee Williams emphasizes their structural significance as the reinforcement of the spoken dialogue:

> The legend of image upon the screen will strengthen the effect of what is merely illusion in the writing and allow the primary point to be made more simply and lightly than if the entire responsibility were on the spoken lines. (*Menagerie,* Production Notes 230)

These structural adaptations apart, the drama version of the plot imparts a meaningful growth to the characters. The most appealingly important is the growth of Amanda from a nagging mother to "The Great Mother" of Neumann's description. "The great Mother" in Erich Neumann is a development through "the archetypal feminine" with all the associated aspects (Neumann 18). The two aspects of "the great mother" prominently represented through Amanda are 'femme fatale' and 'terrible mother', to Laura and Tom respectively. Amanda's suggestions to Laura to assume the ways of 'femme fatale' go nearly unheeded. Laura in the play is an embodiment of puritanical and ascetic shyness. The image that significantly matches her is that of "the cloistered nun, and the chaste virgin" (Thompson 19). There are some obvious suggestions in the course of the play to show the likeness between the cloistered nun and Laura. The frequency of such suggestions increases in the concluding scenes. Near the start of Scene six, for instance, she is described as "a piece of translucent glass touched by light, given a momentary radiance, not actual, not lasting" (*Menagerie* 274). Close to the opening of Scene seven, there is the image of candelabrum along with it's religious connections:

> Amanda: ...But sister is all by her lonesome. You go keep her company in the parlor! I'll give you this lovely old candelabrum that used to be on the altar at the church of the Heavenly Rest.... (290)

The image that brings Laura closest to the puritanical Christian principle of asceticism is that of the mythical unicorn. Of her entire collection of glass menagerie, the dearest to Laura is the unicorn. It is just impossible to miss the fact that unicorn has been the "the traditional emblem of chastity and the lover of virgins" (Frye, *Anatomy of Criticism* 152). The characterization and tragedies of Amanda and Laura in the play have been wrought at a palpably psycho-physical level. Tom's tragedy, in contrast, is convoluted and complex. He is a typically existential man, and his tragedy an existential one. He suffers by failing to integrate the primal, adventurous instincts of "a lover, a hunter, a fighter with the refined creativity of the poet (*Menagerie* 260). He also suffers by failing to live up to the ideals of the "Christian adults."

As the short story plot of "The Portrait of a Girl in Glass" evolves and transforms into the drama of *The Glass Menagerie,* it achieves a multi-dimensional growth. The most significant dimension of this growth has been the structural status and importance awarded to the past. While the story concerns itself with the simple past, the play makes the past a piece of memory with immense bearing on the present and uses it as a dramatic device. The immediate corollary of this development is the coming to life of Laura and Amanda along with her personal past. The playing version of the plot, thus, imparts a meaningful relevance to the past by evoking it in the context of the present. The single beneficiary of the developed structure and the revived past is the theme of the play, which is a family tragedy made out of three individual tragedies. Quite obviously, the broadened structure and the heightened thematic focus demand and cause, at the same time, a more life-like characterization. Consequently, Amanda becomes a more elusive character than her counterpart in the story. Tom in the story is somewhat distant and ineffectual; and, in the play he grows as and into the narrator-character with the important duty of making the final prophecy at the close.

The next case of the translation of fiction into drama is that which connects "The Angel in the Alcove" with a very late play, *Viuex Carré*. The story carries two special marks of identification—it belongs to what can be termed the 'New Orleans' repertoire of the author, and it is from what is generally known as his mature period as a story writer. It belongs to the period when it was still "largely conjectural" whether "he would be a great writer", but "his potential as a story writer" could be seen coming to the noticeable front (Vannatta 23). Very little happens in the story at the actual physical level; but a tremendously consequential movement from the one extreme to the other takes place on the psychological plane. It is a movement from the passionately clutched illusion to the realization of an intolerable reality. Excepting the narrator character, the story features three characters—Mrs. Wayne, a quick sketch artist and the landlady of the rooming house sheltering many such "dead beats" as these two. The story contains two scenes, one after the other, showing Mrs. Wayne and the artist with the landlady. The first is a tragic scene with a comic facade of Mrs. Wayne's maneuvering into the landlady's kitchen to get some stew. The description of this skillfully carried out act is in a comic vein. Yet, there is a tragic current flowing underneath. Mrs. Wayne, quite understandably, is a woman going almost half-hungry all the time for lack of means. Her hunger has added such sharp edge to her olfactory sense that she "gets a sniff of this cooking" even through tightly closed doors (*Collected Stories* 12). Right away, she enters the kitchen of the landlady "with a mottled blue and white saucepan held to her bosom coquettishly as a lace fan"; she carries with her, as always, a series "of horribly morbid or salacious stories" (121). Such is the charm and the enchantment of these stories that the landlady sees her in an unconsciously blind way, almost in a frozen attitude, "removing the lid from the stewpot and ladling out some of its contents into her saucepan"; and, the enchantment breaks only when Mrs. Wayne is quite "out of earshot" (122). In the second scene of the story, the consumptive artist is shown complaining to the landlady about bedbugs "as big as thumbnail!" The complaint brings back on him as a retort, the horrible reality that he has been refusing to see:

> Ho, ho, ho! You spit up blood all the time. I've seen you spit on the stairs and in the hall and on the floor of this bedroom. You leave a trail of it everywhere that you go, a bloody track like a chicken that runs with its head off. You hawk and you spit and you spread contamination. (125)

As the focus of the story moves from Mrs. Wayne to the consumptive artist, there is a violently quick move from the comic to the tragic. There is an interlude of sorts to separate the two. The interlude concerns the "strange goings on" between the narrator-character and the consumptive artist. There is nothing to mention about the happening except its homosexual nature. However, the witnessing of the episode by an apparition of the narrator's grandmother calls for a brief critical attention. It can quite logically and meaningfully be stated that the apparition is nothing more and nothing less than the projection of the narrator's conscience in the form of his grandmother's spirit. The argument obtains validity by the fact that the narrator tries to read an approval or disapproval of the act in the face of the apparition:

> I cocked an eye toward the alcove. Yes, she was there. I wondered if she had witnessed the strange goings on and what her attitude was toward perversions of longing. But nothing gave any sign... I felt that she had permitted the act to occur and had neither blamed nor approved, and so I went off to sleep. (123-24)

A very significant feature of the story is its atmosphere of sickness and malaise. The landlady is "a woman of paranoidal suspicion"; Mrs. Wayne is a "pathological genius" with her "morbid and salacious stories"; the quick sketch artist is afflicted by consumption; and the narrator-character contracts his homosexuality from the artist. This atmosphere is characteristic of the French Quarter of New Orleans which always appears in Williams's writings as the hideout of characters who have been thrown out of the mainstream of life. These are the people who disappear, "the earth swallows them up, the walls absorb them like moisture"; they are destined to disappear like this after suffering "all the wrongs" after coming "into the world" (*Collected Stories* 121 and 127). They fall, invariably, in the class of fugitives. They are relentless drifters under a variety of compulsions. A thematic strand attaches to the situation here—the artists are born to suffer. The strand explains itself by presenting three of the four characters in the story in the loose category of artists. The artistically dispassionate yet sympathetic presentation of these "dead beats" combines with the confessional element in the story to evolve a mature piece of fiction.

"The Angel in the Alcove" the story is related to *Vieux Carré* the play through a common experience forming the basis of both. A particular boardinghouse on Toulouse Street, French Quarter, New Orleans, is the locale evoked in both. Tennessee Williams's mother, Edwina Williams, informs that the owner of the boardinghouse, Mrs. Anderson, had "had a hard time adjusting herself to the bohemian spirit of the *Vieux Carré*" (102). The episode that links the story with the play emerging out of it is about the landlady's sadistic act or malicious prank of pouring hot water through the holes in the floor upon a noisy party underneath. Going by Edwina Williams's account of it, the act caused Tennessee Williams to be summoned as a witness, who saved the situation for the landlady by stating that it was "highly improbable that any lady would do such a thing!" (102). The interesting and important point to note here is that the episode that took place in 1938 connects two works, across genres, separated by a gap of nearly thirty years—the story was written in 1943 and the play in 1976-77.

The distance between the originating experience and its dramatic transcription makes *Vieux Carré* a memory play. The status of the memory is stated in the first statement of the play: "once this house was alive, it was occupied once. In my recollection it still is, but by shadowy occupants like ghosts. Now they enter the lighter areas of my memory" (*Vieux Carré* 05). The statement puts a pall of sorts over whatever follows;

and, therefore, the play assumes the character of a resurrected experience. The twelve scenes of the play have been divided into two parts, the first carrying the first seven and the second the remainder. The two parts are separated by the gap of a year, approximately. The fuller length of the play lends it a greater structural space to accommodate a much greater portion of the life in the middle class boarding houses in the industrial cities. Due to its length and the resultant structural space, the play incorporates a greater number of representatives from the kind of life it portrays. *Vieux Carré* represents the "cloistered heart of the city" of New Orleans along with a "laissez-faire attitude that characterized the mores and amorality of the most colorful segment of humanity" that the author ever encountered (Leverich 277). The structure of the play is such that it fully encompasses a place that seems to be full of love with life along with its wide range of characters, from the artists like Nightingale to the strip teasers like Tye.

En route to *Vieux Carré* from 'The Angel in the Alcove', six new characters join in to make the show more comprehensive. In the order of their appearance, the new recruits are: Nursie, Jane, Mary Maude, Tye, Photographer and Sky. The "rooming house No. 722, Toulouse Street, in French quarter of New Orleans" thus becomes a much peopled, representative boarding house (*Vieux Carré,* Production Notes 04). In contrast to the three scenes in the story, the play has a far greater number of scenes from the 'French Quarter' life. Of the characters that have been borrowed, Mrs. Wayne gets a new name, Miss Carrie; the quick sketch artist gets an elevated status as a painter and also gets the name of Nightingale; and the narrator gets an extended participation in the action. Miss Carrie (Mrs. Wayne of the story version) now has an accomplice in her maneuverings in pilfering of victuals from Mrs. Wire's kitchen. She, along with Mary Maude, fabricates melodramatic narrations to distract Mrs. Wire's attention so as to pilfer out of her pot of cooking gumbo. An amusing point about the entire episode is that Miss Carrie invariably succeeds in her enterprise even in the face of Mrs. Wire's full awareness of her motives. The entire first happening in Scene four is a comic representation of the deception jointly executed by Miss Carrie and Mary Maude. A scratch or two under the surface, however, the episode becomes a semi-tragic presentation of the pathetic poverty prevailing in the boardinghouses of this type.

The greatest beneficiary through the transition from fiction to drama in this particular case is Nightingale. By earning a name and a palpable profession, Nightingale becomes a substantial character in the play. His tragedy is the most poignant of all. The shady goings on in the story involving the writer and the artist get a presentation through a short scene in the play. Rather than a person with queer sexuality, as he appears in the story, he is now a tragic figure helplessly caught in the conflagration of an incurable disease and homosexual desire. On the psychological plane, he suffers from alienation and the inability to face squarely the fact of his being tubercular. His franticness in desperately avoiding a medical confirmation is touchingly encased in the following piece of an angry altercation between him and the writer in scene five:

> Writer: (In a voice quick and hard as knife): I think there has been some deterioration in your condition and you ought to face it! A man has got to face everything...go have your lungs x-rayed...go have your lungs x-rayed... Don't, don't call it a cold anymore or a touch of the flu!
>
> Nightingale (turning with a gasp): You've gone mad, you've gone out of your mind here, you little one-eyed bitch! (He coughs again and staggers out of the light) (*Vieux Carré* 51)

Scene ten of the play adds a significant dimension to his character—his dedicated and unshakeable faith in Christianity. The significance of this dimension of his character gets further enhanced by the fact that it has been added to his being during the transformation of the plot from the fictional mode to the dramatic. Moreover, his passionate religiosity sharpens and sublimates his tragedy:

> Writer: I think that morals are a human invention that he ignores as successfully as we do.

> Nightingale: Christ, that's evil, that is infidel talk. (he crosses himself) I'm a catholic believer. A priest would say that you have fallen from Grace, boy. (91)

Nightingale is not physically evicted like his counterpart in the story; but his last appearance in the play is remarkably suggestive of a funeral service with the writer as the officiating priest and the apparition of the writer's grandmother as the "sainted mother" and "the angel". There is a heavy suggestiveness in the Writer casually dropping a piece of advice about an overdose of sleeping pills—"Maybe this time you ought to take more than one". The suggestion is promptly rejected by Nightingale, as "suicide" is "a cardinal sin" for one who believes in "God the Father, God the Son, and God the Holy Ghost..." However, a kind of euthanasia seems to be taking place immediately afterwards:

> Writer: ... (He opens the pillbox) Press tab to open, push down unscrew the top. Here it is where you can reach it.
>
> Nightingale: Boy with soft skin and stone heart....
>
> (Pause. The writer blows the candle out and takes Nightingale's hand) (*Vieux Carré* 92-93)

For the tubercular artist, this is a far honorable and graceful exit with all its connotations. Upon his 'exit' out of a consumptive body, he is received by the angel of the writer's sainted mother. It is important to note, at this very point, that the simple apparition of the Writer's grandmother in the story attains the angelic elevation and upgradation as the sainted mother in the play.

Jane's portrayal in the play almost falls in the category of Laura and Blanche. Her alienation is as tragic as theirs. She being "a might have been fashion-illustrator of genteel background from upstate New York", Roger Boxill observes in her a "Northern Variant of the fallen Southern gentlewoman" (Boxill 158). She clings to Tye and suffers him in order to put a stop to her own drift. There is a desperation in her clinging to him which, again, brings to mind Laura's unicorn and Blanche's effort to align with Mitch. In the play, she is an embodiment of a double failure, professional and emotional, along with the consequent drift. There can be only one logical end for such character—easing out of life after an escapist addiction. But, human beings cannot "go away and come back" like cats (*Vieux Carré* 104).

The journey from "The Angel in the Alcove" to *Vieux Carré* is from the general to the particular, from the impersonal to the personal. Yet, the scope in the play is sufficiently widened to prepare a new microcosm of life in the French Quarter of New Orleans. The play is nearest to the actual experiences of the author in the particular quarter. Structurally, the play is supposed to be based on memory, like *The Glass Menagerie*. However, the handling of memory as a structural element can be seen wanting in comparison to the masterpiece because of the absence of the surrealistic reinforcing devices like legends and music pieces. The only substantial reinforcement of memory as a structural device is available in the concluding monologue of the Writer (though not as powerful and effective as that of Tom in *Menagerie*). The apparently important advantage of the play over the story is the depth and definiteness of characterization. The obvious result in the present case is the positive loss of the elusiveness of certain key characters. Alongside the new characters joining the play, the old ones gain by their lost elusiveness and increased participation in action. The thematic strands of victimization, loss and alienation get an illustrative focus by this positive development. At the level of pure art, however, the play may seem to stand a few fathoms below the story.

Ominous sounding, "The Malediction" is a story with a heavy socio-political statement. The title suggests that the author means an emphasis on the statement. The drama version of the plot, however, removes this suggestion through the title. The story delineates the inevitable drift of a character towards death after his arrival in a factory town. Lucio, the rootless character, is a little man in search for work and a place to stay. He gets both through Mrs. Hutcheson, who needs him for the kind of companionship which she misses because of her husband's incapacity. Everything goes well for a while, but the tragedy begins to pile up all of a sudden. Lucio receives the news of the death of his brother in an attempt to escape; he then gets laid off along with many others because of the financial cynicism of the stock holders; he tries to ineffectually drown his misery in liquor and is put in jail on charges of drunken wandering. On his release, he returns to the rooming house only to find that he has been replaced by another wanderer by the house owner. He feels he has only one course left—he takes the stray cat that has been his companion for some time and walks into the deep of a river to drown himself.

The story has two obvious facets to it. The one we confront first is the socio-political framework that reaches it's point of climax and highest development in the 'malediction' shouted by the old man against the capitalist owners of factories. The curse, representing the collective agony of the victimized proletariat, earns an added edge and a portentous meaning when the old man declares himself "God Almighty" and raises his curse, like a slogan, with the clenched "fist of God" (*Collected Stories* 158). Though a center of meaning itself, this political framework in the story remains superficial or, at the most, secondary. The focus of the story is the fate of Lucio, who is a typical fugitive in the Williams canon. The fate he suffers, too, is typically reserved for fugitives like him. The narration begins with an archetypal fugitive situation, and goes on to point out a series of fugitives. The first in the series is Lucio himself, "a panicky little man" and a "lonely stranger" who is "scared of his shadow and shocked by the sound of his footsteps" (147). The previous occupant of the room he rents, a Russian, has left more than sufficient traces of his fugitive status, including a stray cat for company. The Russian, though absent here, is one of the frequent tubercular lovers in the world of Tennessee Williams. Following him are the old man and the workers laid off along with Lucio. The laid off workers, "sixty-eight of them", form a horde of sorts. Yet, there are "no angry voices", "no protest" and "no demonstration":

> It was as though these sixty eight factory workers had known from the beginning that this was in store. Perhaps in the wombs of their mothers the veins that had fed them had sung in their ears this song: Thou shalt lose thy job,

> thou shalt be turned away from the wheels and bread taken from thee! (157)

The title of the play, a one-act, growing out of "The Malediction" is potently suggestive of an important shift of focus. *The Strangest kind of Romance* is a title that trains the attention on the personal, though archetypal, tragedy of the protagonist in the one-act. A strikingly meaningful alteration along with the purposeful change of title is the revocation of the names of the characters. In the interestingly resulting situation, only the animal, the cat Nitchevo, retains its name. It is a tremendous loss of identity for these characters who are doomed to interact with one another in this limbo of namelessness. The complexities of Lucio's mind in the story are sufficiently decoded and interpreted by the narrator. But his counterpart in the play, a nameless little man, is trapped in an uncommunicative situation. His predicament, therefore, is effectively conveyed by sifting out communication from the dialogue. The cumulative result of this process is the one-act in four scenes with lots of dialogue but no communication. Here is an instance:

> Little Man: You wouldn't be talking to me
>
> Landlady: I am talking to you—directly!
>
> Little man: Not to me.
>
> Landlady: You! Me! Where is the third party?
>
> Little Man: There isn't a second party.
>
> Landlady: What?
>
> Little Man: You're only talking to something you think is me. (*The Strangest* 184)

The utterance of Little Man here creates a typically existential situation: "I'm not like you, a solid, touchable being (184). People in such situations suffer from "plain old lonesomeness" that cannot be alleviated by any amount of physical company and contact (185).

In comparison to the story, the play capitalizes substantially upon the absence of the Russian. His absence, the fact of his being gone, becomes the cause of the evocative thought about all of his species of "birds of passage". "There must have been a lot" in his species, all of them "birds of passage", suffering "restlessness changes" (176). Having no companionship, these "birds of passage" live by and on an eccentricity. On the move, one way through the cul-de-sac like "passage" to their doom, they leave their "signatures" on the walls of rented rooms as "their little claims of remembrance" (178). Their world is so topsy-turvy with complex emotions, their language so warped and charged, that they can only communicate with animals. One among them, Little Man has a complex emotional and existential situation to explain to Nitchevo, the cat in a travesty of communication:

> ... Nitchevo, don't be nervous. There is nothing to worry about. In winter my hands get stiff, it makes me clumsy... I won't jam up the machine any more... Mr. Woodson grabbed me by the shoulder!... Oh, Nitchevo—I lost my dignity—I cried... (He draws his breath in a shuddering sob). (*The Strangest* 180)

A complex mixture of such feelings as frustration at his own incapability, humiliation and a failing hope come blurting out here, and he makes an abortive attempt to draw some reassurance. Little Man's problem is answered by an elderly member of his clan of fugitives, the Old man: "Independence goes—then pride—then hope. Finally even the ability of the heart to feel shame or despair or anything at all—goes, too. What's left? A creature like me. Whose need of companionship has become a nuisance to people" (189).

The old Man's malediction, unlike that of his counterpart's in the story, has a greater degree of abortive anger. As a consequence, it becomes less of a malediction and more of an abuse: "Go on, go on, you niggardly pimps of the world! You entrepreneurs of deception, you traders of lies! ...glut your bellies on corruption! And when you are too fat to move—that fist will clench, which is the fist of God—to strike!" (192).

The play ends with the suggestion that whatever has been encased herein is just a part in an unending sequence. The little man had been preceded by a Russian; and now he has been followed by the Boxer, yet another of his ilk. The show would go on, right up to the Deluge. Comparing the play with its parent story, it can be observed that the two have their separate distinctions. The story is "richly textured" and "structurally cohesive", while the play "abounds with symbols and metaphors" (Londre 49). The most powerful and meaningful of these metaphors is the wall with signatures of the predecessors of Little Man. Another meaningfully dynamic metaphor is presented by the progress of seasons suggested by the scenes through the two windows in the room occupied by Little Man. The scenes encapsulate a steady progress from autumn to spring, from the opening to the end of the play. A somewhat ethical point scored over the story by the play is the removal of the suicide scene. An end sans suicide suits the structure of the play as a part in an unending sequence. Additionally, the still alive Little Man lends meaning to his replacement, the Boxer, at the rooming house. Thus, against the travestied apotheosis in the story, the play suggests a continual drift and an unending flow of the drifters.

"The Yellow Bird" is the next case in the series of stories serving as plot prototypes for plays later. The story is a heavy blow to Episcopalian puritanism by showing the rebel against it prosper and get to something of a canonized status. Alma is that rebel in the story. Interestingly, she is the daughter of "a Protestant minister named Increase Tutwiler, the last of a string of Increase Tutwilers who had occupied pulpits since Reformation came to England". Before turning into a full-blooded rebel, she displays her independent spirit as the church organist at the congregations of her father. Whenever she feels that her father, "a long-winded speaker", has gone on too long, she breaks "into the offertory hymn in order to turn him off" (*Collected Stories* 221-22). On one such occasion, when she has to practically cut the preacher short by verbal intervention, she breaks the last hitch of shyness restraining her. Pushing thirty and unmarried, Alma all of a sudden breaks into a profligate life style. There is an eruption of sorts to transform her from a restrained minister's daughter to a woman living her life with wild abandon. She takes to smoking, drinking and picking up men from bars or highway. And then, after her father's protests, quits home and goes to New Orleans. There, she settles in the old French Quarter, a place mostly inhabited by 'fugitives', outcasts, queers, victims and others of such classes. She gives birth to a son. "Not knowing" the father of the child, she names him John after the lover she had liked best, a man now dead (227).

The last part of the story has something of an involved symbolism so complex that it remains elusive to attempts at deciphering it. First, it is Alma's dream showing John, her dead lover, "like Neptune out of the ocean" bearing a "cornucopia dripping with seaweed". Following the dream is the suggestion that Alma sleeps forever: "And off he went, and Alma went off with him". Her son, now a grown up sailor, returns from a voyage and sets up a monument showing "three figures of indeterminate gender astride a leaping dolphin. One bore a crucifix, one a cornucopia, and one a Grecian lyre. On the side of the plunging fish, the arrogant dolphin," is inscribed "the odd name of Bobo" (227-28). With its name, the leaping dolphin aligns with the yellow bird, also named Bobo, that Alma's mother was accused of having used as the interlocutor between herself and the Devil. The dolphin and the bird are manifestations of the same symbolic suggestion. Both are anti puritan symbols, as elaborated by the narrator in the concluding sentence of the story.

Summer and Smoke, the play, takes off from "The Yellow Bird" that has been identified by Vannatta as "a generally unique story in which the usual Williams pattern of punishment for pleasure is reversed..." (50). The play, *Summer and Smoke,* is a remarkable improvement upon the story in terms of structural beauty, thematic focus and characterization. Structurally, the play is divided into two perfectly balanced parts with six scenes each. The naming of the two parts as 'Summer' and 'Winter' has as much structural significance as John's anatomy chart and Alma's vision of a tall and elaborate cathedral. Unlike the story, the play provides a good glimpse of Alma's childhood as a girl with a disproportionately large amount of puritanical understanding and sense. She has a ladylike maturity that doesn't match "a child of ten" but goes well with her parentage—she is a "preacher's daughter". She has "a quality of extraordinary delicacy and tenderness or spirituality in her" which sets her "distinctly apart from other children" (*Summer and Smoke,* Prologue 125). With this distinction to her credit, she is able to explain the meaning of 'Eternity', the name of the stone angel, to John whom she loves almost with the depth of a motherly or sisterly affection. This is the beginning of the part of the play, named 'summer', in which "the colder, 'soul' aspect of Alma dominates..." (Griffin 81). Up to the end of the part with Scene six, there can be observed a series of debates and confrontations between Alma and John. At the root of these confrontations lies their conflicting attitudes to life. The part culminates in Scene six where the confrontations between the two reach the point of Climax. Their polarized attitudes get amply delineated in the scene through the presentation of their separate obsessions. Alma's obsession, as the Spanish sense of her name suggests, is the image of "a Gothic Cathedral" with "immense sainted windows, the great arched doors that are five or six times the height of the tallest man—the vaulted ceiling and all the delicate spires—all reaching up to something beyond attainment..." (*Summer and Smoke* 197). Diametrically opposed to this sacred and theological image is John's obsession with "a chart of human anatomy" with all "our insides" portrayed but "the beautiful soul" missing. The two images, one spiritual and the other medical, represent the two extremes of the spiritual and the corporeal. The genuine love of Alma and John for each other is marred by these two conflicting attitudes to love and life. John dares Alma to locate "the beautiful soul" in the anatomy chart; and Alma detests love which is "no better than the coupling of beasts!" (202-03).

The second part of the play, 'Winter', delineates the development of the other side of Alma's "doppelganger," meaning "double person". She climbs down from her spiritual heights to meet John at the other extreme of physicality accentuated by the anatomy chart. Obviously enough, she is inspired to undertake this 'journey' from a high strung spirituality to the opposite extreme of sensual physicality by "the anatomy lecture" of John: "This upper story's the brain which is hungry for something called truth...this middle's the belly which is hungry for food. This part down here is sex which is hungry for love... I've fed all three, as much of all three as I could..." (221). She receives her final, galvanizing jolt when John tells her that he is "more afraid" of her soul than she is of his "body" (222). The journey she has undertaken to meet John at his extreme takes her to the peak of her tragedy, to the realization that "the tables have turned with a vengeance" (247). The penultimate scene of the play, Scene eleven, is a graphic display of Alma's irreversible tragedy. Her conversation with John here is not like the previous ones, a debate or a confrontation. It is an intensely charged exchange of experiences on the journey which the two have just finished. She reaches her destination only to find out that John has traversed to the other extreme:

> John: I have respect for the truth, and I have respect for you...you've won the argument...
>
> Alma: What argument?
>
> John: The one about the chart...I've come around to your way of thinking, that something else is in there, an immaterial something—as thin as smoke... I thought it was just a Puritanical ice that glittered like flame. But now I believe it was flame, mistaken for ice. (243-46)

Instead of meeting midway, the two have crossed over completely. Alma has won the argument, but she has lost John whom she has loved ever since her childhood. This tremendous, irrecoverable loss puts her onto a 'drift' that flows only in one direction—to destruction.

As the story, "The Yellow Bird", grows into the comprehensive drama of *Summer and Smoke,* certain vitally crucial changes can be seen at work. The foremost of these is the arrival of John as a living character with a history as old as that of Alma. He is a substantial character in the play with his 'corporeal' ideology explained through the anatomy chart. This is in vital contrast to his existence in the story as a dead lover capable only of animating Alma's dreams with his cornucopia. Throughout the play, right from the Prologue onward, the two characters interact to put in sharp relief their respective ideology against that of the other. The presence of John as a living character, therefore, provides an impetus to the thematic focus of the play. However, the essence of the theme—a conciliation between body and soul—can best be illustrated by borrowing from the story the image of a leaping dolphin with a trinity astride it: one bearing a crucifix, the second a cornucopia and the third a Grecian lyre. It doesn't need any explication that the comic element of the story has been wholesomely transformed into the tragic. Another notable improvement upon the story is the characterization of Alma in the play. Her persona undergoes a virtual metamorphosis from a socio-religious rebel to a woman with deep spiritual understanding. The difference this metamorphosis makes is immense—Alma, the rebel in the story may or may not excite the sympathy of the reader, but Alma the spiritual lover in the play draws a real catharsis.

"The Night of the Iguana" is a story with some memorable points about it. Its biggest distinction, though, is that it provides the title, locale, some characters and the raw material for Tennessee Williams's last successful presentation in drama. In spite of its secondary status in comparison to the originating play, the story is generally accepted as the author's major offering in the field of short fiction. The story centers on Edith Jelkes who is one of the few memorable female protagonists in Tennessee Williams's fiction. Miss Jelkes is "a spinster of thirty" with "a somewhat archaic quality of refinement", and belongs to a "historical southern family of great but now moribund vitality". The most prominently salient feature of her personality is a duality of instincts. It is a kind of personality not quite different from Alma's in *Summer and Smoke*, who is said to be suffering from "doppelganger". Miss Jelkes, therefore, finds it difficult "to cultivate any interior poise". The two extremes of her personality are manifested through her love of "the dramatic contest of hot and cold color, the splash of scarlet on snow, which was the flag of her own unsettled components" (*Collected Stories* 229-30). In two parts, the story develops out of her contact with two writers, one older and the other younger, of unconventional writings. Apart from the unconventional writings, these writers have a surreptitious relationship between the two, which becomes the source of an acute discomfort to Edith Jelkes. Consciously or unconsciously, her attention gets fixated upon the two writers and their activities. Without knowing it, she begins to indulge in an espionage of sorts. She feels drawn towards the two by their stiff and studied indifference towards her. The reason of their indifference may be entirely obscure to her, but it is more than apparent to the reader. Her interaction with the writers is precipitated by a particular situation used by her as a kind of excuse. The situation is that an iguana has been tied by the hotel owner's son to something underneath Miss Jelkes's room. The story comes to an end with the happenings taking place simultaneously in a symbolic manner. The first is the partial collapse of Edith's spinsterish status, and the other is the release of the iguana. The obvious correspondence between the two, built up and highlighted by the author, is suggestive enough to produce the sense that Edith's spinsterish energy has found a belated release through her physical contact with the older writers. Though the "demon of virginity" wins in the "fierce little comedy of defense" that she puts up against the writer, there is something in her being that gets a delayed but definite release (*Collected Stories* 244).

The story gives the impression as if Williams had decided that "fuller development of his themes and characters would wait for the play" (Vannatta 55). *The Night of the Iguana* the play develops the themes and characters of "The Night of the Iguana" the story to the maximum. Divided into three Acts, the play carries out an admirable exposition of characters and the thematic elements. The dramatic structure of the play heavily depends upon Shannon's memory of a past act of blasphemous seduction and a near re-enactment of it in the course of the play. The re-enactment is thwarted and, at least, stopped from leading to as serious consequences as those of the first. Reverend T. Shannon's memory of the act followed by heresy, and the resultant defrocking, forms the backbone of the play. His relationship with Hannah Jelkes grows and matures indirectly through this memory. Right from her arrival, there has been an obvious chemistry at work between Shannon and Hannah: "Shannon looks at Hannah and Nonno steadily, with a relief of tension almost like that of someone going under hypnosis" (*Iguana* 278). There is something prophetic in a brief expression of Hannah—"It's providential"—that nearly defines this instant relationship. The relationship then begins to grow even in the face of a strong objection by Maxine, the other woman in love with Shannon: "I want you to lay off him, Honey. You're not for Shannon and Shannon is not for you" (*Iguana* 321). The warning comes rather late. Shannon and Hannah have already developed a spiritual and religious dimension about their relationship. Hannah is an animated "Gothic cathedral image of a medieval saint" (*Iguana* 266). It is understandable that Shannon should make his confessions to this "medieval saint". As he makes his informal confession of his past sin, he gets an opportunity to lash it out against the puritanical concept of Christian God. He heaps the blame upon the "theologies" that "accuse God of being a cruel, senile delinquent, blaming the world and brutally punishing all He created for his own faults in construction" (304). Almost by way of benediction, Hannah offers to give him "a sketch of yourself, in words instead of pastel crayons or charcoal" (344). She paints the troubled psyche of Shannon by presenting a somewhat apocalyptic view of his problem:

> Shannon: What is my problem, Miss Jelkes?
>
> Hannah: The Oldest one in the world—the need to believe in something or someone—almost anyone—almost anything—something... Broken gates between people so they can reach each other, even if it's just for one night only. (352)

The tragedy of 'fugitives' or 'victims' like Shannon and Hannah is that they are like iguanas tied not by their tails that they can bite off, but by their throats: "It can't bite its own head to escape from the end of the rope" (*Iguana* 370). Their tragedy can have a finale or an end only if there is a liberator around to "cut loose one of God's creatures at the end of the rope". In this particular case Shannon, the God's man, is the liberator doing this "little act of grace", "so that one of God's creatures could scramble home safe and free" (373).

He 'liberates' Hannah, Maxine, and Miss Fellows among the tourist group he is guiding. His "act of grace" is literal in the context of the iguana he has set free; but in the context of the three women, it has a symbolic significance. He may have been defrocked for preaching his idiosyncratic (or indigenous) gospel (303-04), but he puts it (the gospel) to an exemplary practice by 'emancipating' (344) the women who had been "scrambling" to "cut loose" the puritan "end of the rope" (373). He has exhibited and proved that he is unfit to be a preacher, but has an immense capacity to grow as a 'messiah' whose birth is announced by Doc in *Small Craft Warnings.*

The brief assessment of *The Night of the Iguana* above sufficiently proves that the play is a definite, multi-dimensional improvement upon the story it stems from. The improvement that strikes immediately is the comprehensive redrafting of Miss Jelkes's character to make her one of the bearers of the theme of the play. As long as inside the story, Miss Jelkes remains comic and a frustrated voyeuristic spinster. Out into the play, she gets a sonorous name of Hannah (instead of Edith) alongside a substantial growth in importance. She now gets equated with a medieval saint with her powers of prophetic painting. Thus endowed, she can see through the cynical exterior of Shannon to draw a graphic sketch of his loneliness. The play's main concern, as stated by Tennessee Williams, is to deal with the problem of living "beyond despair and still live" (qtd. in Londre 147). The play does suggest a solution to this problem, that to live "beyond despair" one needs to make human contact, to come out of isolation and believe in something or someone". In this context, the symbolic significance of iguana also grows in due proportion. The situation involving iguana, its being tied and released, has barely a sensual significance in the story. In the play, however, the situation becomes symbolic of a comprehensive spiritual experience. The release of the "God's creature" here is loaded with as much significance as spiritual emancipation. From the story to the play is a transit in which an intrinsic but unhealthy aspect of the plot gets dropped off. The aspect relates to the nature of the relationship between the two writers in the story. The writers do not figure in the drama version of the plot. Instead, we have a troupe of some interestingly meaningful characters like Shannon and Maxine. The entire thematic structure of the play depends upon these two and Hannah, apart from Nonno, who serves as the catalyst in the "vibrations" between his grand-daughter (Hannah) and Shannon. As one of the last successes of Tennessee Williams, *The Night of the Iguana*, thus, draws the best out of the delicate structural parallel between the two varieties of journey. One of the two is a simple journey of tourists guided by Shannon; and the other is a spiritual journey being guided jointly by Nanno and Hannah.

The reputation of "Three Players of a Summer Game" overwhelmingly depends upon the play that comes out of it—*The Cat on a Hot Tin Roof*. Independently, it is just a story that draws a few character sketches with dispassionate nonchalance. The nonchalantly drawn portraits include Brick Pollitt, Margaret Pollitt, Isabel Grey and her daughter. Beyond the portraits, there is little binding action to involve the characters in a feasible and interactive relationship. Even the titular summer game, croquet, takes place less frequently than it is awaited. When it happens, after all, it turns into Brick Pollitt's drunken antics. There is something strategic about the narrative in the sense that the narrator has a fixed position, most probably outside one of the neighboring houses. The narrative is shaped in such a manner that the visible action is restricted to the lawn of Isabel Grey's house. There is no glimpse of the interior of the house or whatever happens there. Brick Pollitt in the story is an alcoholic with some vague guilt heavy upon his heart. He is a regular visitor to Isabel Grey, quite possibly to escape from his over domineering wife. The death of Dr. Grey, Isabel's husband, has only resulted in an increased frequency and duration of his stay at the house. The more he recedes into his alcoholism, the firmer becomes his wife's grip on him and his property. By virtue of Brick's power of attorney, Margaret takes control of all his business affairs and holds his "ten-thousand acre plantation as firmly and surely as if she had always existed for that and no other purpose". A little further, there is a view of Brick's tortured psyche which pushed him into alcoholism and an affair with Isabel:

> ...it's the most precious thing that a woman can give to a man—his lost respect for himself—and the meanest thing one human being can do to another human being is take his respect for himself away from him! I had it took away from me. (*Collected Stories* 311)

At the two extremes of this statement are the two women in the story. Margaret, Brick's wife, is the woman who has imbibed all his pre-marital "assurance and vitality" as if she has "her lips fastened to some invisible wound in his body" (306). She, being the kind of woman she is, likes Brick at his liquor, rendered dull and inactive. With her femininity and meekness, Isabel is a complete antithesis to Margaret. The end of this two part story shows a man, completely consumed by a strange nexus between his wife and liquor, being driven away limp and dull in a car. The man, unmistakably, is Brick; and the person driving the car is his wife, Margaret. Margaret is at the driving wheel, physically and symbolically: "It was exactly the way that some ancient conqueror, such as Caesar or Alexander the Great or Hannibal, might have led in chains through a capital city the prince of a state newly conquered" (325).

Out of this series of word portraits and the accompanying metaphysical commentary grows *Cat on a Hot Tin Roof* which can be called "a near classical tragedy, in which a larger than life 'king' of his domain, Big Daddy, with his son Brick, relentlessly pursues the truth..." (Griffin 143). As the story gets transformed into the drama of *Cat on a Hot Tin Roof,* it takes into the mainstream several new characters. Of these new characters, missing in the story version of the plot, the inevitably important is Big Daddy. The play also thrives on Gooper, Sister Woman, her Children and an absent character, nick-named Skipper. Even Brick Pollitt and Margaret are reshaped and given a substantial identity. The characters profitably left out are Isabel and Mary Louise, but their ouster has been more than compensated by the recruitment of Sister Woman and her train of noisy children. The joint family that thus emerges is under the threat of a common crisis in the form of an unavoidable death of Big Daddy by cancer. The crisis rises to an ironical status in Act II, where Big Daddy is seen trying to stave off the smarmy and apparently sycophantic efforts of Mae (Sister Woman) to put up a birthday celebration. With his experience gained through his extensive travels and interaction with humanity, Big Daddy is able to see through the designs of Mae (and Gooper). His outburst at Big Mama is a more revelatory evidence of his perspicacity in reading the real intents carefully brushed under the birthday celebration:

> ...Well, I'm just about to tell you that you are not just about to take over, you are not just about to take over a goddam thing... I've had the goddam exploratory operation, and nothing is wrong with me but a spastic colon—made spastic, I guess, by disgust. By all the goddam lies and liars that I have had to put up with, and all the goddam hypocrisy that I lived with all these forty years that we been living together! (*Cat* 40)

Big Daddy is not alone in his pursuit of truth; he has a mate of sorts in Brick who is fighting his own, separate battle against 'mendacity'. Both Big Daddy and Brick are disgusted. Their modes of reaction against mendacity and disgust, however, are different. Brick deciphers two enigmas, himself and Big Daddy, by just two short sentences: "Mendacity is a system that we live in. Liquor is one way out and death's the other" (69). 'Liquor' is the key word to decipher Brick; and 'death' to unravel the mystery of Big Daddy, who is dying of cancer. It is necessary here to call attention to the ironical tragedy of Big Daddy. He is a man celebrating his "sixty fifth birthday" with the hope that he has "got fifteen years or twenty years left in" him (68). He realizes that all his wealth and prosperity cannot earn him an extra second of life:

> ...Guess, Brick! Guess how much I'm worth! Close on ten million in cash and blue chip stocks, outside, mind you, of twenty eight thousand acres of the richest land this side of the valley Nile! But a man can't buy his life with it, he can't buy back his life with it when his life has been spent..." (*Cat* 45-46)

Big Daddy's tragedy is simple enough to be straightened out to understand. Brick, however, remains an elusive character with his elusive tragedy. His tragedy has multiple contours. That he would remain unexplainable is suggested in the first description of his appearance in Act I:

> ...He has the additional charm of that cool air of detachment that people have who have given up the struggle. But now and then, when disturbed, something flashes behind it, like lightning in a fair sky, which shows that at some deeper level he is far from peaceful.... (*Cat.* Stage Directions 02).

The elusiveness of Brick's character has caused some scholars to train their criticism at Tennessee Williams, the author of the character. Prominent among these scholars are Benjamin Nelson and Signi Falk. Benjamin Nelson feels that the "situation" of Brick has been "left unexplained", with the result that the "true quality of (his) experience cannot be grasped" (211). Much more defining is the remark of Signi Falk: "Williams writes as if he himself did not know the physical and moral condition of his hero and the reason for his collapse" (107). The "mendacity" that has been troubling him cannot be as straight as his queer relationship with Skipper. It can't even be the fact that his wife, Margaret, has had an affair with Skipper.

For a closer analysis of Brick's vague tragedy, it is necessary to trace its history in "The Three Players of a Summer Game", the story version of the plot. Something that has been eating into his vitals comes to be expressed in some of his drunken ravings. In one such raving, he admits that he has had "his respect for himself...took away from" him. He has been morally and psychologically castrated by none other than his wife. For a while, he puts on a bold demeanor and declares that he would prove that he is "a man with his balls back on him" (*Collected Stories* 311, 313). This is illustration enough that Brick's problem gets understandable contours and creates a truer picture through its antecedents in the story. As in the case of Brick Pollitt, the story serves as an explanatory prelude to the play in many other respects. It is worthwhile to note that the game of croquet, so elaborately compared by the narrator to art, functions as a broad metaphor. The metaphor can even throw light on some of the dark areas in the play. Within the story, the metaphor applies to the situation among Brick, Isabel and Margaret—the 'three players'. However, the 'game' is always played away from Margaret, at Isabel's residence. For Brick, therefore, it means "running together out of something unbearably hot and bright into something obscure and cool" (*Collected Stories* 308). For Brick, the two extremes are respectively represented by Margaret and Isabel. Applied to the play, *Cat on a Hot Tin Roof,* the metaphor explains the calculated but insufficiently veiled moves of Mae and her husband. Brick is 'retired hurt' on his crutch, and the players now are Big Daddy, Margaret and Mae (Sister Woman). At another level, the metaphysical plane, the game suggests the losing or lost struggles of Big Daddy and Brick. A vital alteration made in the play version of the plot is the transformation of Margaret. She is no more a "Caesar or Alexander the great or Hannibal" (*Collected Stories* 325). She is now a woman supremely charged with attractive and charming feminine attributes; she is now "a pretty young woman" with a voice that "is both rapid and drawling" (*Cat* 01). She is conscious of her feminine capability and uses it as a weapon to get the better of Brick. The ultimate result of this weapon is that she now achieves a much more seemly, though delayed, victory over Brick. At some obscure but vulnerable spot, she has even wounded Big Daddy by her weapon. Her facelift and recreation is one of those aspects of the play, which make it a magnificent achievement and improvement upon the story from which it grows.

The repertoire of Tennessee Williams includes two more cases of the transformation of fiction into drama. The first of these two is the dramatization of "Man Bring This Up Road" as *The Milk Train Doesn't Stop Here Anymore*, and the second is the conversion of "The Kingdom of Earth" into a play with the same title. The common factor and an important fact about the two cases is that these preparatory stories belong to the later period of the author's writing career. Neither of them grows into memorable drama. It is possible to contrast them from such excellent preparatory works in fiction as "Portrait of a Girl in Glass", "The Yellow Bird", "The Night of the Iguana", and "Three Players of a Summer Game".

"Man Bring this Up Road" features an encounter of sorts between two persons at the two opposed extremes of age and financial capability. The persons involved are Mrs. Flora Goforth, a millionaire aged seventy, and Jimmy Dobyne, an artist in his thirties whose art is yet to be recognized. Professedly, Mrs. Goforth is a rich patrona of arts living in isolation in "her siege on the Divina Costiera of Italy", and is "diligently sought after by that flock of young people who fly to Europe in summer with one large suitcase and a small one, a portable typewriter or a paint box..."; she has deliberately left the approach to her "siege" a "mortal hazard" to test the physical capability of these amateur artists (*Collected Stories* 347). The fact immediately grows into a mystery but is solved and settled a little later. When Jimmy Dobyne reaches her deliberately isolated "up the road" mansion upon the crag, he is "ravenously hungry, the hungriest" he can remember ever being in life (351). The situation in the story is not as straight as it appears at this level. A little further, it is revealed that Mrs. Goforth is not as much a patrona of arts as she appears. A lonely, affluent woman in her seventies, she needs these artists to keep her illusion of vitality and attractiveness going. The artists that reach her are drifters in search and need of sustenance and recognition. Eventually, it amounts to a give-and-take situation: the archetypal drifter needing succor and Mrs. Goforth needing the distraction from the consciousness of her lost youth and charm.

The Milk Train Doesn't Stop Here Anymore is, as the longish title suggests, a broadening of the issue in the parent story. The process is facilitated by the incorporation of at least two disparate structural devices into a single braid. The author makes an announcement regarding this structural innovation in the 'Author's Notes' preceding the play:

> I have added to the cast a pair of stage assistants that function in a way that's between the Kabuki Theatre of Japan and the chorus of Greek Theatre. My excuse, or

> reason, is that the play will come off better the further it is removed from conventional theatre" (*The Milk Train* 03).

In almost an imitation of the ancient Greek theatre, the 'Prologue' features the 'Chorus' with their action and conversation that resemble a commentary on what is to follow. The vital and seminal piece of information is provided by 'One', a member of the Chorus: that what follows in the course of the six scenes of the play is "presentation...of the two final days of Mrs. Goforth's existence" (*Milk Train*, Prologue 07). Immediately following this piece of information is a cry of pain by Mrs. Goforth in the background, which is accompanied by "the sound of distant Church bells" (*Milk Train*, Prologue 08). The information by 'One' is right away confirmed and verified by a cry suggesting death and the church bells suggesting funeral service. Chris in the play is the replacement for Jimmy in the story. The replacement has much more to it than just a change of name. Apart from being a tramp artist, Chris is a saintly figure reminiscent of St. Christopher. But his apotheosis, his sainthood, stems from an inversion of ordinary medical ethics. At the climax of the play, Scene six, he recounts his experience of helping "a very old gentleman" easing out of life "light as a leaf". The act may shock a sensibility fed on conventional ethics. But Chris doesn't find it different from an ordinary deed of generosity. Moreover, his deed gets a spiritual sanction by an ascetic Hindu hermit:

> Mrs. Goforth: Did you tell the old Hindu, the Swami, when you got to his place, that you'd killed an old man on the way and—
>
> Chris: I told him that I had helped a dying old man to get through it... He said, "you've found your vocation", and he smiled. It was a beautiful smile. (*Milk Train* 114)

The presence of Chris, thus, imparts an unmistakable spiritual status to the play. The spirituality here, obviously, is related to the phenomenon of death. Chris becomes the carrier of the message in the play by his references to the Hindu concept of death as just an event in a nearly everlasting cycle of life. His curious mission as a 'saint' is to help people die peacefully.

Technically and thematically, the play, thus, is a remarkable improvement upon the story in its history by virtue of the spiritualization of death. From "Man Bring This Up Road" to *The Milk Train* is, therefore, a philosophical movement from carnality to spiritual sublimation.

Though after a lapse of time, "The Kingdom of Earth" lends itself to reorganization and reconstruction in drama like the earlier events of cross genre transformations analyzed in the preceding paragraphs. The key characters in the story, as in the play later, are Chicken and Myrtle. The story follows the method of first person narration by Chicken, the protagonist. Consequently, what we get in the story is the perception of the 'Kingdom of Earth' by him. He is a character who would not subject himself to spiritual struggle being preached by Gypsy Smith, an archetypal Episcopal priest. He feels that he is "not cut out for" salvation and, therefore, has committed himself to "personal satisfaction" instead of "straining and struggling for something" which is beyond reach (*Collected Stories* 368). He does suffer a brief period of struggle after the arrival of Myrtle, the wife of his half-brother Lot. At the end of the story, everything is settled for him: Lot is dead, he has "hitched up" with Myrtle and has stopped worrying "about them spiritual gates the preacher said to keep shut" (*Collected Stories* 378). *Kingdom of Earth* the play is an overhauling and a fair expansion of "Kingdom of Earth" the story into a work with sociological concerns. There is a complete shift of focus from the spiritual struggle against the demands of flesh to the issue of the unfair system of inheritance. With the arrival of Lot and Myrtle, Chicken feels himself deprived of his fair right to possess the house he has been living in and taking care of all these years. The presence of Myrtle leads to a situation that may render the understanding between Lot and Chicken redundant. In the course of the play, Myrtle slowly and steadily moves away from Lot and ultimately ends up as a companion to Chicken. The movement incorporates physical, ethical, spiritual, and social descents for Myrtle. Everytime Lot asks her to retrieve the written understanding between him and Chicken, she has to 'descend' to the kitchen in the lower floor; as she steadily develops an attraction towards Chicken, she descends to a different ethical plane. As she drifts from the materialistic love for Lot to the carnal one for Chicken, she 'descends' to the least spiritual situation; and as she chooses to align herself with Chicken, she 'descends' to a relationship that would be branded illegitimate by the society. The dramatization of the story in this case, therefore, can be seen as a viable effort at the presentation of the actual 'Kingdom of Earth' as an existing counterpart to the hypothetical 'Kingdom of Heaven'.

The foregoing discussion and analyses of the cases of transformation more than accentuate the fact that Tennessee Williams has often used the characters and the themes and the situations of his stories, as, to quote Ren Draya, the "drawing board" for improvement and amplification into drama (in Tharpe 648). The use of the characters and the themes and the situations of the stories to draw up drama has been manifest and obvious in the cases studied above; and yet, in all probability, there would be many more cases of subtle transformations not so easily discoverable. Additionally, an important and common aspect of the entire series of transformations is a noticeable movement from the personal to the impersonal. Writing stories had been purely and "plainly a catharsis" for the author (Leverich 146). When he creates drama out of the stories, he engages himself in an artistic activity keeping himself detached from the components that have gone into the making of stories. As far as the above analyzed metamorphoses are concerned, it would be appropriate to treat Williams's fiction as a run-up to his major artistic achievement in his drama. However, apart and away from all these transformations—manifest and analyzed, and subtle and unanalyzed—Williams's short stories have the force and capacity to be independently reckoned as genuine manifestations of "the Southern Gothic tradition along with Flannery O'Connor, Eudora Welty, Carson McCullers, Truman Capote, and others" (Vannatta xi). Here is a quote from Jeffrey Walker (in Gordon Weaver) to tersely conclude the entire discussion of fiction-to-drama transformations in Tennessee Williams canon in terms of the gains in the process, in terms of the preparation of the 'great outpouring' in drama, and also in terms of the significance of the author's short fiction as independently artistic in the tradition of the said Southern Gothic:

> It is clear that Williams's reputation as a major American literary figure rests in his dramatic achievements. Yet the early stories are important, too, especially as the best of them mirror the themes of his most remarkable plays, for they establish his place in the Southern renaissance (in Weaver 25)

5

Quest for "the Right Word": Plays into Plays

> "I am not interested in style", she went on, "it's such a waste of time to do things over and get the right cadence and always just the right word." ("The Important Thing")

Speaking to John Gruen in the course of an interview, Tennessee Williams said, "I know that there is nothing else I could do but write. I don't believe that there's such a thing as born writer, but I—I couldn't face a day without writing. The day would seem so completely empty to me that by the time the evening came I would feel like shooting myself" (qtd. in Devlin 112). The statement points to the fact that writing was a compulsion to Tennessee Williams; his very survival depended on the act of writing. A graphic picture of this compulsion has been sketched by Gilbert Maxwell, a poet from Atlanta, who had an opportunity of watching the author from close quarters. Referred earlier in a different context, Maxwell's memory of Williams's frenetic writing every morning at New York during 1940 works fine, too, in the present context: "...while the rest of us were showering, using electric razors, shouting back and forth from bedroom to bath above a raucous radio, he sat typing ninety words a minute, plainly deaf and blind to all the bedlam. After half an hour he whisked a last sheet from the typewriter, sat back and sighed" (Maxwell 43-44). Apart from being a compulsion, writing was also a passion for him. A good evidence and testimony of the passion is afforded by the creative reincarnations of his short stories into plays. The reincarnations have already been extensively analyzed and critically evaluated in the preceding chapter. To take an input from George W. Crandell, a greater evidence of his passion is provided by his "habitual practice of revision" resulting in "thousands of pages of draft material, written over long periods of time" (in Voss 15-16). At the one end of these "thousands of pages of draft material" is an experience mutating into a potential object, and at the other is a finished work with the original experience transformed into a universal one. All these mutations constitute a sizeable group of individual histories climaxing in finished plays. Robert Bray catches the secret behind these often successful revisions constituting the individual histories of many of his plays. Writing to introduce *The Reading*, a previously unpublished one-act, in the 11th issue (2010) of *The Tennessee Williams Annual Review*, Bray writes that "Williams's plays often began with a single, compelling image—his clay that he might remold for years" (4). To add weight to his argument, Bray refers to Williams's own word about it: "If a play grips me, I will continue to work on it until I reach a point where I can no longer decide what to do with it. Then I'll discontinue work on it" (qtd. in Bray 4). It would not surprise one, therefore, to know that, apart from the famous and often studied examples like *The Glass Menagerie* and *The Streetcar Named Desire,* many of Williams's plays have had individual histories ultimately traceable to earlier versions or drafts. The most significant of these plays are *Orpheus Descending, Eccentricities of a Nightingale, The Rose Tattoo, The Night of the Iguana, Small Craft Warnings, Out Cry* and *Vieux Carré.*

To begin with the first in the list above, *Orpheus Descending* has a long and remarkable history dating back to an unnamed play, provisionally labeled *Opus V*, and from there to the landmark *Battle of Angels*. Introducing the play to Audrey Wood through the letter enclosed with the draft of the play, Tennessee Williams wrote: "You won't like the pathological characters or violent theme but I'm hoping my final treatment of it will please you somewhat better. After I've married the banker's daughter or received the dramatic fellowship I may be in a mood to write something sweet and simple. Jesus, I hope so!" (qtd. in Leverich 330). Along its long history, with *Shadow of My Passion* as its "working title", the play later came to be named *Battle of Angels*. According to Tennessee Williams, the play was "a huge advance over its predecessors" and was packed with "practically all that I have felt about life" (qtd. in Lahr 16). The catastrophic failure of the play and its rejection by the Boston audience in December-January 1940-41 has already been discussed in Chapter III in the context of the manifest non-conformism of our author. The dramatization of the theme of the irreconcilability of flesh and spirit proved an unmanageable material for the prudish Boston people. Drawing on Tennessee Williams the man, of whom we have learnt much in the first three chapters of this study, it would not be an exaggeration to state that the author had put himself into the play. He had such an immense faith in the elements and the constituents and the possible messages of *Battle of Angels* that he stuck to it even after that shattering rejection. His conviction about the 'purity' and authenticity of the play and its themes led him not to give it up and to continue working upon it over the years. Understandably, nothing can be more authentic than lived—enjoyed and suffered—experiences. In "The History of a Play", he calls *Battle of Angels* "first of these plays to release and purify the emotional storms of my early youth", of which "the stage or setting" had been "the country of my [his] childhood" onto which he "projected the violent symbols of my [his] adolescence" (in Bak 16). Williams's faith in the play and whatever it represents gets a strong assertion in its reincarnation in *Orpheus Descending*, a play that came as the result of nearly sixteen years spent in revisions of the original material in *Battle of Angels*. The play came in March 1957 with several structural changes, but with little moderation by way of the message and contents. The most important structural alteration, to begin with, is the incorporation of the Prologue within Act I. In the original play, *Battle of Angels,* the Prologue has a separate existence outside the play proper. The separation and distance of the Prologue from the play proper in *Battle* is also suggested by a gap of time. Interestingly, the play is set in a flash-back situation with the Prologue making a commentary of sorts on the tragedy that took place at the mercantile store a year ago. The gap of time, the things and articles connected with the tragedy, the shadow in the light of oil lamp, an ancient Negro (the Conjure Man) as the caretaker—all these create an atmosphere of somber nostalgia about the old mercantile store now turned into a museum, thematically and structurally. The Conjure Man is the link between the past and the present by virtue of his status as being perched on the dividing line between the real and the unreal. This is how he is described in the 'Prologue' by Eva and Blanche, two chorus-like characters:

> Eva: He's part of the exhibition.
>
> Blanche: Don't call it that!
>
> Eva: Oh, the memorial then! What's the difference? This Conjure Man, as they call him: He was on the place when everything happened that happened. (*Battle of Angels*. Prologue 08)

The highly symbolic and aesthetic significance of the Conjure Man comes to the fore in his symbolically meaningful gesture of 'elevating' and holding "above his head" the snakeskin jacket of Val Xavier who has been hounded to death (117). His gesture suggests consecration of Val and the things associated with him. Whatever has been left unexplained in the Act is clarified in the Epilogue, where the Conjure Man is presented as a mystic priest:

> ...Faintly, as from some distance, there comes the sound of chanting from a Negro Church. The store itself is like a pillaged temple... The Conjure Man sits with immobile dignity...crouches forward...and, unfolding the brilliant snakeskin jacket once more, he goes to the back wall and hangs it above his head in the shaft of sunlight through the door. He seems to make a slight obeisance before it" (*Battle*. Epilogue 119, 122).

The snakeskin jacket thus earns the status of a relic, and its dead owner, Val Xavier, that of a messiah. The reduced appearances of the Conjure Man in the revised and reinvented version of the play altogether cut off the romantic, heathen and mystic symbolism. It makes substantial sense to logically assert that *Orpheus Descending* descends from the symbolic loftiness of the antecedent play due to the curtailed presence of the character. His absence also leads to the dropping of the 'Prologue' and the 'Epilogue', making *Orpheus Descending* a compact play in comparison to *Battle of Angels*. In the entire process, the Conjure Man suffers huge disparagement of his status and his symbolic significance eases significantly. He is no more a priest at the "pillaged temple" now. He only carries superstitious talismans with him and is skilled at giving "Choctaw cry". However, the revised and renamed play emphasizes the application of certain strands from the Greek mythology. The broad contours of the Greek myth of Orpheus find an easy and well defined application in *Orpheus Descending*. Val in the play is presented as a present day incarnation of the mythical Orpheus. His development from a young man of twenty-five with virile grace and freedom of body to a man who does not wear Levis or a T-shirt is a remarkable piece of alteration. More remarkable is the fact that he now carries a guitar covered with inscriptions. From a certain point onward, the play becomes a degraded ritual of Orpheus going to Hades to bring back Eurydice. The dry goods store where Val descends resembles Hades in this degraded ritual; and Jabe resembles the authority in Hades, Death. Lady Torrance in the play has a travestied likeness with Eurydice. The ritual is carried out to its fullest potential. Val Xavier fails to rescue the Lady just as Orpheus had failed to draw Eurydice out of Hades. As required by the ritualistic replay of Orpheus myth, a highly 'Purgatorial' scene is created towards the end of the play. Jabe, "Mr. Death", who has throughout created abnormal feelings by his "knocking", is seen at his worst: "Jabe appears on the landing...a strained purple robe hangs loosely about his wasted yellowed frame. He's death's self, and malignancy" (*Orpheus* 344). There are 'Voices of Men' evoking the image of the numberless souls suffering in Hades. Then, there is the concluding shout of Sheriff who is the symbol of authority in present day Hades. The tragic end of Val, by falling prey to the angry mob, is reminiscent of Orpheus's end by being torn to pieces by women in an orgiastic trance.

Carol Cutrere in *Orpheus Descending* is the Cassandra of *Battle of Angels*, and suggests a corrupted clone of Cassandra in Greek mythology. Like her prototype, she prophesies doom and disaster and is never believed. All her warnings are wasted upon people that never take her seriously. Two of her prophesies relate to Val and Lady, the two characters around whom the play moves. Her first prophecy, "a warning of danger" to Val, is just dismissed in Act II (294-295). In Act III (333), she informs Lady about Val's plan to leave, but is ignored by Lady. However, the most important fact about her mythological status is her Tiresias like characteristics—she is as good as sexless and has the capacity to look deep into the past and the future. One of her statements in Act III links the distant past with the present and, thus, brings her closest to Tiresias:

> Something is still wild in this country! This country used to be wild, the men and women were wild and there was a wild sort of sweetness in their hearts for each other, but now it's sick with neon, it's broken out sick, with neon, like most other places. (*Orpheus* 334)

At some level, she also evokes the image of a sexless being doomed to suffer the act of sex:

> The act of love making is almost unbearably painful, and yet, of course, I do bear it, because to be not alone, even for a few moments... It's dangerous for me because I'm not built for childbearing. (294)

Orpheus Descending makes a significant departure from the original in bringing in the idyllic memory of a paradisiacal romance between Lady and David. As Myra and David Anderson do in *Battle of Angels,* the two do not have as much resemblance with Adam and Eve of Eden. *Orpheus Descending* carries the horrible image of Eden broken in and destroyed by Jabe and his horde, a satanic being with his fallen crew:

> Jabe: (With a muted ferocity): ...Her daddy 'The Wop' was just as much of a live one till he burned up...He had a wine garden on the north shore of Moon Lake. The new confectionary sort of reminds me of it... We burned him out, house and orchard and vines and 'The Wop' was burned up trying to fight the fire. (320)

The play, by its scuttling of the Biblical myth, develops a meaningfully symbolic value. Eden, the original Biblical or the corrupted modern, is a place under a potential threat. There cannot be a sufficient guard against this threat. The Eden of Adam and Eve was broken into by Satan leading to the eviction of Adam and Eve; and the Edenic vineyard in the play has been destroyed by Jabe to displace Lady and David. *Orpheus Descending*, thus, pictures the negative and destructive potential of mankind more graphically than its predecessor. Set against this negative, hatred-driven force are the twin images of Biblical innocence in love and Orphean capacity of survival. In spite of an improved structure making the message clearer, the play failed to move the audience still unwilling to draw the cathartic pleasure by deciphering the not so complex symbolism. It must be granted, though, that the play read is more pleasurable than the play performed. The onstage failure of the play flows from "a conglomeration of pagan and Christian symbolism and myth which obliterates all else in its intensity and confusion" (Nelson 230). The following observation of Nelson nearly captures the reason that may have probably lead the play not to evoke much response while in performance:

> For more than two acts, *Orpheus Descending* offers us the spectacle of two almost distinct dramas vying for dominance; but in the middle of the final act, the morality play emerges the dominant and the character of Lady Torrance and the story of her reawakening to life is lost in the symbolic hysteria which engulfs the proceedings. (230)

The history of *The Eccentricities of a Nightingale* spans over a longer period than that connecting *Battle of Angels* and *Orpheus Descending*. At the originating end of this history is "The Yellow Bird", a short story written in 1947; in the middle, *Summer and Smoke*, a play arriving in 1948; and, at the concluding end is located *The Eccentricities of a Nightingale,* which was published in 1964 but could not be produced until 1971. From "The Yellow Bird" to *The Eccentricities of a Nightingale*, thus, is a journey covering seventeen years. If we bring in an interestingly vital piece of information from Donald

Spoto, the period of the journey gets stretched to twenty-eight years:

> ...in a paper on Goethe that he submitted in the spring term of 1936, he embarked on a passionate (if tangential) plea for the presentation of human dignity in the mechanical age....The original draft of his play *Summer and Smoke,* just a decade later, bore the title *Chart of Anatomy,* and its conflicts are very close to a revision of this early student enthusiasm for Goethe. (48)

On the evidence of the anatomy chart being an important thematic and structural element in *Summer and Smoke*, as also in its successor, it can reasonably be said that *The Eccentricities of a Nightingale* has a history of twenty-eight years of making beginning with Tennessee Williams's term paper on Goethe in 1936. The other constituent elements of the play come from "The Yellow Bird", a short story en route the metamorphosis from the anatomy chart to *Summer and Smoke.*

Though it may have failed on stage production, *Summer and Smoke* is a beautiful play with an admirably balanced structure and a nicely executed theme. The play begins with a Prologue, which is a telescopic view of the childhood of Alma and John, the joint protagonists in the play. The theme begins to germinate even at this level of the dramatic past of the play. Alma is very much a Preacher's daughter even in her love for John. As the play moves deeper into 'A Summer', the first part, the diametrically opposed attitudes of the two are accentuated by the fact that the name of the angel of the fountain, Eternity, moves Alma while John remains untouched. John's early carnal bent is displayed in his childhood in his act of kissing Alma and running away. As a child, he has not been able to respond to his mother's death and does not at all have any remorse at having been harsh to his dying mother. As the play proper begins, John is already a practicing doctor and Alma an amateur singer on stage, known as the Nightingale of Delta. One must note here that the play thrives on the structural and thematic contrast that grows from the difference between Alma and John. The opposite of Alma, the 'Nightingale of Delta', is starkly available in John who has been presented as "a promethean figure, brilliantly and restlessly alive in a stagnant society" (*Summer and Smoke* 132). The contrast between their natures is further accentuated and underlined by the contrast between anarchy and order in God's Creation. The natural inclination of John is towards anarchy, while Alma is fixated upon order. But order is not all about Alma; her repressed urges make her a case of "Doppelganger" (144). Their divergent inclinations assume irreconcilable proportions in the crucial arbor scene in the first part where the two are seen engaged in an exclusive debate, which envisages two exclusive symbols: "Gothic cathedrals" with immense stained windows and "a chart of human anatomy" (197, 202). The cathedrals symbolize the spiritual longing to reach "something beyond attainment", and the chart symbolizes bodily hungers.

The second part of the play, named 'A Winter', presents the denouement for the complication that has reached the high point of tension at the conclusion of the first part. Throughout the part, Alma is seen in her descent from the isolated peak of spiritual striving. On her way down from that peak, she meets Rosa and Nellie, her complete foils. But her descent leads her to her tragedy. In spite of her spiritual anguish, she comes down to John's plane only to find that he has already abandoned his chart of anatomy and has moved to the destination of denial and austerity. At the end, the play turns out to be quite an Aristotelian tragedy with neither John nor Alma responsible for their cathartic suffering.

In the Author's Note to *The Eccentricities of a Nightingale,* Tennessee Williams says: "Aside from the characters having the same names and the locale remaining the same, I think *The Eccentricities of a Nightingale* is a substantially different play from *Summer and Smoke,* and I prefer it. It is less conventional and melodramatic" (*The Eccentricities*. Author's Note 07). Of the structural changes, the most striking are the removal of the Prologue, the reorganization of the scenes into three Acts with titles, and the addition of an Epilogue. The total number of scenes in *Summer and Smoke*, twelve, is reduced to nine in *Eccentricities of Nightingale*. The titles of the Acts clearly appear undisguised clues to the simple enough symbolism of the play. Unlike in the former, Alma and John are grown up at the start. The exclusion of the Prologue takes away a glimpse of their childhood. Since the play has been built up on the contrasting natures of the two, the exclusion of the Prologue seems to be doing some damage to the revised play. However, the exclusion may be seen as bringing increased focus upon the present. Scene three of the second Act of *Eccentricities of Nightingale* is the parallel to Scene four of the first part in *Summer and Smoke*. The presence of Rosa as a catalytic foil to Alma has been done away with in the revision. Instead, we have the hawk like observation of Mrs. Buchanan. It can be easily surmised that Rosa's absence from the scene in particular and the play in general removes the background against which can be seen the proportions of Alma's character. The most striking shift from the original is marked by the third Act. The shift is so remarkable that Alma is completely stripped of her particular characteristic that becomes the vital backbone of her tragedy in the original version of the play. The most poignant scene of *Summer and Smoke* is the eleventh, which, quite surprisingly, does not get a replication in the revision. The loss caused by the absence of the scene, or a parallel to it, is suffered equally by Alma and John. The famous statement of Alma in Scene eleven in *Summer and Smoke*, which encapsulates her tragedy, gets omitted, muffling and obscuring the intensity of her tragedy in some ways. The omitted statement is about her having made an exhaustive journey from her spiritual alienation only to find out that "the tables have turned with a vengeance". John undergoes a serious diminution of personality due to the omission of his statement about having discovered that Alma's "Puritanical ice...was flame, mistaken for ice" (246-47). Both John and Alma suffer a serious diminution of their status as protagonists due to the removal of the vital details of their experiences on their different journeys in opposite directions. While Alma and John descend from their exalted status as protagonists, the revised play, too, climbs down from the Aristotelian cathartic heights.

In this transition from *Summer and Smoke* to *The Eccentricities of Nightingale*, certain characters get dropped. Those totally absent are Rosa and Nellie; and the one reduced to an off-stage presence is John's father. It has already been observed that Rosa and Nellie in *Summer and Smoke* have a catalytic influence over Alma. Since there is no replacement for the two in the revised version, an absent character is introduced to exert that much needed influence. Aunt Albertine, a cavalier person who eloped with a traveling salesman, is unconsciously a model for Alma now. Aunt Albertine's story is quite sensitively narrated by her in the last scene of the second Act. Immediately following the scene, Alma is in the company of John begging him for something that she had denied him in the past: "Give me the hour, and I'll make a lifetime of it" (*The Eccentricities* 99). The tragedy of the play, whatever of it is left in the transformation from *Summer and Smoke*, is contained in this scene. First, there is a declaration by John of his disinterestedness in Alma, and then an expression of his inability to appreciate the fact that Alma can be much less elusive than smoke: "I see through my microscope. But you are not one of those creatures. You are a complex being. You have that mysterious something, as thin as smoke, that makes the difference between the human and all the other beings!" (*The Eccentricities* 99). Alma's eccentricities and the something "as thin as smoke" about her have been traced to some other source by John M. Clum in his study of "the evolution of the queer Alma":

> ...*Eccentricities of a Nightingale* comes closer than most of Williams's plays to translating the subversiveness of the stories onto the stage. Four stories are particularly important to understanding the evolution of the queer Alma of *Eccentricities of a Nightingale*: "The Important Thing" (published 1945), "One Arm" (1945, published 1948, the year of the publication of *Summer and Smoke*), "Something about Him" (published 1946), and "The Yellow Bird" (published 1947). The queer Alma has much more in common with the central characters of these stories. (Clum 37)

The Epilogue in *The Eccentricities* is a parallel to the last scene of the original. This is where Alma is seen on a drift having lost John and having got "the hour" to "make a lifetime of it" (*The Eccentricities* 99). It does not require much effort to understand that whatever is so natural to *Summer and Smoke* by way of conclusion is somewhat superfluous in *The Eccentricities.* In spite of the danger involved in making qualitative statements, it can be said that the Epilogue does more damage to the organic beauty of the play than bring any emphasis upon Alma's tragedy.

As announced by the author in his note preceding the play, *The Eccentricities of a Nightingale* is less conventional and less melodramatic than its predecessor. Yet, the antagonism of natures between Alma and John, which forms the thematic and structural substance of the two versions, is depleted to the detriment of the revised version. The puritanical spirituality of Alma in *Summer and Smoke* virtually becomes an eccentric nervousness in the later version. John in the revised version is no more than a caricature of his original. Most of all, it is the "angel of the fountain" named 'Eternity' that suffers disparagement through the revision. The Prologue in *Summer and Smoke* calls attention to the angel in such a manner that it comes to a metaphysical life and becomes an observer of the interaction among the humans doomed to their individual fates. By way of summing up the discussion of the transition from *Summer and Smoke* to *Eccentricities of Nightingale*, it can be conclusively observed that "Williams got it right the first time around" (Griffin 102). The critics may have had their differing opinions on and about *Summer and Smoke,* but Tennessee Williams knew it instinctively that plays like this were doomed to fail: "I suppose people just don't care enough about Almas and Roses and Sandras of this world as they ought to, or I was not able to put it into sufficiently eloquent words to make them care that much" (qtd. in St. Just 54).

The Rose Tattoo opened for its premiere at Chicago in December 1950. On 3rd February 1951, it opened at New York and was a resounding commercial success. Before coming on stage, *The Rose Tattoo* went through a series of revisions and change of titles. Beginning as a comedy titled *The Eclipse of May 29, 1919*, the play was given as many as eight, "temporary titles: *The Vigil Light, Novena to a Rose, A Candle to a Rose, A Rose for our Lady, A Rose from the Hand of our Lady, Perpetual Novena to a Rose* and *Stornello*" (Spoto 161).

Without denying the relationship of *The Rose Tattoo* with the comedy, a recent research has come upon a couple of manuscripts as the preliminary one-act sketches for *The Rose Tattoo*. One of the two manuscripts is complete and is published in the sixth number of *The Tennessee Williams Annual Review* in 2003. Both the complete and the incomplete manuscripts of the sketch, entitled *Il Cane Incantato della Costiera*, are a part of the Tennessee Williams collection at the University of Texas in Austin. The one-act sketch titled in Italian "has many anticipations of the later play, though the names Paul and Clara are probably derived from D.H. Lawrence's *Sons and Lovers*, (without in any way resembling the novel's characters)" (Parker, Introduction. *Incantato*). The 'sketch,' as it has been called by Brian Parker, shows a brief interaction between Clara and Paul. At the opening, Clara is shown "seated in a tight fitting pale blue silk dress in the exact center of a small sofa in the parlor of a shot gun cottage" (*Incantato* 01). She is waiting for her first date after the death of her husband. Ironically, her fifteen year old daughter (an absent character) is having her 'first real date' too. The parlor where Clara sits is lighted brightly "with three or four lamps in addition to the bulb suspended from the ceiling. It is full of hot colors, pinks, oranges, vivid greens, purples, the palette of Matisse" (*Incantato* 01). When Paul Mangiacavallo arrives, he strikes with his obvious sensuality of total appearance—such as would not be incompatible with the general gaudiness of the parlor. There is a subtle and steady movement in the course of the short play. The movement is from a false rejection of Paul's overtures by Clara to a natural acceptance. Much of her false initial rejection of Paul emanates from her consciousness of the prying neighbors. Her desire for Paul is potent, yet she has to act prudishly for certain reasons—she claims that the memory of her dead husband still animates her heart, she is aware of the fact that her daughter is passing through the crucial stage of adolescence, and she feels that she has to keep herself upright and blameless in the face of the prying neighborhood. But pretensions do not have sustenance and life, and she is seen at the end of the 'sketch' in a rayon kimono with scarlet poppies on it, suggestively ready to receive Paul. During this transition from the start to the end, there is a shift from bright light to lack of it. The turning out of lamps by Clara, indicates her decided movement away from prudery; and, it also indicates the lessening of her care for the prying neighbors. The structurally highlighted issue of Clara's daughter's date calls for a special attention. She remains an absent character throughout with a near constant presence. Her indirect presence is first evoked by Clara remembering her daughter when Paul gifts her a box of chocolates. Clara brings her in again while talking about the aquarium that had been attacked by a cat. A little later, a reference to her again comes up when Clara informs about her daughter on her "first real date tonight" (*Incantato* 07). The last reference to her comes up when Clara talks about a white voile dress stitched specially for her. As stated earlier, the structural importance of the absent daughter lies in the fact that her *real* date presents the background against which is projected Clara's *unreal* one with Paul. By implication, it is a situation in which the unseen is real and that which meets the eye is phony. Through a little extension of the same phony design, it can be proved that whatever passes in the course of the 'sketch' is either unreal or a flawed imitation of the real. The points about the 'sketch' that need to be remembered follow in the order of their occurrence: Paul is a truck-driver and a prospective lover of Clara; throughout, there is an implied presence of the prying neighbors; the voyeuristic middle-aged man who likes to watch Clara's daughter dress and undress; the details of a smashed goldfish bowl; and the electric piano that goes out of control. These are the points that get carried over and on to the full-length play with some vital changes.

The Rose Tattoo, a comprehensive enlargement and broadening of the 'sketch' has been designated "my love play to the world" by Tennessee Williams (*Memoirs* 162). The "love play", which incidentally is the author's first full-length comedy, has a vital and earthy woman full of unrequited energy to play the protagonist. The atmosphere that is created around this protagonist, Serafina, is accordingly sensuous. The play, thus, gets located in a "village populated mostly by Sicilians", "somewhere along the Gulf coast between New Orleans and

Mobile" (*The Rose Tattoo*. Author's Production Notes 17). To fill up the gaps in the sensuousness of the ambience, there is the fulsome resonance of the singing of a Sicilian folk singer. Very coherently constructed around this sensuous ambience is a heathen structure with "a little statue of the Madonna in a starry blue robe and gold crown" that has a "vigil light in its ruby glass cup" (17). The presence of seven life size mannequins has a far-reaching symbolic significance that is made clear by the two particular dummies facing each other in a posture of altercation. One of the two-represents a widow and the other a bride. The first scene of the play shows Serafina in her marital bloom which she prefers to call "glory". Marriage means for her a physical nearness which she mixes with sex and religion. Remembering her happy days with Rosario (after his death) she says: "I did, I give him the glory. To me the big bed was like a religion. Now I lie on it with dreams, with memories only" (64). The Act with the scene has a swiftness of movement; and by the end of it, Serafina becomes widowed and her daughter grows up into a woman: "I have been grown for two years!...grown enough to be married, and have a—baby!" (103). The two succeeding Acts move at two levels dealing with two different strands. There are two relationships growing side by side—Serafina's with Alvaro and Rosa's with Jack. By the time the four Scenes constituting the two Acts are over, the two relationships reach their respective consummation—Rosa goes away with Jack and Serafina has "two lives again" in her body (113). In the course of the play, there are two contradictory movements taking place simultaneously. These movements happen at two different levels. At the surface, Serafina is rendered a widow by the death of Rosario; but at a slightly subtle level, the major part of the play is concerned with her conversion from a widow to the bride of Alvaro. This conversion does not have a religious and social sanction. However, it draws its validity through an approval from the image of Madonna, the Virgin Mother. It is urgent that we take note of the fact that the two love relationships in the play have been linked to childbearing. The fact is the undeniable proof of the 'ethicality' of the relationships from the religious and social points of view. Pregnancy and childbearing have not been looked upon as the unwanted byproducts of sex that has been treated in the play as an exposition of a union at a deeper and spiritual level. For a logical illustration, it would be worthwhile to cite a conversation of Rosa and Jack, the two vitally central figures in the two relationships:

> Jack: Honey, on that island I almost forgot my promise. Almost, but not quite, do you understand, Honey?
>
> Rosa: Forgot the promise!
>
> Jack: I made it on my knees in front of our Lady. I've got to leave now, Honey.
>
> Rosa: (clasping him fiercely) you'd have to break my arms to!
>
> Jack: Rosa, Rosa! You want to drive me crazy!
>
> Rosa: I want you not to remember,
>
> Jack: You're a very young girl! Fifteen-fifteen is too young!
>
> Rosa: Caro, Caro, Carissimo!
>
> Jack: Hold some of it back until you're grown
>
> Rosa: I've been grown for two years.... Grown enough to be married, and have a baby! (*The Rose Tattoo* 103)

The core sentiment in this piece is pure sincerity and the ebullient emotion of uncorrupted love. As stated earlier, the uncorrupted love is not distanced from the idea of motherhood. Like Rosa, Serafina would not shun motherhood, though it comes as the culmination of her relationship with Alvaro. The close of the play, thus, enters into a referential relationship with the start where the two mannequins, "a widow and a bride," "face each other in violent attitudes" (18). The struggle comes to be decided in favor of the bride at the conclusion of the play.

The validation of Serafina's relationship with Alvaro is one of the points of improvement upon the 'sketch' *Incantato*, out of which *The Rose Tattoo* grows. That which is an illicit dalliance in the sketch, with nothing except corruptible desire at the root, gets metamorphosed into an intrinsically pure union blessed by the Virgin Mother. One of the flimsy points of similarity between the sketch and the play is the nickname or surname Mangiacavallo shared by Paul and Alvaro. Additionally, both

Paul and Alvaro are truck drivers and have comical appearances; both wear suits that accentuate their comical appearances and sensual attitude. Far from this similarity at the surface, the two have differences that distinguish them as two strikingly different characters. As opposed to Paul, Alvaro is far more sensible and vulnerable. Moreover, he has the big responsibility of three dependents: "One old maid sister, one feeble minded grandmother, one lush of a pop that's not worth the powder it takes to blow him to hell" (79). His feminine vulnerability is in spite of his resemblance to "Mediterranean types" and "glossy young bulls" (69).

Philip C. Kolin finds Alvaro a significant member of what he calls (in the title of his essay) "The Family of Mitch" and labels him "the quintessential comic unsuitable suitor, the generic embodiment of the type" whose unsuitability lies in his being the "ungentlemanly caller" in the "larger psychic narrative of replication in *The Rose Tattoo,* which contributes to the cycle of uninterrupted/incomplete sexuality" (in Voss 140, 142). An important point of structural difference between the sketch *Incantato* and the play is the case of Rosa. Throughout the sketch, she remains an absent character with repeated references to her first real date and her taste for chocolates. In the play she turns up along with her sailor boyfriend, Jack. Her presence in the play with Jack runs parallel to the growth of her mother's relationship with Alvaro. Each of the two gives meaning to the other. Rosa's love for Jack assumes a double romantic value because of Jack's profession. He is a sailor who has been "initiated into the court of Neptune and gets to wear gold earrings"; "he is a shellback" (57). The sincerity of his relationship with Rosa is manifested in his vow to respect the 'innocence' of Rosa. The vow, though almost extorted, is made with utmost meaningfulness and its significance is meaningfully enhanced by the fact of Jack's apparent freedom from ordinary connections. The voyage that is imminent offers him the opportunity to break away; yet he doesn't—he gives "that little gold ring" of his ear to Rosa to put on her finger, and he has to "keep" her heart "forever! And ever! And ever!" (105).

Conclusively, it can be said that the play celebrates "the Dionysian element in human life, its mystery, its beauty, its significance" ("The Meaning of *The Rose Tattoo*" 55). The statement of the author with its reference to the myth of Dionysus revives the interest in the pagan nature of the play. The image of dead Rosario is constructed alongside the pagan god. If Dionysus is the floral god, Rosario is (to Serafina) "my rose of the world"; if Dionysus is a fruitful god, Rosario is "the apotheosis of sexual prowess and fertility"; if Dionysus dies a violent death, Rosario dies by burning (Thompson 55). By his death, Rosario rises to the level and status of the pagan god. However, he has his demythicised and humanized version in Alvaro, who has the body of Rosario with a clownish face. Alvaro thus becomes an image of Rosario who, therefore, carries the double but scuttled references to Dionysus. Though the force of the principle propagated by the pagan god suffers through the succession from Rosario to Alvaro, it needs to be seriously noted that Dionysus as a pagan god is accompanied by other symbols and rituals that create a proportionately consistent atmosphere to extend legitimacy to the myth. Prominent among these are the goat chased by the Strega and the urn containing the ashes of Rosario's cremated body. The goat being chased can easily be interpreted as a sacrificial figure; and the urn of ashes has its connection with the practice of idolatry, as pointed out by Father De Leo, the Christian priest in the play. It is possible to get an obvious glimpse of Tennessee Williams's personal theology in the course of a brief interaction between the Father and the Doctor attending upon Serafina. The theology seeks a humanization of religion:

> Father De Leo: One thing I want to make plain. The body of Rosario must not be burnt.
>
> The Doctor: Have you seen the 'body of Rosario'?... Wouldn't you say it was burnt?
>
> Father De Leo: Of course the body was burnt. When he was shot at the wheel of the truck, it crashed and caught fire. But deliberate cremation is not the same thing. It's an abomination in the sight of God.

> The Doctor: Abominations are something I don't know about ...Father De Leo, you love your people but you don't understand them. They find God in each other. And when they lose each other, they lose God and they're lost. (*The Rose Tattoo* 30)

The potent Dionysian element in the play—the pagan symbols and rituals and a religion sympathetically accommodating the human element—are all, apart from the other issues discussed earlier, remarkable improvements and expansions of *The Rose Tattoo* over *Incantato della Divina Costiera.*

Describing the genesis of the *The Night of the Iguana,* Ronald Hayman writes:

> When Marian Vaccaro arrived in Havana, Tennessee took her to a male brothel. Together they went back to Key West, where they stayed with Frank and Tennessee worked on the play he was to call *The Night of the Iguana,* taking the title of a story he had sketched out in September 1940 when he was staying at the Hotel Costa Verde in Acapulco, after the summer season was over and before the winter season had begun. Most of his work on the story was done between April 1946 and February 1948 (182).

It is possible to be more precise about the start of the work by another reference, to a letter written by Tennessee Williams to Margo Jones: "I started working on another long play today: just the opening shot. But I shall not push it hard until after '*Streetcar*' is in. I call it Quebrada, meaning 'The Cliff'. The scene is a hotel at Acapulco built on a cliff..." Dated 15 August 1947, the letter has been preserved at the Tennessee Williams Collection at the University of Texas at Austin, and has been quoted by Brian Parker in "Introduction to A One—Act version of *The Night of the Iguana*", published in 2001 issue of *The Tennessee Williams Annual Review* (Parker, A One Act Version of *Iguana* iii).

The above references jointly verify the long history of the evolution of *The Night of the Iguana* from the story to the full length play through a lot of revision work. Somewhere along this journey of evolution lies the one-act version of *The*

Night of the Iguana, first published in the fourth volume (2001) of *The Tennessee Williams Annual Review*. This previously unpublished material carries the central issue and characters brought to a greater development in the full length version of the play. The key characters in the one-act (as in the full-length play) are Mrs. Faulk, Shannon, Hannah Jelkes, her Grandfather, Judith Fellowes and Jake Latta. The one-act shows Shannon as a tourist guide conducting a group of teachers and students of a Baptist Female college. Like many of his ilk through the width and breadth of Williams's creative world, Shannon is a vulnerable being cracking up under the pressure of a strong streak of 'difference' in his being (viii). His difference in the present context is his attitude to the tour and the members of the touring party. His only defense against situations of victimization is his charm: "Shannon has lived on his charm, he's operated on that, and he can still turn it on when he's in a tight corner and his charm seems the only way out" (ix-x). It can even be suggested here that he resembles the non-human vulnerable creatures in God's world. If chameleon can change color, if fowls can fly, Shannon can "turn on" his charm. He has been granted this mechanism of defense by God because he does not have the aggression indicative of a more sustainable instinct to survive. His resemblance to the nonhuman vulnerable in Nature defines the point behind his being "cracked up". Paradoxically, he finds himself in trouble strictly because of this charm that has caught the fancy of a 'straight' member of the touring party being conducted by him for Drake Tours. The 'straight' member, Josephine Totter, must have found herself out of place with the "Lesbians in Texas" to develop a relationship with Shannon (xx). The 'charm' of Shannon fails to impress the lesbian Judith Fellowes, but it must have meant a lot to Josephine. It would not be unwarranted here to point out that the author has nearly placed the lusty and voluptuous Mrs. Faulk over Miss Fellowes who has an alternative sexuality.

In the course of the one-act, Shannon is constantly under attack from Miss Fellowes for two reasons—he has developed a relationship with a member of the group under Miss Fellowes; and he has not stuck to the itinerary and the schedule. The entire one-act has been constructed upon this attack from Miss Fellowes, her telegraphic complaint to the firm, the arrival of a substitute for Shannon and his termination. The storyline appears flimsy up to Shannon's termination; but it assumes a philosophical substance thereafter. An unseen iguana serves as the catalyst in the process of the gathering of substance. Symbolized by the tethered iguana, the one-act now turns on a theme that depicts the situation of being "at the end of the rope". Apart from the iguana, the other beings holding on to the leash of life are Shannon, Hannah and her grandfather. While Shannon's case has been evident, those of Hannah and her grandfather become evident through Shannon: "They're at the end of the rope: she's gone up to the annexe to hustle her water-colors with the ladies up there. Ha ha!—If that's not the end of the rope I don't know where the rope ends" (xv). Hannah's survival is entirely dependent upon her ability to sell her quick crayon sketches. Her grandfather, it is apparent, is just pulling on to finish his poetic swansong. When he does finish it, he says his last prayer to God and dies. The theme of difficult survival, or of being "at the end of the rope," gets a gruesome yet graphic expression in a speech of Shannon in the third and the last scene of the one-act:

> There's a lot of hungry people in the world; many have died of starvation but a lot are still living and hungry... when I was conducting a party of—ladies? Yes! Ladies... one of my ladies said, 'Oh Larry, What is this?'...I didn't use the four letter word for what the great mound was...the smell was unmistakable! Then she noticed, and I noticed, too, a pair of very old natives of this nameless country, practically naked except for a few filthy rags, creeping and crawling about the mound of—and—occasionally stooping to pick...bits of undigested—food—particles." (xxix-xxx)

The picture of starving people picking up "undigested food particles" from the carcass of some dead creature is horribly nauseating; yet the same picture evokes a shocking image of the situation of being on the periphery of survival. The sacked Shannon and the impoverished Hannah, in all probability, are the two beings "creeping and crawling" around the "mound" of decadence around them in search of something to subsist on.

The Night of the Iguana makes substantial extensions and improvements over the one-Act version. In the transition from the one-act to the full length play, the major gainers are Shannon, Hannah and the 'Iguana'. Lawrence T. Shannon of the one-act becomes Reverend Shannon in the play, Hannah becomes the confessor and the spiritual guide to Shannon, and the 'Iguana' earns an added religious perspective to its symbolic value. Shannon's background as a priest defrocked on the charges of the seduction of a congregation member is another significant addition. The alleged charge grows in proportion when aligned with the nature of the faith he preaches. Rather than a priest, he becomes a crusader against Puritanism from the very pulpit. Puritanism, in his opinion, paints God as an "angry petulant old man...a bad tempered childish old, old, sick, peevish man" failingly trying to "put together a jigsaw puzzle" (*Iguana* 303-04). In his present position of a tourist guide, he considers himself a "minister of God with a cross" conducting the "tours of God's world" (*Iguana* 304). He has experienced the "Majestic apocalypse of gold light", and has seen "God Almighty paying a visit to the world he created" (*Iguana* 305). Through and by virtue of this apocalyptic vision, Shannon rises to the level of a prophet, or to a travesty of that rise. It would not be an exaggeration to say, therefore, that the evolution of Shannon's character is the most remarkable of the three cases of evolution in the play.

From the one-act to the full play, Hannah grows as a spiritual character. Her spiritual importance, to Shannon in particular, has been highlighted by her description in ecclesiastical terms:

> Hannah is remarkable-looking—ethereal, almost ghostly. She suggests a Gothic cathedral image of a medieval saint, but animated. She could be thirty, she could be forty. She is totally feminine and yet androgynous-looking—almost timeless". (*Iguana* 266)

The apotheosis of Hannah as a "medieval saint" has the important purpose of extending legitimacy to Shannon's variety of faith. Apart from her role as the mentor of Shannon in his psychological rebirth, Hannah also functions as the saintly confessor to him. Her picture of him, a "character sketch...in words instead of pastel crayon or charcoal", is that of a being suffering a "voluptuous kind of crucifixion to suffer for the guilt of the world" (*Iguana* 344). As observed by Hannah, Shannon's 'voluptuous crucifixion' has at its core a masochistic tendency to enjoy panic. Her observation and a candid appraisal of Shannon's manner of atonement has an element of chastisement: "...who wouldn't like to suffer and atone for the sins of himself and the world if it would be done in a hammock with ropes instead of nails, on a hill that is so much lovelier than Golgotha, the place of the skull, Mr. Shannon?" (*Iguana* 344). Her ministrations of Shannon have a strong element of motherliness. It would not be inappropriate, therefore, to state that Hannah almost evokes the image of Mother Mary. Her evolution during the transition from the one-act to the play proper runs parallel to the meaningfulness of her name. In the play, her name becomes a true indicator of her status—'Grace'.

The gross symbolic value of the iguana gets overwhelmingly increased in the play. As long as in the one-act, the creature symbolizes the effort and the instinct to survive in the physical, Darwinian sense. The full-length play, however, overhauls the symbolic value of the iguana to make it broader and more sustainable. The broadening is largely due to the religious aspect added to it. The added or superadded religious aspect nearly sends into oblivion the simpler physical meaning suggested by the struggle of the iguana to escape. Quite obviously, the play looks upon the iguana's scuffle and struggle as a kind of spiritual yearning to get to a meaning of one's existence. Shannon has been shown a meaning of his existence by Hannah. By virtue of her approval of his theological findings, he has nearly risen to the level of a prophet. It has already been explained that Hannah as a "medieval saint" has the authority to extend legitimization to Shannon's findings. He has been ordained by her to propagate his new found religion, which does not portray God as a "petulant" and "peevish old man". Now, he is required by Hannah to play the liberator, the messiah, to the iguana.

He refuses initially, but he does cut it loose eventually. Before its liberation, however, the iguana attains its status as "one of God's creatures" (370). At this stage, Shannon's elevation as a prophet and messiah reaches the point of final recognition. If the Son of God descended to the earth to cut man loose from his original sin, Shannon (as the messiah) is required to perform some ritual commemorating the mercy of God. He does perform the ritual: "We'll play God tonight like kids play house with old broken crates...Now Shannon is going to go down there with his machete and cut the damn lizard loose...because God won't do it and we are going to play God here" (370). There are two acts of liberation happening simultaneously—cutting loose of the iguana and the completion of Nonno's long awaited swansong. For both, the iguana and Nonno, the suffering and the scuffling comes to an end. The iguana runs "back to its bushes", and Nonno dies (370).

It is clear enough on the basis of this discussion that *The Night of the Iguana,* the full play acquires a scriptural value over and above its one-act version. This particular scriptural value of the play, however, cannot be categorized under the format of the major faith of Christianity. There cannot be any dispute about it because the play significantly diverges from the Christian faith at the point where the vision of God is presented as a tyrannical, "peevish" and "petulant" old man. Moreover, there is evidence enough to prove that the faith recommended in the play is closer to Buddhism, a moderate oriental faith. One of the major principles of Buddhism is distance from extremes. By raising a protest against the puritanical extremes, the play makes a call for moderation like that recommended in Buddhism. The most incontrovertible evidence of the play's Buddhist leanings is there in a combination of two apparently disjointed religious references. The first of these is a description of Hannah as a "medieval saint"; and the other is her presentation as "Miss... Thin-Standing-up-Female-Buddha" (347). Combined meaningfully, the two otherwise separate references grow into a theological philosophy that Shannon is going to propagate. This Orient-inclined philosophy finds a vision of God in "Lightning and Thunder" (305). The full play *The Night of the Iguana,* thus, grows into a major scriptural and theological development out of the earlier one-act.

The intermission between *Confessional* and *Small Craft Warnings* is remarkable for the comparatively lesser time gap between them. In one of her illustrative commentaries on Tennessee Williams's letter to her, Maria St. Just writes: "Begun in 1967, *Confessional* had first been produced at the Maine Theatre Arts Festival in July 1971, directed by William Hunt. Tennessee expanded the play into *Small Craft Warnings* for its New York premiere the following year" (251). Separating the beginning of *Confessional* from the production of *Small Craft* is, thus, a period of five years. A one-act in two scenes, *Confessional* is a series of eight 'confessions' in a row by the eight of the nine characters included in the frame of the action. The ninth character, a policeman, has a fringe existence with a very brief appearance. For structure, the one-act provides the "evocation of a bar on the beach-front in one of those coastal towns between Los Angeles and San Diego" (*Confessional*. Stage Directions 153). The bar attracts a group of "regulars" that can be treated as an acceptable travesty of a church congregation. Each of the eight members of this congregation makes his or her confession by coming down to "an area in the downstage center that can be lighted in a way that sets it apart from the bar" (153). The personae in the one-act have their individual aberrations or tragedies to recount during their individual confessions. These "regulars" at the bar have a superficial interaction; each one of them is a lonely drifter thrown together in the confessional territory of the bar. Their loneliness is a common theme running through their individual confessions. Another common point about their confessions is the absence of regret or a sense of wrong doing. Each one of them either expresses their compulsion, or complaint, or abortive anger. The first in the series is the confession of Bill, a male prostitute, who would sell sex to both male and female clients. His 'confession' is all about his plan to survive after Leona has thrown him out of her trailer; it is about his designs to seduce Young Man by applying a little threat. A remarkable thing about his confession is that it does not have an iota of shame regarding his method of survival: "They can't help the way they are. Who can? Not me. Left home at fifteen, and like Leona says, I've never done a lick of work in my life and I never plan to" (*Confessional* 162). Following immediately is the deprivation and compulsion: "But a man unmarried, forty-seven years old, employed as a short-order cook at a salary he can barely get by on alone, he can't be choosy. Nope he has to be satisfied with the Goddam scraps in this world" (162).

Of the eight of them, the more important and meaningful confessions are by Doc, Young Man, Boy and Monk. The confession of Doc is an enunciation of abortive anger at the "irreverent paraphernalia" desecrating the "holy mysteries of birth and death." Birth has been rendered desecrated and unholy by "Rubber gloves, boiled water, forceps, surgical shears" and death by "the wheeze of an Oxygen tank, the jab of a hypodermic needle, ...tubes in the arms and the kidneys, absorbent cotton inserted in the rectum to hold back the bowels discharged when the—being stops" (169). All these "expedients," he feels, "take away the dignity" of birth and death. It does not require much exercise to understand that Doc's is an anger against a distortion of the intrinsic beauty of Nature and all its manifestations like birth and death. Doc is a visionary; he wants that all coercive and cruel religions be discarded to make way for a generous and compassionate faith. He has "figured that the God is a black man with no light on his face", that He is a "Negro miner in the pit of a lightless coal mine..." (169). His call to deliver a "new Messiah," therefore, has an incontrovertible validity (170).

The confession of Young Man and Boy highlight the essential tragedy of homosexuals. Both the confessions seem to be making at least one point, that the people with differently directed sexuality need sympathy and compassion rather than the otherwise. Young Man's confession provides the view of the pathetic world of homosexuals:

> The Young Man: ...There's a coarseness, a deadening coarseness, in the experience of most homosexuals. The experiences are quick, and hard, and brutal, and the pattern of them is practically unchanging. Their act of love is like the jabbing of a hypodermic needle to which they're

> addicted but which is more and more empty of real interest and surprise. This lack of variation and surprise in their —"love life"—spreads into other areas of—sensibility.... (*Confessional* 178)

The psyche of a beginner entering the coarse world of homosexuality is no less scarred. The Boy's 'confession' is all about the vicious circle of liking the 'coarse' pleasures and deriving a sense of guilt out of it. It can be presumed that Boy represents the earliest stage of that differently directed sexuality:

> Tonight was—initiation. It scares me because I liked it, and liked him, too. I'll never turn into the bad-word flower shop man, but I'll probably have an experience like that again, and next time I won't make the mistake of showing an excitement and pleasure. (181)

Boy and Young Man, thus, represent the two stages in that kind of alternative sexuality. The Boy represents the "initiation" and the Young Man shows the horrible decadence of the sensibility of homosexuals.

Monk, the bar owner, functions as the confessor for all these 'confessions' turning on the themes of abortive anger, frustration, decadence and the compulsions of survival. The characters of the one-act find in him, consciously or unconsciously, a catalytic synthesizer. As stated earlier, the bar here travesties the Church. There is every sense, therefore, in treating Monk as the 'officiating' priest. His confession displays his priestly sympathy and generosity. He does not have any "moral objections to them as a part of humanity", and he has "got an affection for, a sincere interest" in his regular customers at the bar (182).

Small Craft Warnings is a play in two Acts emerging from *Confessional*. Structurally, the expanded version is a definite development over the one-act. The development is visible in a more proportionate division of action and a more natural methodology for the individual confessions of the characters. Under the changed methodology, the character does not walk downstage to the lighted confessional area; but the light focuses upon him or her where he or she sits or stands. A positive fallout of the changed system is the enhanced fidelity to the conventional dramatic structure. As the one-act *Confessional* develops into *Small Craft Warnings,* it lends the bar an additional character and significance. While *Confessional* evokes the image of a travesty of Church, *Small Craft Warnings* evokes the image of an amphibian territory. The bar, thus, could be suggestive of a territory between existence and evanescence. The opening stage directions underline the imminence of ocean with all its associations: "The curtain rises. The sound of ocean wind is heard. The stage is lighted at a very low level. The scene is a somewhat nonrealistic evocation of a bar on the beach-front..." (*Small Craft* 225). A concomitant of the ocean wind is the fog that may be looked upon as "the signature element in *Small Craft Warnings*: it sits, permeates, isolates, freezes. Fog represents stasis, suspension, the sense of nothing happening, the perfect signifier for the lack of dramatic action, or story..." (Kolin, *Undiscovered Country* 112).

As far as the absence of dramatic action or story is concerned, *Small Craft Warnings* is closest to its original draft. The play is just a series of soliloquy like speeches or confessions thinly connected by the place of their happening—the bar—and the minimum interactions made compulsory by the situation. The eight characters that matter are all alienated except for the synthesizing influence exerted by Monk. His influence, though, remains limited in the sense that he only functions as the passive listener to their travails. Each of these characters has his or her unique tragedy that cannot be shared. Their "confessions" or soliloquies are the same as in the one-act. A meaningful difference, however, is that two unnamed characters of the One-Act version now get names in the longer version. The 'Young Man' and the 'Boy' of the one-act are Quentin and Bobby in the expanded version. The names, Quentin and Bobby, have a strong suggestive quality to indicate the dominant characteristics of the characters they represent. The name Quentin suggests the 'quaintness' of the character's sexual preferences; and the name Bobby suggests the recipient of those preferences.

As in the one-act, *Small Craft Warnings* has all the confessions made in the first part. A vital point of difference crops up in the second part, which converts a Scene in *Confessional* into an Act in *Small Craft Warnings.* While the second scene in *Confessional* is merely an appendage, the analogous second Act in the play *Small Craft Warnings* is indispensable. The Act makes a huge difference with its cultivation of some community spirit. The lack of communication so apparent in the previous Act is diluted to a significant extent. The difference is immediately underscored at the very start of the Act by the "group singing" of the characters. When Leona returns to the Act, she has already lost much of her vitriol against Violet. A substantial part of the Act is a blank with "an off-stage quarrel between Leona and a night watchman on the beach. Their overlapping ad-lib dialogue continues in varying intensity as background to the business on stage..." (*Small Craft* 273). The "off-stage quarrel"—the "ad-lib dialogue"—reaches the audience while there is no verbal business on stage. The second Act in *Small Craft Warnings,* thus, emerges as an indispensable structural support to the first Act. By the time the Act ends, Violet has moved to a safe and motherly haven up the "narrow flight of stairs" that is "like the uterine passage to life" (*Small Craft* 276).

Briefly describing the relationship between *The Two Character Play* and *Out Cry,* the Publisher's Note introducing *Out Cry* states: "*Out Cry* opened at Lyceum Theatre in New York on March 1, 1973 ... An earlier version of *Out Cry* was presented in Chicago on July 1971... A still earlier version, under the title of *The Two Character Play,* was offered...on December 12, 1967." (*Out Cry*. Publisher's Note 05). The version of the play produced in 1973 under the title *Out Cry* is not the final version. The culminating climax of revisions and changes comes with *The Two Character Play*. The two versions cannot be said to have much difference: both originate "from the state of lunacy", both explicate a situation of "disorientation" and both represent the "two sides of one person" (Hayman 203).

Felice and Clare are the two characters, brother and sister, in *Out Cry.* The two grapple throughout with such psychic experiences as fear, shame, confinement, rejection, and desertion. Fear dominates the play right from the start, which is even accentuated by the author through the description of a particular piece of stage property:

> At curtain rise, Felice stands motionless as a hunted creature at the sound of pursuers... He is staring from the raked platform...at a huge, dark statue upstage, a work of great power and darkly subjective meaning,... Then he leaps off to the pediment of the sculpture that towers over him and begins a fierce, demonic effort to push it away. It is too heavy...he shouts for assistance. (*Out Cry* 07)

The statue appears a "chained monster" to him. By every perceptible means, the "monster" is an outward projection of the fear in Felice's mind that he is unable to move. A very early utterance of Felice provides a view of his psyche:

> Places! – Fear... (He has glanced upstage and at the "chained monster".) Fear! – The fierce little man with the drum inside the rib-cage. – Compared to fear grown to panic that has no limit – short of consciousness blowing out and not reviving again – no other emotion a living, feeling creature is able to have, not even love or hate.... (*Out Cry* 08)

Clare, the other character in the play also feels the looming presence of fear: "It dominates, it towers over the stage, what play on earth could be performed under this? Not even Medea or Oedipus Rex?" (10).

As the play progresses, fear begins to grow as a compendium with such concomitants as confusion, shame and confinement. Felice and Clare are two characters distanced by confusion which emerges from their situation of confinement and desertion—a confinement and desertion that is not physical. They have been psychologically confined by their sense of shame. The following bits of their conversation exhibit the intermingling of confinement and shame:

> Clare: ...Oh, Felice, I want to go, today I want to go out, I want to walk on the street—like a favorite of nature in public view without—shame...
>
> Felice: Oh?—You want to go out calling? ...Clare. So! Go! (He opens the door for her)
>
> Clare: Why have you opened the door?

> Felice: For you to go out calling.
>
> Clare: ...I'd never dream of going out without you in your—disturbed—condition.
>
> Felice: And you in yours. (*Out Cry* 33-34)

The urgency to "go out calling" and the inability to do so results in the situation of confinement the two characters in the play suffer. The net result of this conflict is a confusion that is felt by the two quite alarmingly. The shame of Felice and Clare is the product of a secret related to the death of their parents. The two failingly try to prove that the deaths had been accidental; whereas the common perception has been that the deaths had occurred through murder and suicide. The common perception, which is the truth, has led to the confiscation of the insurance money. The truth of the common perception is made clear in Part II of the play where Felice tries to concoct the "absolute opposite of the truth" to draw the insurance money. The "absolute opposite" is that "mother with the revolver" first killed "Father and then herself" (43-44). The opposite of the "absolute opposite", then, leads to the truth—that father, with the revolver, first killed mother and then himself. The truth, or "the absolute opposite" of it, has been the source of their shame as well as the paranoid state of the mind expressed by Clare in Part I:

> My brother and I are surrounded by so much suspicion and malice that we almost never, we hardly ever, dare to go out of the house. In the nighttime people stop and linger on the sidewalk and whisper charges, anomalous letters of obscenities are sent us. (*Out Cry* 35)

The scuttled and made defunct play in the play, entitled *The Two Character Play,* has an intrinsic relationship with Felice's efforts to concoct "the absolute opposite" of the truth regarding the two deaths. He tries, right from the start, to recreate their story by writing and trying to produce *The Two Character Play,* in which he would put himself and his sister as characters. Right from the start, therefore, the play has a stultified play within the play that confronts the audience. The stultified play is brought to the forefront in *The Two Character Play,* presented off-Broadway on March 1, 1973 and included in the fifth volume of *The Theatre of Tennessee Williams*. Evidently, the revised version has more to do with the convoluted and troubled psyches of the brother and the sister. The first evidence of the fact that the play tries to bring to the fore the stultified play of the earlier version is provided by the opening stage directions where the "statue of a giant" (Chained monster" in the earlier version) is deprived of prominence. To note the contrast, let's place side by side the concluding lines of the opening Stage Directions in the two versions:

(a) Then he leaps off to the pediment of the sculpture that towers over him and begins a fierce, demonic effort to push it away. It is too heavy to be moved by a man alone. He shouts for assistance. (*Out Cry* 07)

(b) He draws a piano stool into the light, sits down to make notes for a monologue on a scratch pad. (*The Two Character Play* 309)

It is obvious here that the description in *Out Cry* is concerned with the fear of Felice, whereas the attempt in *The Two Character Play* is to highlight the 'monologue' Felice intends to present. Even his first statement is a part of the proposed play read aloud. As he reads, it can be observed that he is facing the usual creative confusion. The play he is writing has to have fear as its central theme:

> Felice: (Slowly, reflectively, writing): To play with fear is to play with fire. (He looks up as if he were silently asking some question of enormous consequence) No, worse, much worse, than playing with fire. Fire has limits. It comes to a river or sea and there it stops, it comes to stone or bare earth that it can't leap across and there is stopped, having nothing more to consume. But fear—Impossible.... (*Two Character Play* 309).

Fear and fire, thus, fall into the same category; the former being more destructive and consumptive than the latter. The inner, real, play that is accentuated here serves to underscore the psychopathic condition of the two characters. Their psychopathic condition is characterized by claustrophobia and a manic degree of fear. The inner play promises to be therapeutic and cathartic. But the acuteness of the malaise is such that defeat is almost a foregone conclusion. And defeat is what Felice and Clare face at the end, where the imitation of their parents' death is almost carried out:

> [He moves a few steps toward the revolver, then picks it up and slowly, with effort, points it at Clare. Felice tries very hard to pull the trigger: he cannot. Slowly, he lowers his arm, and drops the revolver to the floor. There is a pause...in both their faces is a tender admission of defeat. They reach out their hands to one another...] (*The Two Character Play* 370).

The difference between *Out Cry* and *The Two Character Play* is quite elusive and difficult to exactly locate. The absence of a definite difference makes the two plays "fairly equal contenders on the page"; the two do not differ "substantially in terms of content or literary style" (Londré in Kolin, *Undiscovered Country* 97). In spite of the apparent and genuine similarity, there can be located some subtle points of difference between the two versions. *Out Cry* can be seen as a drama of schizophrenia in which Felice and Clare are indistinguishable from each other. Moreover, the inner play in *Out Cry* remains elusive, vague and inseparable from the apparent play. In *The Two Character Play,* the two characters are fairly separate from each other and their identities are sufficiently distinguished. Further, the revised version brings to the fore the inner play in such a manner that it becomes distinct from the apparent outer play. A positive outcome of the clarified distinctions is a distinguishable gap between the brother and sister both in the inner play and the outer.

Vieux Carré as a play is a creative depiction of Tennessee Williams's experiences in a shabby rooming house on 722, Toulouse Street in New Orleans. From the autobiographical point of view, therefore, the play is a reminiscing of a period in 1938-39. Talking of its genesis, the play is related to a very faithful, though comic, slice of the New Orleans experiences in a one-act entitled *The Lady of Larkspur Lotion.* Chronologically, the one-act is closer to the experiences than the later full-length play *Vieux Carré*, which is an enlargement of the one-act version into an artistic work attempting to figure graphically the transience of failed artists and dreamers. As it appears in the sixth volume of 'The Theatre of Tennessee Williams', *The Lady of Larkspur Lotion* is a fairly short one-act running barely into nine pages. In fact, it can be called a strand that merges into *Vieux Carré* along with the antecedent short story entitled "The Angel in the Alcove". *The Lady of Larkspur Lotion* concentrates upon a character who has nearly converted her lies to an illusion that she believes to be the truth. The character is Mrs. Hardwick Moore, and her lies about a non-existent lover, an imaginary rich rubber plantation man in Brazil, have been so frequently and insistently repeated that they nearly assume the shape of an illusion. The sustenance of the illusion is entirely dependent upon the persistence of the lies. The fact here is a horrible opposite of the lies—Mrs. Moore subsists upon whatever she can earn through prostitution. Her complaint about cockroaches only incurs the anger of the Landlady, Mrs. Wire, who has suffered many 'deadbeats' like Mrs. Moore. The argument between Mrs. Wire and Mrs. Moore brings to the scene the Writer, another derelict clinging to a dream. It is understandable that there should be vibes between Mrs. Moore and the Writer, simply because the two belong to the same clan of derelicts. Both have their elaborate dreams—Mrs. Moore of a rich lover, and the writer of a "780-page masterpiece". That the "masterpiece" is just a dream, an ambition beyond realization, makes the Writer a more miserable character than Mrs. Moore who has been pushed into prostitution for survival:

> Writer: (in a tired voice): Ah, well, now, what if I am? Suppose there is no 780-page masterpiece in existence... supposing there is in existence no masterpiece whatsoever! ... Suppose I wanted to be a great artist but lacked the force and the power! Suppose my book fell short of the final chapter, even my verses languished uncompleted! Suppose the curtains of my exalted fancy rose on magnificent dramas—but the houselights darkened before the curtain fell! Suppose all of these unfortunate things are true... suppose that I live in this world of pitiful fiction!... I tell

> you this—now listen! There are no lies but the lies that are stuffed in the mouth by the hard knuckled hand of need, the cold iron fist of necessity, Mrs. Wire! (*Larkspur Lotion* 87).

The speech, almost double the length of what has been reproduced here, pronounces the theme and the thrust of the play. What the Writer pleads for indirectly is a sympathetic attitude towards the misery of the 'fugitives' like himself and Mrs. Moore. The eccentricity of the Writer's dream is expressed by his identification of himself with "Chekhov! Anton Pavlovich Chekhov!" (*Larkspur Lotion* 89).

Vieux Carré incorporates *The Lady of Larkspur Lotion* along with the important strands and characters from the antecedent story "The Angel in the Alcove". Mrs. Wire of the one-act reappears in the play along with the Writer, and Mrs. Moore is replaced by two younger women. However, the limelight in the play *Vieux Carré* is hogged by Nightingale, who doesn't appear in the one-act. Nightingale in *Vieux Carré* is, as has been illustrated in the previous chapter, a reincarnation of the unnamed consumptive artist in the story. Quite obviously, the consumptive artist's material presence in the play makes a bold statement about the increased dimensions of the theme. Through the Writer and Nightingale, the play delineates the stilted psyche of a failed artist. Around this picture of a failed artist, so common in Tennessee Williams, are the other portraits of the typical failures in life. The crux and concern of the play comes summed up in the concluding conversation between the Writer and Mrs. Wire:

> Mrs. Wire: Now watch out, boy. Be careful of the future. It's a long way for the young. Some make it and others get lost.
>
> Writer: I know... (He turns to the audience) I stood by the door uncertainly for a moment or two. I must have been frightened of it...
>
> Mrs. Wire: Can you see the door?
>
> Writer: Yes –but to open it is a desperate undertaking...!

(As he first draws the door open, he is forced back a few steps by a cacophony of sound: the waiting storm of his future – mechanical racking, cries of pain and pleasure...)

They're disappearing behind me. Going. People you've known do that: they go.... The earth seems to swallow them up, the walls absorb them like moisture...their voices are echoes, fading but remembered.... (*Vieux Carré* 116)

Vieux Carré relates to *The Lady of Larkspur Lotion* in as much as it comprehensively weaves around and enhances in proportion the life and characters experienced and encountered by Tennessee Williams on 722, Toulouse Street, New Orleans, in late 1930s. Taking into account the recent discovery of *The Reading*, a one-act play of the author written around the time of *Larkspur Lotion* and first published in the 2010 issue of *The Tennessee Williams Annual Review*, the particular history of *Vieux Carré* gets an additional extension. It is so because *The Reading* too grows from Williams's "acquaintance with Jane and Tye", two of the characters of the play, during "his second visit to New Orleans in 1941" (Bray 4). *The Reading*, thus, becomes, according to Bray, the "part of a larger scheme – in this case, the full length *Vieux Carré*" (03).

The thrust of this chapter and the preceding has been the study of the range and the magnitude of the characteristics creating the spectrum of successive stages of reincarnations and revisions of thematic, structural, ideological and conceptual material. Tennessee Williams creates these reincarnations and makes these revisions as he progresses from short stories and sketches to early plays or one-acts to full plays later. These reincarnations and revisions also show the interrelationships among the writings representing the different stages in Tennessee Williams's evolution as an author. The chapters, thus, create a 'nerve center' of sorts to interconnect the three successive stages in the career of the author: the earliest stage as a storywriter, the intermediate stage as a dramatist and the mellow stage of revisions. Apart from all these cases of intensive interrelationships, it is quite possible to find several independent strands running through many of Williams's works.

For example, two very prominent independent strands running throughout the repertoire of Tennessee Williams are brother-sister bond and mutilation. These free-floating strands quite often create an interrelationship among works otherwise quite diverse.

An interesting illustration is the connection growing between *The Glass Menagerie* and *The Two Character Play* on account of the brother-sister relationship in them. It is already a piece of preknowledge now that *The Glass Menagerie* emanates from the short story entitled "The Portrait of a Girl in Glass", and *The Two Character Play* from its antecedent in *Out Cry*. By including other works incorporating brother-sister bond, the sequence can be substantially enlarged. Two short stories readily come in—"The Vengeance of Nitocris" and "The Resemblance between a Violin Case and Coffin". All included, it becomes a sequence of six works actively and passively linked by the free-floating strand of brother-sister bond. Parker observes "solipsism that exists in sibling love" as a connective link between two of the works in this sequence—*The Glass Menagerie* and *The Two Character Play* (Parker, *The Circle Closed* 521). Claudia Cassidy, a strong believer in *The Two Character* Play, and consequently, in its antecedent in *Out Cry*, calls the play "in some ways a sequel to *The Glass Menagerie*" (qtd. in Williams and Mead 308). Judged from Cassidy's point of view, the last long play by Williams tries to say whatever may have remained unsaid in *The Glass Menagerie*. Once all other characters have been dispensed with, *The Two Character Play* succeeds in concentrating upon the tragedy of the brother and sister alongside the nature of their relationship. The close of the play suggests a better, and arguably the only end to the tragedy and the undefined relationship—a murder followed by a suicide.

In its various manifestations, mutilation nearly connects the entire range of Williams's writings. From ostensible and physical forms to subtle psychological varieties, mutilation is available in the author's works with a striking consistency. It is worth taking a glance at the consistently available instances of mutilation through the fiction and drama of Tennessee Williams. To begin with, in the fiction of the author, it is a-now-familiar instance of the brutal dismemberment of the Pharaoh in "The Vengeance of Nitocris", referred and investigated earlier in this study. Following that early instance of mutilation, there are examples occurring with consistent regularity: John's incurable amnesia in "Something by Tolstoi"; the rape of a little white girl in "Big Black: A Mississippi Idyll"; the self-deprecatory shyness of Bud in "The Accent of a Coming Foot"; the paralysis coupled with old age in "Sand"; the demented seclusion of Tina in "The Dark Room"; the unnatural pursuit of flesh in "The Mysteries of Joy Rio"; the abortive passion of the consumptive artist in "The Angel in the Alcove"; Oliver's loss of an arm and a vital balance in "One Arm"; the chillingly suicidal masochism in "Desire and the Black Masseur"; and the crazed old age in some late short stories of the author. The presentation of the varieties of mutilation is equally consistent and regular in Tennessee Williams's drama. Present in a fairly recognizable form in the major dramatic presentations, the phenomenon becomes all the more pronounced in the drama of the author. *The Glass Menagerie, A Streetcar Named Desire, The Cat on a Hot Tin Roof, Orpheus Descending, The Rose Tattoo* and *Suddenly Last Summer* are the major dramatic presentations that project either psychological or physical varieties of fragmentation and mutilation. *Orpheus Descending* and *Suddenly Last Summer* are two outstanding examples in the sense that both suggest a total and brutal fragmentation of body. The latter of the two even makes a brush with cannibalism, and thereby enters into a somewhat thematic relationship with the short story entitled "Desire and the Black Masseur". It is important to note here that in both the cases, cannibalism functions as a sort of punishment or penance for altered sexuality. Cannibalism, here, entails the futility of "trying to define and contain human desire, of trying to construct and control the human subject through sexuality, and displays the destructive consequences of these attempts" (Saddik, "The (un)Representation of Fragmentation" 348). Anthony Burns in the story and Sebastian Venable in the play do not show any desire to contain their sexuality; they only give a horribly masochistic twist to it. For a comparative look, we put two examples of extreme masochism side by side. This is how Anthony Burns reaches the finale of his penance or self-inflicted punishment:

> The Negro masseur leaned over his still breathing victim. Burns was whispering something. The black giant nodded. "You know what you have to do now"? the victim asked him. The black giant nodded. He picked up the body, which barely held together, and placed it gently on a clear swept table. The Giant began to devour the body of Burns. (*Collected Stories* 211)

Sebastian's penance is more easily understood because he surrenders himself to the targets of his pedophilia:

> Catherine: The band of naked children pursued us up the steep white street in the sun that was like a great white bone of a giant beast... They had devoured parts of him. Torn or cut parts of him away with their hands or knives or maybe those jagged tin cans they made music with, they had torn bits of him away and stuffed them into those gobbling fierce little empty black months of theirs (*Suddenly Last Summer* 422).

Up to *Suddenly Last Summer* and other works around it, mutilation remains an explainable phenomenon. But the later repertoire of Tennessee Williams brings in some convoluted varieties of it. Such late one-acts as *The Mutilated* and *The Gnädiges Fräulein* are the representative examples exemplifying those complex and convoluted varieties of fragmentation and mutilation.

The entire discussion in this chapter and the one immediately preceding, proves a major point about Tennessee Williams's habits of explaining and magnifying of themes, characters, narrative or dramatic techniques and other elements of creative writing through a series of revisions. As has been seen, the revisions very often transcend the dividing line between the genres of fiction and drama. Apart from the aesthetic dissatisfaction characteristic of a genuine writer, there is something very subtle behind this tendency of the author to revise. Speaking to Joanne Stang about this subtle element, Tennessee Williams says: "Finishing a play, you know, is like completing a marriage or a love affair...you feel very forsaken by that, that's why I love revising and revising, because it delays the moment when there is this separation between you and the work" (in Devlin 108). The statement of Tennessee Williams unmistakably brings to the fore the throbbing, live and personalized relationship between himself and his work. Revising, thus, becomes a mechanism of existence for the author. It would not be extravagant at this point to suggest that writing and revising for the author have been indicative of both an obsession with and an escape from himself. Taking John Lahr's opinion in another context as the base—that "Williams is at his most alert, eloquent, humorous, vulnerable, and forthright while talking about the one pure thing in his life: his work"—one can draw a more subjective conclusion to explain the continuous and almost unending revising and revisions in Tennessee Williams (xiv). The subjective conclusion would be that Williams's unstoppable revisions were spurred by his unstoppable search for elusive "purity", which is always an unattainable aesthetic height.

To close the circle, it should further be concluded that many strands and experiences suffered and enjoyed by the author come to be repeatedly replicated and reinforced through the revisions. Revised and replicated and reinvented, the experiences steadily make a movement away from the personal to the impersonal as they enter into newer artistic combinations in successive versions from the stories to the early plays, and from there to the mature.

6

The "Broken Language": The Absurd and the Abstract; the Modern and the Postmodern

> Speak out the broken language of your hearts, and we'll supply the sense where it seems to be needed.
>
> (*The Purification*)

In a fresh and new-in-many-ways biography of Tennessee Williams, published in 2014, John Lahr authentically informs, "On March 31, 1945, at the Playhouse Theatre on Forty-Eighth Street, on the unfashionable side of Broadway, in New York City, the curtains rose on the sold out opening night of *The Glass Menagerie* ten minutes late, at 8:50 p.m." (01). Thanks to the "chic, diminutive agent" of the author, Audrey Wood, the play, thus, was the inauguration of an illustrious career on Broadway, New York. (Lahr 01). In the Production Notes to this memorable, much archived and written about success, Tennessee Williams writes:

> Being a 'memory play', *The Glass Menagerie* can be presented with unusual freedom from convention. Because of its considerably delicate or tenuous material, atmospheric touches and subtleties of direction play a particularly important part. Expressionism and all other unconventional techniques in drama have only one valid aim, and that is a closer approach to truth (229).

Prefacing his first Broadway success, and in many ways his inauguration into Modern American Drama, these remarks almost constitute the manifesto of his creative career in theatre. Whatever follows from this point to *The Two Character Play* (in mid-1970s) makes the movement up the scale in the use of the "unconventional techniques" loosely falling in the zone of 'Expressionism'. Tennessee Williams's use of expressionistic conventions, however, has an earlier start with *Stairs to the Roof*. That early play of the author is about the vague dissatisfaction of a wage earner, Benjamin Murphy. Dissatisfied, perhaps, with his meaningless existence, he finds a kindred soul in a co-worker, The Girl, and decides to climb the "stairway to the roof" at the factory. At the point of the climactic end, Benjamin Murphy and The Girl are taken away by a mysterious Mr. E. "to another world to begin the story of man anew" (Nelson 68, 73). Williams's variety of expressionism begins early, comes of age in *The Glass Menagerie* and reaches its point of high development in *Camino Real*. The progress is nearly analogous in the author's short fiction where such stories as "The Knightly Quest", "Happy August the Tenth" and "Sabbatha and Solitude" represent the high mark of his expressionistic creations.

Away and apart from his major Broadway successes, which have often been understood in the context of the functioning of expressionism in them, the following paragraphs discuss two less talked of but representative cases of the use of expressionism in Tennessee Williams's repertoire, one each from drama and fiction—*Camino Real* the play and "Yellow Bird" the story. Different from *The Glass Menagerie, A Streetcar Named Desire* and *Cat on a Hot Tin Roof, Camino Real* is sufficiently distanced from reality (at least the normal manifestations of reality) to be designated as a uniquely expressionistic play. Almost measuring the uniqueness of the play, Louis Broussard makes a qualitative statement that "nothing like *Camino Real* had appeared on the stage for over thirty years" (Broussard 07). More than corroborating the view of Broussard, Mary Ann Corrigan says that the "technique and subject matter" of *Camino Real* recalls "the Expressionistic extravaganzas popular in the American theatre during the 1920s" (in Tharpe 396). Quite conscious of the difference of the play, Tennessee Williams makes the following observations in the 'Author's Foreword' attached to its Broadway premier:

> More than any other work that I have done, this play has seemed to me like the construction of another world, a separate existence. Of course, it is nothing more nor less than my conception of the time and world that I live in.... A convention of the play is existence outside of time in a place of no specific locality.... This sort of freedom is not chaos nor anarchy. On the contrary, it is the result of painstaking design, and in this work I have given more conscious attention to form and construction than I have in any work before.... (*Camino Real.* Author's Foreword 119-21)

The play has an epigraph from Dante's *Inferno* appended to it to signify that it presents Tennessee Williams's conception of the modern world where "the spring of humanity has gone dry" (128). The dramatic action in the play is obviously the dream of Don Quixote who goes to sleep in the Prologue to wake up only in the later part of the last 'Block'. Instead of proper Acts and Scenes, there are sixteen 'Blocks' in the play announced by the Gutman who has a dual existence inside and outside the 'dream'. The Gutman is both the presenter and the interlocutor. To start, he announces "Block One on the Camino Real"; and, to end, he informs the audience that "the curtain line has been spoken" (*Camino Real* 131, 233). The Prologue in the play takes place immediately before daybreak. Don Quixote, followed by Sancho Panza, enters the stage questing for the lost ideals of truth and valor. Before the entry of Kilroy, the key character, at the close of Block Two, there is some rioting by the street people over the shooting of the Survivor. The rioting, however, is cut short by a distraction caused by the announcement of moonlight fiesta by the Gutman. Already, characters from the dead past are in action—Jacques Casanova, a seventeenth century rogue, and Marguerite Gautier, a courtesan from the romantic era. Since the play is stated to be outside the linearities and logicalities of time, only Kilroy's entry and departure follow a chronological system. Everything in the play except Kilroy's visit is illogical, suggested by the simultaneous presence of Casanova, Marguerite, Lord Byron and Don Quixote. It is important to note here that Casanova and Marguerite in the play have been shorn of their respective notorieties. Casanova cannot love and Marguerite is inefficient as a courtesan. Their stultified status is revealed in their conversation:

> Marguerite: You know what it is: that I am one of those aging – voluptuaries – who used to be paid for pleasure but now have to pay! – Jacques, I won't be followed. [...]... your vocabulary is almost as out of date as your cape and your cane. How could anyone quit this field with honor, this place where there's nothing but the gradual wasting away of everything decent in us. (*Camino Real* 171-75)

In the course of the sixteen Blocks of Camino Real, Kilroy enters, gets robbed by pick-pockets and the Loan Shark, has a series of encounters with the inhabitants and then departs. He is a former boxer, now fallen on bad days because of a heart problem which requires him to "give up liquor and smoking and sex" (143). By the end of the play Kilroy "has survived humiliation, two chases, robbery, a fertility ritual in which he is the 'chosen hero', and even death itself, followed by resurrection" (Griffin 127). Inside this framework of Kilroy's visit, characters defying time barriers appear and disappear in an illogical manner. This illogicality regarding the appearance of characters is strictly on account of the play being a fantasy "outside of time". Towards the end of the last Block (sixteen), Kilroy along with Don Quixote is seen leaving Camino Real. Before the two leave, "the violets in the mountains have broken the rocks", the dry fountain has started "flowing loudly and sweetly", and the final message has been delivered:

> Quixote: Don't! Pity! Your! Self!
>
> (He takes out a pocket mirror and combs and grooms his beard and moustache.) The wounds of the vanity, the many offences our egos have to endure, being housed in bodies that age and the hearts that grow tired, are better accepted with a tolerant smile—like *this*! —You see? (He cracks his face in two with an enormous grin). (*Camino Real* 231-32)

In reference to the elusive structure and the characters of the play, Benjamin Nelson observes that the characters signify "attitudes rather than individuals and thus their plights become abstraction" (Nelson 183). Such observations are "representative of those who insisted on realism when the play was produced" (Griffin 127). The observation of Nelson and the reaction of Alice Griffin point to the important fact that *Camino Real* demands unconventional perspectives for analysis. That it is so has been clearly and heavily stated in the Foreword and the Afterword of the play. In the Afterword, Tennessee Williams suggests that *Camino Real* be approached in the manner the works of "Michelangelo, Velasquez, and Rembrandt" would be approached:

> ...How much art his hands were blessed with or how much mine are, I don't know, but that art is a blessing is certain and that it contains its message is also certain and I feel, as the painter did, that the message lies in those abstract beauties of form and color and line, to which I would add light and motion.... (*Camino Real*. Afterword 122)

The play assumes its added significance when illustrated from the perspectives of expressionism. As the curtain goes up, it is "an almost lightless stage" and "there is a loud singing of wind, accompanied by distant, measured reverberations like pounding surface or distant shellfire." The "day break" has to be seen as "a white bird caught in a net and struggling to rise". The plaza which is sought to be represented on stage has two rows—the "left is the luxury side of the street" and the right is the "Skid Row which contains the Gipsy's gaudy stall, the Loan Shark's establishment..., and the 'Ritz Men Only' which is a flea-bag hotel or flophouse..." "Downstage right and left are a pair of arches which give entrance to dead-end street". The only way out of this modern-day inferno is a great flight of stairs that mount the ancient wall to a sort of archway that leads out into "Terra Incognita" which is "a wasteland between the walled town and the distant perimeter of snow-topped mountains" (*Camino Real*. Prologue 125). The slight action that fills this evanescent setting is the presentation of Kilroy's visit and his experiences. The characters populating the setting and carrying forth the action are archetypal figures drawn from history, literature and legends. They are, as the author specifies, "archetypes of certain basic attitudes and qualities" (*Camino Real*. Author's Foreword 119). As such, the play is a tribute of sorts to dreamers, artists and idealists who routinely turn to a lost past for sustenance and inspiration. Understandably, therefore, the characters in *Camino Real* seem indistinguishable from such unforgettable characters in Tennessee Williams's canon as Amanda, Alma, Blanche, Hannah, Brick and Shannon. The dialogue in the play is inconsistent and unbelievable; it alternates between extreme colloquialism and pretentious profundity. The play heavily depends upon symbolic settings and props to create a horrifying image of modern life. The seen and heard images in the play are archetypal and, hence, immediately decipherable into meaning. The theme of the play is as expressionistic as the setting, symbols and characters. It can aptly be summed up by borrowing John Gassner's general observation: "For the expressionist, the stage was to be a means of projecting the disintegration of modern man and twentieth century society" (109). In the process, *Camino Real* serves as a station on the journey from birth to death—"it is a port of entry and departure" where it is impossible to have "permanent guests" (*Camino Real* 176). There is so much of expressionistic material in the play that Mary Ann Corrigan finds it entering into kinship with the expressionistic works of the German exponents of the genre:

> Like Strindberg's *A Dream Play*, in which a bud on top of a castle mired in dung suddenly bursts into flower just before the play ends, *Camino Real* extends its ray of hope only in the last minute. Both plays are monuments to the overwhelming strength of evil in the world. The happy end to the quest seems almost tacked on. The Terra Incognita appropriately remains hidden behind a high wall, unknown, insubstantial, without artistic realization. In his failure to give form to his "solution", Williams is no different from his German Expressionist forbearers. (in Tharpe 408)

Many of the stories of the author use explicitly expressionistic modes of narration. As a representative case, we can take up the concluding part of "The Yellow Bird". Pointing to the suddenly changed character of the narrative in that part of the story, the author asks the reader to look upon it from a different perspective—"Now from this point on the story takes a strange turn that may be highly disagreeable to some readers, if any still hoped that it was going to avoid the fantastic" (*Collected Stories* 227). The conclusion of the story shows Alma in her deathbed waiting for her son to return. The one who returns is not the son but the dead father "like a Neptune out of the ocean". He bears a cornucopia dripping with seaweed and his bare chest and legs" have acquired "a greenish patina such as a bronze statue comes to be covered with" (227). The dead father, John the first, goes "off" and Alma goes "off with him" (227). The son, John the second, does return sometime later and sets up a monument which is "a curious thing" showing a "leaping dolphin" with "three figures of indeterminate gender astride" it. One of the three figures carries "a crucifix, one a cornucopia and one a Grecian lyre" (228). The story, thus, becomes a narrative exposition of the expressionistic conventions. The juxtaposition of 'Crucifix', 'Cornucopia' and 'Grecian Urn' is an index of the indeterminacy and indefiniteness of postmodernity. The brief resurrection of the dead lover of Alma, his body resembling weather beaten bronze statue, and the departure of dying Alma with him only convey an expressionistic meaning. The culmination, of course, comes in the description of the monument of a very complex symbolic value.

As the explicitly expressionistic creations discussed above clarify, Tennessee Williams's art—both fictional and dramatic —is in direct line of descent from the system devised by the symbolists. At the very surface of his art can be seen a fascination with the past, a liking for dream reality, a penchant for mixed dramatic forms including music and a steadfast rejection of realism in an attempt to create congenial surroundings for the omnipresent fragile 'fugitive' in Tennessee Williams. Also noticeable in his art is a significant aspect of the symbolist philosophy—a concern with the mystery of life. Like the symbolists, the author can be seen tortured by the thought of the imminence of death, and haunted by the unavoidability of isolation. A particular group of Williams's plays quite explicitly evinces the influence of the symbolist aesthesis. The plays are: *Slapstick Tragedy* (a double-bill including two short plays, *The Mutilated* and *The Gnädiges Fräulein*), *Kingdom of Earth, In the Bar of Tokyo Hotel* and *The Two Character Play*. Among the stories apparently influenced by symbolism are: "The Knightly Quest", "The Field of Blue Children", "Sand", "The Yellow Bird" and "Sabbatha and Solitude". It must be noted here that the antirealistic and the unconventional in Williams incurred the displeasure of the critics of the time and prompted the author to react in an incensed but expository manner in a conversation with C. Robert Jennings:

> I hope I'll never become one of those quarrelsome old writers who go after critics....They knock you down with all the ammunition, they've got plenty....They want to judge you on traditional form when you're trying to move to something freer, like presentational theatre when you depart from realism and put style on the presentation itself....All my great characters are larger than life, not realistic. In order to capture the quality of life in two and a half hours everything has to be concentrated, intensified. (in Devlin 239-40)

Williams's symbolism "derives from Wagner's concept of synthesis and the ideas of his symbolist followers whose goal was to create a new syntax of poetic conventions that transcended ordinary Language" (Larsen in Tharpe 416). Almost in the manner of Wagner, Tennessee Williams seeks a synthesis of poetry, music, dance, mime and other constituents of design. The plays and stories listed above follow the symbolist conventions: they grapple with the conflict of flesh and spirit, they deal with the dualism of life and death, they reach back into the past, they underscore a sense of isolation, they use nature and colors to evoke emotions and they put up a resistance to realism.

Indicating the bent and character of the revival of interest in Tennessee Williams in early 21st Century, Verna Foster states:

> Greater understanding of the grotesque elements in Williams's work has aided in the critical re-evaluation of several of his late plays in recent years. The grotesque,

> present even in Williams's earlier, more realistic drama, overtly informs later plays such as *The Mutilated, The Gnädiges Fräulein, The Two Character Play* and *In the Bar of Tokyo Hotel,* works in which Williams invents a dramatic style that draws on the dramaturgy of the theatre of the Absurd (as well as on his earlier experiments in dramatic form). (in Kolin, *Undiscovered Country* 156)

When it comes to the experimentation in the later writings of the author, his art can be seen falling in line with the European literary forms. European writers' efforts to deal with art and existence can be seen finding a parallel in Tennessee Williams's perception of an artist in a sadistic world, his style of filtering experience, his eclectic sense of social engagement and in his unstoppable effort to transcend the negative states of existential absurdity. At the core of many of his late fictional and dramatic writings is, essentially, the Absurd point of view. The Absurd artist has to transcend the negative awareness of the Absurd human condition. He also has to be aware that there is a danger of falling into highly secularized (non-religious) and non-redemptive vision. He is sometimes required to externalize his own personality in order to be able to deal with the external phenomena. There is always a feeling of inextricability, of exile and of being captive. As such, there is an apparent absurdity in the Absurd artist's relationship to his environment and to himself as a part of the social surroundings. The later fiction and drama of Tennessee Williams shows him as an explicitly Absurd artist. In her article entitled, "Confronting the Late Plays of Tennessee Williams" in *The Tennessee Williams Annual Review* 6 (2003), Allean Hale remarks in this context: "As with Beckett, his (Williams's) new plays were abstract, with characters who were more than the embodiment of an idea than real people and who might simply be named MAN and WOMAN or ONE and TWO" ("Confronting the Late Plays"). In a situation of alienation, which is a form of the Absurd and the abstract, the first and the foremost casualty is dialogue. At this level, such one-acts of the author as *Talk to Me Like the Rain* and *I Can't Imagine Tomorrow* come very close to a representative play of the genre of the Absurd—Samuel Beckett's *Waiting for Godot.*

The eagerness of Estragon in *Waiting for Godot* to communicate his nightmare to Vladimir is matched, if not surpassed, by Man's desperation for dialogue in *Talk to Me Like the Rain.* It would be worthwhile here to cite pieces of conversation to illustrate this argument:

> Vladimir – I felt lonely.
>
> Estragon – I had a dream.
>
> Vladimir – Don't tell me!
>
> Estragon – I dreamt that –
>
> Vladimir – DON'T TELL ME!
>
> Estragon – (gestures towards the universe). This one is enough for you? (Silence) It's not nice of you Didi. Who am I to tell my private nightmares to if I can't tell them to you?
>
> Vladimir – Let them remain private... (*Waiting for Godot* 45-46).

The failure of Estragon to elicit a response from Vladimir is matched by Man's fervent appeal to Woman for conversation in *Talk to Me Like the Rain:*

> Man: Well, talk to me like the rain and—let me listen, let me lie here and - listen - ....It's been too long a time since—we've leveled with each other. Now tell me things. What have you been thinking in silence?—While I've been passed around like a dirty post card in this city...
>
> Woman: I—
>
> Man: You've got to, it's necessary! I've got to know, so talk to me like the rain and I will lie here and listen, I will lie here and—
>
> Woman: I want to go away. (*Talk to Me* 269).

A similar absence of communication characterizes the relationship between the aged couple in the short story "Sand". The willful and passionate effort of Rose to elicit some response from Emiel, her paralyzed husband, fails miserably. Their isolated life now, ironically, draws its sustenance by rooting itself in the happy past of their youth. There is a constant conflict between the happy past and an unrelentingly apprehensive present:

> And then one day she hears a heavy thud. She drops the soup ladle. She stands motionless by the Kitchen stove.... In a moment she will hear the crinkling of the newspaper or the clank of the pipe bowl against the glass tray. She waits for these. Still there is nothing. Something inside of her congeals. Grows hard and cold as a rock (*Collected Stories* 52).

Written in 1936, the story clearly indicates the course Tennessee Williams's art would be taking in the years to come.

The point deserving emphasis here is that the strains of the Absurd and the abstract get manifested in the fiction of the author much earlier than his drama. The expressionistic and Absurd metaphor of journey to suggest an unavoidable transition or metamorphosis can be seen coming into play in some of Williams's stories and plays. In a story written in 1936, entitled "Ten Minute Stop", the author uses an enveloping metaphor of a bus journey as a parallel to replicate the existential problem of belonging. The bus journey of the protagonist, Luke, from Chicago to Memphis helps him sort out and solve his existential problems. The stop that the bus takes en route to Memphis brings a sudden realization of his status to Luke:

> Ten Minute stop in a strange town—home for me, but for you—just a ten minute stop! I get you, thought Luke. *I don't belong*. I'm not one of the actors. That's why I'm able to sit here and look at the show. No, I'm not really a part of it. Not one of the dramatis personae. Not dark enough, not light enough. Not enough—what do they "call it? Centrifugal force? Specific gravity? (*Collected Stories* 58)

The key expression here is "Centrifugal force" that invariably drives the lighter, insubstantial elements towards and out of the periphery. The experience is not far from that of the Absurd. It is an experience terribly incomprehensible and weird. The resultant mental condition of the sufferer of the experience would be exactly like that of 'Woman' in *Talk to Me Like the Rain*:

> Then I will know—looking in the mirror—the first time has come for me to walk...with the strong wind beating on me, the white clean wind that blows from the edge of the world, from even further than that, from the cool outer edges of space, from even beyond whatever there is beyond the edges of space. (272)

Her wish to dissolve and disappear in an unnatural way has, again, an Absurd element at its core:

> I'll walk alone and be blown thinner and thinner! ...And thinner ... Till finally I won't have body at all, and the wind picks me up in its cool white arms forever, and takes me away! (272)

Beate Hein Bennett notices prominent "sense of exile" that the protagonist suffers because of the "dichotomous demands upon his own self both as artist and as man.... The deep seated dilemma of existential commitment to be a probing, analytical artist in a society which demands above all social commitment in the form of synthetic approval of its criteria is what relates him to the European artist" (in Tharpe 431-32). A special instance of the combination of the "sense of exile" with the elements of the Absurd occurs in "The Knightly Quest". Written in 1965, "The Knightly Quest" may well be reckoned among Tennessee Williams's late works. The elements of the Absurd in here, therefore, are not accidental but deliberate and pointing towards a specific meaning. The story, a novella in fact, is a quest for a world, a space, where there are no infringements upon individual liberty. If there are any, the consequences may be as devastating as graphically narrated in the novella. The story has Gewinner Pearce, an inveterate romantic, at the core of its plot. The start of the story shows him returning from a period of interminable roaming and drift due to a curtailed allowance. Not liking the confinement in the town, Gewinner only needs an allowance, a stipend of sorts to keep away and out of it. Gewinner has returned after a long period "on the go since the spring of his sixteenth year, since a morning in the spring when his tutor companion, the late Dr. Horace Greaves, had convinced Father and Mother"...that he "could be better instructed in humanities while traveling here and there among foreign lands and seas" (*Collected Stories* 406). What he encounters on his return is a strangely changed town, from what it had been before his departure "on the go". From the time Gewinner left it to the time of his return, the town has changed into a jingoistic stronghold because of a project dedicated to develop some mysterious weapon of mass destruction. 'The Project' at once creates a sense of fear, a curious interest and a definite amount of unnecessary jingoism. It is so because of the way in which 'the project' is being guarded and the way its purpose is being kept under wraps. While passing by, it appears to be "an enormous penitentiary for criminals of the most dangerous nature" with "its grounds" having been "enclosed by a tall metal fence" and being patrolled by "uniformed men with dogs". 'The Project' has been set up "for the development of a thing to blow them all off the map of the world for good and all and forever!" (*Collected Stories* 401). The characters appear in a steady flow as the story moves on. Those who matter are Violet (Gewinner's sister-in-law), Braden Pearce (his brother), Mother Pearce (his mother), Billy Spangler (the restauranteur spying for 'The Project') and Gladys (the girl employed at Billy's restaurant). The town has turned into an inferno of sorts because of the paranoid jingoism spewing from the 'Project.' The story steadily assumes the character of a socio political 'dystopia' even from the start. At places, the story seems to have the same sense of chilling suspicion which is characteristic of *Nineteen Eighty Four*, a classic 1949 dystopia by George Orwell. The following description, for example, gives the first hint of the extent of paranoid distrust:

> Oh, I do love you, Prince, cried out Violet. To think you honestly don't know what the Project is for!
>
> Why, Prince, it's for the development of a thing to blow them all off...
>
> Who is them?
>
> Why, them is them, who else! Are you serious, Prince, or are you just putting me on about it?
>
> He heard a quick scratching sound and saw that she had snatched a little appointment book from her purse and

> was scribbling down something. She tore the page out and pressed it into his hand.
>
> The message was: Change the subject, I think this car is bugged...Violet snatched the paper back from him, crumpled it, thrust is into her mouth, ground it beneath her teeth, swallowed, gagged...swallowed again, this time successfully. (*Collected Stories* 401-02)

This early passage in the story gives a clue about and sets the stage for what is to follow. As has been clarified by Violet's action, the characters in the story constantly suffer the torturous thought of forever being under the scanner. The resultant mental condition of the people of the town has been narrated in one of the intense passages in the story:

> But as I saïd already, one thing that wasn't mentioned, but that everybody thought about in secret, was the ever-menacing idea of "*the spy*". It interfered with really close and warm relationships among members of the Project community. You never knew, did you? No matter how simple and good a guy might seem to be, who knows but what he was a counterspy, taking notes on you all the time and the notes going into the files of the office that had the big wide-open blue eye painted on the opaque glass of its entrance, and nothing more (*Collected Stories* 432).

In a situation not different from Orwellian *Nineteen Eighty Four*, families and relationships have been shorn off all they can be worth. The above passages bear a testimony to the fact that the story almost paints a chilling picture of the other half of the world than the one projected in the Orwellian dystopia.

In the story, the dystopia turns upon its perpetrators as Gewinner Pearce, Violet and Gladys put their heads together. The three are romantic humanists who would not entertain any encroachments upon individual liberty. They are 'Quixotic' figures in the sense that Don Quixote in Tennessee Williams is the ideal and the iconic humanist. He is forever in search of an elusive utopia. Tennessee Williams believes that America (the Southern States in particular) started off as utopia, but was made into something quite opposite through a subtle coup carried out by 'the businessmen':

> Of course, America, and particularly the Southern states, is the embodiment of an originally romantic gesture. It was discovered and established by the eternal Don Quixote in the human flux. Then, of course, the businessmen took over and Don Quixote was on exile at home: at least he became one when the frontiers had been exhausted. But exile does not extinguish his lambent spirit. His castles are immaterial and his ways are endless and you don't have to look into many American eyes to suddenly meet somewhere the beautiful grave lunacy of his gaze or to observe his hands making some constrained but limitless gesture.... He gets along badly with policemen. He is much too American for them. (*Collected Stories* 444)

It is easy to conclude that America, "built of paranoia by men who thought themselves superior to the common lot," cannot be the destination or the place of habitation for quixotic beings (444). One may confront a problem here—where would the quixotic beings, the Fugitives, the characters in exile, go? They have nowhere to go because neither half of the world can accommodate them—neither the half of "the businessmen" that Williams presents in the story, nor the Orwellian half like that in *Nineteen Eighty Four*. They can only depend upon "the getaway spaceship" that would carry them far away to "weightless Ozone" where their watches would be "timed by light-years". They have a destination far beyond human imagination—"the spot marked x on the chart of time without end". (*Collected Stories* 454-55)

The exile, the ouster in the story discussed above is due to the inability to adjust of such characters as have been cast in the mold of "Quixote de la Mancha", who, ironically enough, "has never been broken"; he lives on, though in exile, because the "long skeleton of him too elastic and springy" (*Collected Stories* 444). The sense of 'exile', however, may spring from a very shattering and absurd experience of mutilation or incompleteness. Apart from the poignant short story entitled "One Arm", discussed earlier, there is the double-bill Slapstick tragedy that deals with the issue of mutilation. The double bill carries two short plays entitled *The Mutilated* and *The Gnädiges Fräulein*. In the first of the two, the apparent mutilation is the mastectomy that Trinket has undergone. The deformity or sense of incompleteness caused by the mastectomy is Trinket's guarded secret, and yet it constantly eats into her sense of being. Hers, though, is a mutilation that would only serve as a symbol—the real mutilation is pervasive and affects whoever is a part of life on this earth. The fact is clarified by Celeste in one of the most poignant statements in the play:

> ...forget your mutilation, it is not the end of the world for you or the world. Hell, I'd say, we all have our mutilations, some from birth, some from long before birth, and some from later in life, and some stay with us forever. (*The Mutilated* 87)

These deformities or mutilations take a heavy toll upon the sensitive, the victimized and the quixotic drifters. The second part of the double-bill Slapstick Tragedy, *The Gnädiges Fräulein*, seems to be focusing on the cruel and relentless manner in which mutilations are wrought upon the fugitive and the victimized. The play is nearly an exposition of Antonin Artaud's 'theatre of cruelty'. There have been two distinctly diverse approaches to the play—traditional biographical and post modernistic. From the traditional viewpoint, the play only lends itself to biographical interpretation in which Fräulein would be looked upon as the self-portrayal of the author and the cocaloony birds as the caricature of the critics constantly preying upon the author. A contemporary approach to the play reveals it as a kind of anti-mimetic presentation which would be a critique of the theatre itself. This contemporary approach to the play is represented by Linda Droff in her article published in the 1999 issue of *The Tennessee Williams Annual Review*. She explains that the absence of conflict and plot annihilates the concept of the well-made and constructed play. She feels that the drama in the *Gnädiges Fräulein*, "like cubist painting, or pop art, engages in self-conscious play with representations that already exist" (Droff 15). *Slapstick Tragedy*, the double-bill containing *The Mutilated* and *The Gnädiges Fräulein*, brings us round to the issue of experimentation in Williams's late writings (especially drama). Commenting upon the brand of playwriting suggested by such plays as *Fräulein,* Allean Hale states:

> Fräulein is certainly the most experimental of Williams's new direction plays written after *The Night of the Iguana.* When reviewers compared it to Black comedy, the playwright declared that he had invented Black comedy. Others labeled it "Theatre of the Absurd". This Williams denied, saying that he could never see human existence as meaningless. Indeed, he was now much nearer to European drama stylistically, the declamatory style of Brecht, the buffoonery of Ionesco, the cruelty of Genet. Molly and Polly, eternally rocking while they wait, seem first cousins to Beckett's Vladimir and Estragon. (in Kolin, *Undiscovered Country* 43-44).

An aspect of the experimentation in *The Mutilated* is a remarkable and rewarding combination of the Ancient Greek theatre with the conventions of the Modern Japanese theatre. Two essential requirements of the play are that "the sets" should be "as delicate as Japanese line drawings," so abstract, so spidery, and that "a band of Carollers" comprising" all the characters in the play" would appear "preceding the play, after various scenes, and at the end of the play" (*The Mutilated.* Production Notes 79). The immediate suggestion here is that the author would like to bring together the conventions of the Japanese Kabuki Theatre and the classical system of Chorus in the Ancient Greek drama. Another suggestion here is that the author would find the chorus in Greek drama as much unconditional as the tenets of the Japanese theatre. Other plays explicitly evincing the influence of the Kabuki theatre are: *In the Bar of Tokyo Hotel, The Gnädiges Fräulein, I Can't Imagine Tomorrow* and *Confessional* (the one-act from which comes *The Small Craft Warnings*). The experimental devices employed by Tennessee Williams clearly indicate his belief in a theatre that stretches its effects "through caricature and the grotesque", to an "unendurable" point of "paroxysm". The author (in his late writings at least) seems clearly to subscribe to the theory of Ionesco which states that drama essentially "lies in extreme exaggeration of the feelings, an exaggeration that dislocates flat everyday reality" along with a "disarticulation of language". Williams appears to believe, like Ionesco, that "we need to be virtually bludgeoned into detachment from our daily lives, our habits and mental laziness, which conceal from us the strangeness of the world" (Ionesco 24-25). The argument earns a substantial amount of endorsement from Annette J. Saddik when she pointedly states that the "sensibility of Williams' late work" gets appropriate description through such "terms" as "Extreme, excessive, grotesque, carnivalesque, tragicomic, campy, cartoonish, pop art, burlesque, slapstick, Grand Guignol" (*Tennessee Williams* and *The Theatre of Excess* 10).

The entire creative canon of Tennessee Williams can be seen entering into a relationship of intertextuality through the central thread of "Orphean quest for unification of man's animal and intellectual dimensions. Williams is never able to reconcile the split between man the artist and man the thinker. The body in its full, free life always becomes either a brutal punishment or an agent of tragedy. The Orphic dilemma, expressed by the ancient warning, soma sema (the body, a tomb), is one of the consistent mythopoeic themes in Williams's work" (Davis in Tharpe 196-97). In Davis's view, the protagonists in Williams's writing "suffer dismemberment in their attempts to live the full life of the body" just in the manner "the half-crazed Maenads tear Orpheus to pieces" (197). This prominent Orphean conflict runs parallel in the short stories and the plays of the author—from "The Vengeance of Nitocris" (1928) to "The killer Chicken and the Closet Queen" (1977) in stories, and from *Battle of Angels* (1940) to *The Two Character Play* (1973) in plays.

Nicholas Pagan observes a greater depth and scope in the intertextuality and interconnectivity created by the Orphic myth in Tennessee Williams. He feels that the "retitling" of *Battle of Angels* as *Orpheus Descending* "automatically connects the play to all the pretexts that concern the legend of Orpheus". Pagan concentrates upon "the relation between Williams's texts and Virgil's and Ovid's pretexts" (47-48). An additional connection of relationship between William's *Battle of Angels* and *Orpheus*

Descending with Ovid's *Metamorphoses* is created by the outstanding similarity of Myra in *Battle of Angels* and Lady in *Orpheus Descending* with Myrrha of *Metamorphoses*. Ovid's Myrrha turns into a tree as a punishment for her incestuous relationship with her father. With a little shift, Williams's Myra (in *Battle*) imagines herself as a Christmas tree, potently capable of reproduction: "Yes, and I'm glad, I'm glad, I'm planning a celebration! I'm going to wear Christmas ornaments in my hair! Why? Because I'm not barren. I've gotten death out of me and now I've taken life in!" (*Battle* 114). The hanging of Christmas ornaments in hair is reminiscent of her childhood act of decorating the fig tree in the backyard of her house. Tree, thus, becomes an enduring imagery in giving a firm root to the intertextual network between Ovid's *Metamorphoses* and Williams's twin plays exclusively dealing with Orpheus myth. The intertextual network actually proliferates to create a relationship between *Metamorphoses* and other texts by Williams. The proliferation, of course, is afforded by the tree imageries. The 'texts' by Williams entering the context are *The Case of Crushed Petunias* (An 'American Blues' play), *The Night of the Iguana, The Glass Menagerie, 27 Wagons Full of Cotton* and *Summer and Smoke.*

There is yet another element in Tennessee Williams that lends itself to the creation of an intertextual network with Virgil and Ovid; and that is the persistent element of violence. In his Foreword to *Sweet Bird of Youth,* Williams writes:

> In my first published work, for which I received the big sum of thirty-five dollars, a story published in the July or August issue of "Weird Tales" in the year 1928, I drew upon a paragraph in the ancient histories of Herodotus to create a story of how the Egyptian queen, Nitocris, invited all of her enemies to a lavish banquet in a subterranean hall on the shores of the Nile,...and opened sluice gates... into the locked banquet hall, drowning her unloved guests like so many rats... I don't have to tell you that it set the keynote for most of the work that has followed (*Sweet Bird*. Foreword 10-11)

Tennessee Williams is here making a reference to his first story, "The Vengeance of Nitocris". Talking of this, Nicholas Pagan says that the "key note is surely a kind of violence very similar to the Orphic violence described by Ovid and Virgil"; and further specifies that "most versions of the Orphic legend begin with the violence entailed in the ravishment of Eurydice and end in the dismemberment of Orpheus" (52). Though Virgil speaks of the Thracian maids tearing Orpheus, limb from limb and hurling him piecemeal over the fields, Ovid offers a nearer pretext for Williams's texts by describing the women rushing upon Orpheus with their implements and tools covered with leaves. The point to note here is that trees (their leaves covering the weapons) as much participate in Orpheus's destruction as they do in Bacchus's vengeance upon his (Orpheus's) assailants. In Tennessee Williams, trees are consistently associated with mourning in the form of painful nostalgia. In *Battle of Angels,* Val nostalgically remembers the cypress trees in the Witches Bayou while Myra recalls her happy childhood in the company of the fig tree in the back yard of her father's house. *Orpheus Descending* only enhances these associations. At the close of *The Glass Menagerie,* Tom thinks of the life left behind as the cities sweeping behind him like "dead-leaves, leaves that were brightly colored but torn away from the branches" (*Menagerie* 313). To quote Nicholas Pagan again, "trees, branches, leaves and other arboreal references indicate one way in which Williams's texts may allude not only to one another, but also in particular to Ovid's *Metamorphoses,* and to a lesser extent Virgil's *Georgics* and even Dante's *Inferno* (53).

C.W.E. Bigsby suggests yet another avenue of approach to Tennessee Williams. The approach invariably leads to the treatment of his writings from the psychological point of view. Putting Tennessee Williams and Arthur Miller on a comparative perspective, Bigsby states that the two are concerned with the "erosion of private space" in the social world. "Needing to believe in the integrity of a resistant self, they (the two playwrights) shift the threat of collapse onto the form of the play (*Death of A Salesman* and *Camino Real*) or onto a dramatic symbol which must stand for that collapse (the unicorn in the

The Glass Menagerie, the dried up fountain in *Camino Real,* the concentration camp in *After the Fall*)" (*Critical Introduction to Twentieth-Century American Drama.* Vol. Two. 06). It is possible to envisage two ways in which Williams's writings can be approached from this perspective—general psychological and theory specific. The first of the two, quite often discussed, brings into focus the archetypal conflict between the corporeal and the spiritual. The other approach, however, has the potential to proliferate into several strands. In a thought provoking essay published in the 1999 issue of *The Tennessee Williams Annual Review,* Lindy Levin makes "A Jungian Analysis of *The Night of the Iguana*". The crux of the essay is revealed in the following pivotal remark:

> The duality of human nature is expressed in contradictory images of light and dark, man and beast, and epitomizes the split in personality between the known and unknown parts. The dark side of human nature is portrayed in religion as the demonic, in psychology as the unconscious, and in Tennessee Williams's play, *The Night of the Iguana* as the shadow. (Levin 87)

In the Jungian theory of the unconscious, the shadow is defined as "the negative side of the personality, the sum of all those unpleasant qualities we like to hide" (Connie Zweig, qtd. in Levin 87). The shadow in this sense, better defined as the dark side, refers to the aspects of the self that are disowned in an attempt to adapt to the norms. The disowned aspects of the self may vary from society to society, leading to different forms of psychological derailments. The model that the society holds up may be fastidiously rigid in accommodating individual impulses. In the course of time, the impulses may be forgotten through repeated denial, but it is impossible to remove them from the unconscious psyche. Thus, these individual impulses may be unimaginably destructive in their disguised forms. There can be various ways in which they can unfold in the course of one's life. For instance, these impulses get a manifestation in the form of a "spook" in the case of Shannon. He, of course, means a resurgent sexual impulse whenever he talks of the "spook" that "doesn't attack before sun-down" (*Iguana* 62-

63). A different but analogous situation occurs in the short story "The Mysteries of the Joy Rio". In the fourth and the concluding part, the story takes a weird turn to show the ghost of the protagonist's mentor descending upon the theatre to claim his protégée. Pablo Gonzales, the protégée, has almost reenacted the life and experiences of his master, Emiel Kroger. It would not be out of place to insinuate that he has been stalked by the shadow of his master. So much so that the shadow, in fact the ghost, of his master comforts Pablo into a painless death. In both the cases, of "Joy Rio" and *Iguana*, the shadow has been a palpably felt projection of all that has been repressed and denied. According to the Jungian system, what Pablo or Mr. Shannon have is a dark side like each one of the inhabitants of this planet. But this dark side is "a condition of life in our world, not a sin" (Eichman 136). If followed a little further, Eichman's theory awards the cases of Pablo and Shannon a therapeutic status—because both Pablo and Shannon can be seen in the process of "healing" their "dark nature" which could help them reclaim "vast amounts of personal power and ability" (136). The "condition" of the dark side of life gets a physical representation in "The Dark Room", a short story, where the present and yet absent protagonist, Tina, shuts herself in a dark room of the house. While she remains there unclothed, refusing to come out, she admits only her lover into the room. The various manifestations of the dark side of a person's psyche in Williams's writings have actually been the presentation of the "Crazy blue devil" that went round the author all day (Leverich 174).

The discussion here gets poised to enter the phase of conclusion by veering round to the issue of the characteristic autobiographical strands in Tennessee Williams's writings. Various critical studies have repeatedly taken up the biographical approach to the author's art. The representative ones have been those by Benjamin Nelson (*Tennessee Williams: The man and His work*), Signi Lenea Falk (*Tennessee Williams*), and Francis Donahue (*The Dramatic World of Tennessee Williams*). Even his authentic biographers like Lyle Leverich (*Tom: The Unknown Tennessee Williams*) and Donald Spoto

(*The Kindness of Strangers: The Life of Tennessee Williams*) have confirmed the general autobiographical character of his work. Nancy Marie Tischler (*Tennessee Williams: A Rebellious Puritan*), Benjamin Nelson (*Tennessee Williams: His life and His Work*) and Esther M. Jackson (*The Broken World of Tennessee Williams*) corroborate the view of the author's biographers. The greatest pointer to the autobiographical character of his works comes from Tennessee Williams himself in his controversial autobiography entitled *Memoirs*. However, a very objective and a very powerful reiteration of the fact of the autobiographical character of Williams's writings, and (therefore) the justification of the 'autobiographical' approach to his works, comes in his newest biography (2014) by John Lahr:

> As early as 1939, having just acquired an agent, a Rockefeller grant, and a career path, Williams vowed to write plays that were "a picture of my own heart." Over the decades, as that outcrying heart opened, faltered, and atrophied, Williams stuck to his game plan: "to be simple, direct and terrible... I will speak truth as I see it...without concealment or evasion and with a fearless unashamed frontal assault upon life." The plays are his emotional autobiography, snapshots of his heart's mutation. So, to tell the story of the plays is to tell the story of the man, and vice versa. (xiv)

In his perceptive *Critical Introduction to Twentieth-Century American Drama*, C.W.E. Bigsby proposes a new direction to take for an understanding of the author's art—the direction of a "deconstructive vision" to appreciate "the sense of dislocation of logic and continuity as a major force in Williams's work" (*Vol. Two* 80). The direction suggested by Bigsby would definitely lead one to all those various situations in which Tennessee Williams has repeatedly questioned the 'me' of his writings. A possible conclusion here can be that the entire mass of his writings is an existential search for his own self. As the author embarks on this existential search for the self, he goes through several personal and creativity related conflicts. He prefers to talk about and picture his search in terms of the metaphor of a romantic and quixotic journey into the unknown. The metaphor of the quixotic journey comes to its full bloom in *Camino Real* (play) and "The Knightly Quest" (novella/story). Both the works have been discussed in detail earlier in this chapter. Of the conflicts he has to go through, the most prominent is that between physical impulses and religious Puritanism. The character and nature of the conflict has been encapsulated in the title of Nancy Marie Tischler's book *The Rebellious Puritan*. The conflict, often resulting in various forms of violence, runs throughout the literary creations of the author. The violence may vary from the sadistic extreme in "The Vengeance of Nitocris" to the masochistic in "Desire and the Black Masseur". The most appealingly poignant forms of the conflict and violence, though, can be seen in *The Glass Menagerie, Sweet Bird of Youth, A Streetcar Named Desire, The Night of the Iguana* and *The Two Character Play*. A concomitant of the conflict and violence in the works of Tennessee Williams has been a persistently pervasive atmosphere of gloom and confusion. All his major protagonists are bound to suffer the gloom and brave the confusion.

As the author delineates his characters and themes, a broad framework of social and religious iconoclasm emerges from his works. Though not always so, the personae in Williams's fiction and drama employ this iconoclasm as the manner and method of coping with the gloom and confusion they are doomed to suffer. The religious iconoclasm of his characters, who have been the faces of the alter ego of their author, gets a broad and explicatory manifestation in such works as "The Vengeance of Nitocris", "One Arm", "The Yellow Bird", *The Battle of Angels*, *Orpheus Descending* and *The Night of the Iguana*. The iconoclasm of the author also gets a socially relevant manifestation in the form of politico-economic protest, material enough for Allean Hale to designate Tennessee Williams a "Proletarian Playwright" in her article in the inaugural issue of *The Tennessee Williams Annual Review* in 1998 (13). The subtext of the designation obviously hints at a communist reading of the author's works. The legitimization of the designation comes from such works as "The Malediction" and its dramatization in *The Strangest Kind of Romance* (Play). Even *The Glass Menagerie, Cat on a Hot Tin Roof* and *Sweet Bird of Youth* can be subjected to a study from the politico-economic viewpoint of communism. Allean Hale points out that the Marxist streak in Williams's writings has much to do with his association with "Clark Mills, surnamed McBurney", French scholar, poet and intellectual, who had affiliations with the Communist Party through his father, "a freight agent for Union Pacific Railroad," and one sister, Adeline, who "was a social Welfare worker" (*Proletarian Playwright* 14). The scholar further points out that *Candles to the Sun,* which marks "Williams's start in professional theatre", has "a good Marxist ending" by showing "the individual giving into the group for the good of the cause" and also by showing the workers singing "Solidarity forever", a characteristically Proletariat song (18). As the author mellows, he distances himself from such ostensibly social protest. Yet the continuing and persistent Orphic strand in his works incorporates various forms of iconoclasm at the levels of the substrata.

It has been an established critical belief that writing short stories has been a sort of catharsis for Tennessee Williams. It has also been believed and observed that many of the author's short stories have served as the pre-texts for his major successes in drama. It is common knowledge that such masterpieces as *The Glass Menagerie, Cat on a Hot Tin Roof, Summer and Smoke* and *The Night of the Iguana* have all had their origin in corresponding short stories. While the importance of the stories from the viewpoint of inter-genre transformations cannot be ignored, it has to be borne in mind that many of the author's short stories have been the acknowledged classics of the genre of short fiction. Writing the Introduction of Williams's *Collected Stories*, Gore Vidal Observes:

> No, he is not a great story writer like Chekhov but he has something rather more rare than mere genius. He has a narrative tone of voice that is totally compelling. The only other American writer to have this gift was Mark Twain; a very different sort of writer (to overdo understatement); yet Hannibal, Missouri, is not all that far from St. Louis, Missouri, and each was a comic genius. In any case, you

> cannot stop listening to either of these tellers no matter how tall or wild their tales. (xx)

In his dedicated study of Williams's short fiction, Dennis P. Vannatta even awards a station to the author as "the short story writer in the Southern-Gothic tradition, along with Flannery O'Connor, Eudora Welty, Carson McCullers, Truman Capote, and others" (Vannatta xi). Both of these theories about Tennessee Williams's short fiction—that it serves as the pretext for the author's drama and that it has its own position of dignity in its own genre—have the sanctity of established facts.

No less sanctified has been the theory about the author's persistent revisions within the genre of drama. The obvious result has been a series of plays that have been evolved out of their predecessors in the same genre. It has already been illustrated in our study that Tennessee Williams as a creative artist has had the aesthetic desire for improvement. The aesthetic desire, or the artistic dissatisfaction, has always been a major motivating force for the revisions. There has been yet another factor behind the revisions—the general animus of the Broadway drama critics. At some unconscious level, all these revisions appear to be the manifestation of the author's earnestness to justify himself and the validity of the general nature of his art. Quite a good number of his plays have had a history often stretching back to short stories, with one-act versions falling en route. Apart from the direct connectivity created by overt revisions, many of his works (including short stories) have a relationship engendered by several free floating strands running through the creative repertoire of Tennessee Williams. The most noticeable among these are: rose as an imagery, mutilation in its various forms, the conflict between the body and the soul and some social and religious taboos. More important among these is the locale of New Orleans as an "image" in the works of the author. In the creative world of Tennessee Williams, "New Orleans is his special metaphor for the modern world.... This special metaphor is pervasive and ubiquitous, but it is specifically manifest in such plays as "*A Streetcar Named Desire* (1947), *Suddenly Last Summer* (1958) and *Vieux Carré* (1977) as well as in minor plays" (Barranger 38).

There is still a lot of scope and 'undiscovered country' in Tennessee Williams in terms of the potential for the use of postmodern standpoints of study. Some studies coming in the past two decades have created a fresh interest in the author by putting his works (called 'texts' in the critical jargon of the context), fiction as well drama, in perspective with the postmodern literary and critical canon. Much remains to be reconceived in postmodern terms in Tennessee Williams. One of the postmodern streams of critical theory is intertexuality, which has been the major concern and thrust of the present study throughout in seeking the broad spectrum of interrelationships in the short fiction and drama of Tennessee Williams. That Tennessee Williams is not passé is better proved by the testimony of Ralph S. Voss who points out that "the production and/ publication of 'new' works by Williams...in 1999, coupled with New York revivals of ....*Small Craft Warnings* in 1999 and *Stairs to the Roof* in 2000, all attest to a revival of interest in Williams's play". He further points out that "the textual studies, bibliographies, and reference works published in the last decade of the twentieth century have enabled students and other scholars to identify and locate primary and secondary resources with considerable ease" (Voss 15).

That the plays and other writings of Tennessee Williams have the proverbial element of universality, arguably of space and certainly of time, is borne out by the special section entitled 'Williams Then & Now', pages 27-41, remembering Tennessee Williams in the September 2011 (28.07) issue of *American Theater* with reports of various innovative productions of his plays along with critical views that mean much more than simple words of homage to the author in his birth centenary year. The section documents the continued presence of and enduring interest in Tennessee Williams at theatres and academia. A representative case is the view of Lisa D'Amour, who says that she "can't imagine writing plays or teaching playwriting without Tennessee in my life" ("Williams Then & Now" 40). The views of Amiri Baraka quoted in that issue of *American Theater* add another dimension of universality to Williams's plays: "I cannot think of a single Williams play that is not about the struggle for power. The fact is that the poetic power of Tennessee's work does not lessen its political import, it enhances it" (41). It does not require any elaboration to understand that 'power' has been a perennial issue all along human history, and will always remain so. There have always been and will always be physical as well as psychological issues of power governing us; and, there have always been and will always be physical as well as psychological 'fugitives' and 'drifters' in the territories—physical as well as psychological—governed by power. Deal as it does with the 'fugitives' and 'drifters' either easing out of those physical and psychological territories of power or with the 'moths' going down to perish, the art of Tennessee Williams earns a coveted amount of immunity from all corrosive effects of time. To put it cryptically yet meaningfully, "when he died at the age of seventy-one, Tennessee Williams was young" (Saddik 163).

Bibliography

Primary Sources

(Tennessee Williams's Works)

I. Fiction

Williams, Tennessee. *Collected Stories.* London: Secker & Warburg, 1985. Print

The in-text references cite the following stories from the collection: 'The Vengeance of Nitocris', 'A Lady's Beaded Bag', 'Something by Tolstoi', 'Big Black: A Mississippi Idyll', 'The Accent of a Coming Foot', 'Twenty Seven Wagons Full of Cotton', 'Sand', 'Ten Minute Stop', 'The Field of Blue Children', 'In Memory of an Aristocrat', 'The Dark Room', 'The Mysteries of the Joy Rio', 'Portrait of a Girl in Glass', 'The Angel in the Alcove', 'Oriflamme', 'The Vine', 'The Malediction', 'The Important Thing', 'One Arm', 'Desire and the Black Masseur', 'The Yellow Bird', 'The Night of the Iguana', 'The Poet', 'Rubio Y Morena', 'The Resemblance between a Violin case and a Coffin', 'Three Players of a Summer Game', 'Hard Candy', 'Man Bring This Up Road', 'The Mattress by the Tomato Patch', 'The Kingdom of Earth', 'Grand', 'The Knightly Quest', 'Happy August the Tenth', 'Miss Coynte of Greene', 'Sabbatha and Solitude', 'Completed', 'The Inventory of Fontana Bella'.

———. *The Roman Spring of Mrs. Stone.* Harmondsworth: Penguin, 1969. Print.

———. "Isolated". *The Tennessee Williams Annual Review* 1 (1998). 35-36. Print.

———. "A Playwright's Prayer". *The Tennessee Williams Annual Review* 06 (2003). n.pag. Web. 15 December 2014.

II. Plays

Williams, Tennessee. *Sweet Bird of Youth; A Streetcar Named Desire; The Glass Menagerie.* Penguin Plays. Ed. E. Martin Browne. Harmondsworth: Penguin, 1982. Print.

———. *The Rose Tattoo; Camino Real; Orpheus Descending.* Penguin Plays. Ed. E. Martin Browne. Harmondsworth: Penguin, 1983. Print.

———. *Cat on a Hot Tin Roof.* In *Five Plays by Tennessee Williams.* London: Secker & Warburg, 1962. Print.

———. *Out Cry.* New York: New Direction, 1973. Print.

———. *Battle of Angels.* In *The Theatre of Tennessee Williams* Vol. I. New York: New Directions, 1971. Print.

———. *The Eccentricities of a Nightingale* and *Summer and Smoke.* In *The Theatre of Tennessee Williams* Vol. II. New York: New Directions, 1971. Print.

———. *Suddenly Last Summer.* In *The Theatre of Tennessee Williams* Vol. III. New York: New Directions, 1971. Print.

———. *The Night of the Iguana.* In *The Theatre of Tennessee Williams* Vol. IV. New York: New Directions, 1972. Print.

———. *The Milk Train Doesn't Stop Here Anymore; Kingdom of Earth; Small Craft Warnings; The Two Character Play.* In *The Theatre of Tennessee Williams* Vol. V. New York: New Directions, 1976. Print.

———. *27 Wagons Full of Cotton; The Purification; The Lady of Larkspur Lotion; The Last of My Solid Gold Watches; Portrait of a Madonna; Auto Da Fé, Lord Byron's Love Letter; The Strangest Kind of Romance; The Long Good-bye; Hello from Bertha; This Property is Condemned; Talk to Me Like the Rain and Let Me Listen; Steps Must be Gentle* (all one-act plays). In *The Theatre of Tennessee Williams* Vol. VI. New York: New Directions, 1981. Print.

———. *Vieux Carre; The Red Devil Battery Sign*. In *The Theatre of Tennessee Williams* Vol. VIII. New York: New Directions, 1992. Print.

———. *In the Bar of a Tokyo Hotel; I Rise in Flame, Cried the Phoenix; The Mutilated; I Can't Imagine Tomorrow; Confessional; The Frosted Glass Coffin; The Gnädiges Fräulein* (all one-act plays). In *Dragon Country*. New York: New Directions, 1970. Print.

———. *Il Cane Incantato della Divina Costiera: A One Act Sketch for The Rose Tattoo*. In *The Tennessee Williams Annual Review* 06 (2003): n.pag. Web. 15 January 2015.

———. *The Night of the Iguana (One-Act Version)*. In *The Tennessee Williams Annual Review* 04 (2001). iv-xxxv. Print.

III. Autobiography, Essays/Prose

———. *Memoirs*. New York: Doubleday, 1975. Print.

———. "Preface to My Poems", "The Meaning of '*The Rose Tattoo*'" and "Too Personal?". In *Where I Live: Selected Essays by Tennessee Williams*. Ed. Christine R. Day and Bob Woods. New York: New Directions, 1978. Print.

———. "The History of a Play (With Parentheses)" and "Facts About Me". In *New Selected Essays: Where I Live*. Ed. John S. Bak. New York: New Directions, 2009. Print.

Secondary Sources

Adler, Jacob H. "Williams's Eight Ladies". *Southern Literary Journal* 8.1 (1975): 165-69. Print.

Adler, Thomas P. *A Streetcar Named Desire: The Moth and the Lantern*. Boston: Twayne Publishers, 1990. Print.

———. "The Search for God in the Plays of Tennessee Williams". *Renascence* 26.01 (1973): 48-56. Print.

Bak, John S, ed. *New Selected Essays: Where I Live*. New York: New Directions, 2009. Print.

Barranger, Milly S. "New Orleans as Theatrical Image in Plays by Tennessee Williams". *Southern Quarterly* 23.02 (Winter 1985): 38-54. Print.

Beckett, Samuel. *Waiting for Godot: A Tragicomedy in Two Acts*. New Delhi: Oxford University Press, 1989. Print.

Bigsby, C.W.E. *A Critical Introduction to Twentieth-Century American Drama*. Vol. 1 (1900-1940). Cambridge: Cambridge University Press, 1982. Print.

———. *A Critical Introduction to Twentieth-Century Drama*. Volume 2 (Williams/Miller/Albee). Cambridge: Cambridge University Press, 1984. Print.

———. *Modern American Drama 1945-2000*. Cambridge: Cambridge University Press, 2001. Print.

Bloom, Harold, ed. *Tennessee Williams's A Streetcar Named Desire* (Critical Interpretations Series). New York: Chelsea House, 1988. Print.

———. ed. *Tennessee Williams*. Bloom's Major Dramatists: Comprehensive Research and Study Guide Broomall, PA: Chelsea House, 2000. Print.

Boxill, Roger. *Tennessee Williams*. New York: St. Martin's Press, 1987. Print.

Bray, Robert. "A Reading of *The Reading*". *The Tennessee Williams Annual Review* 11 (2010): 03-06. Print.

Broussard, Louis. *American Drama: Contemporary Allegory from Eugene O'Neill to Tennessee Williams*. Norman: University of Oklahoma Press, 1962. Print.

Clum, John M. "The Evolution of the Queer Alma". *Modern Drama* 39.01 (1996): 31-50. Print.

Clurman, Harold. "THEATRE: Tennessee Williams' Rose". *The New Republic* 124.8 (February 19, 1951): 22. Print.

Colanzi, Rita. "Caged Birds: Bad Faith in Tennessee Williams". *Modern Drama* 35.3 (1992): 451-65. Print.

Corrigan, Mary Ann. "Memory, Dream, and Myth in the Plays of Tennessee Williams". *Renascence* 28 (1976): 155-67. Print.

Costello, Donald P. "Tennessee Williams's Fugitive Kind". *Modern Drama* 15.01 (1972): 26-43. Print.

Day, Christine R. and Bob Woods, eds. *Where I Live: Selected Essays* by Tennessee Williams. New York: New Directions, 1978. Print.

Dean, Anne. *Language as Dramatic Action*. Cranbury, NJ: Associated University Presses, 1990. Print.

Debusscher, Gilbert. "Minting Their Separate Wall's: Tennessee Williams and Hart Crane" *Modern Drama* 26.4 (1983): 455-75. Print.

———. "Tennessee Williams's Dramatic Charade: Secrets and Lies in *The Glass Menagerie*". *The Tennessee Williams Annual Review* 03 (2000): 57-68. Print.

Devlin, Albert J, ed. *Conversations with Tennessee Williams*. Jackson, MS: The University Press of Mississippi, 1986. Print.

[The following interviews from the collection:

"*The Life and Ideas of Tennessee Williams*" with Jean Evans; "*Williams: Twenty Years after 'Glass Menagerie'*" with Joan Stang; "*Tennessee Williams*" with John Gruen; "*Will God Talk Back to a Playwright?*" with David Frost; and, "*Playboy Interview*" with C. Robert Jennings]

Donahue, Francis. *The Dramatic World of Tennessee Williams*. New York: Frederick Ungar, 1964. Print.

Droff, Linda. "Theatricalist Cartoons: Tennessee Williams's Late 'Outrageous' Plays." *The Tennessee Williams Annual Review* 02 (1999): 13-33. Print.

Eichman, William Carl. "Meeting the Dark Side in Spiritual Practice". *Meeting the Shadow*. Ed. Connie Zweig and Jeremiah Abrams. New York: G.P. Putnam's Sons, 1999. 134-37. Print.

Eliot, T.S. *The Waste Land and other Poems*. London: Faber & Faber, 1973. Print.

———. "Tradition and Individual Talent." *English Critical Texts*. Eds. D.J. Enright and Ernst De Chickera. Delhi: Oxford University Press, 1975. 293-301. Print.

Falk, Signi Lenea. *Tennessee Williams.* Boston: Twayne Publishers, 1978. Print.

Fedder, Norman J. *The Influence of D.H. Lawrence on Tennessee Williams.* The Hague: Mouton & Company, 1966. Print.

Fleche, Anne. *Mimetic Disillusion: Eugene O'Neill, Tennessee Williams and U.S. Dramatic* Realism. Tuscaloosa: University of Alabama Press, 1997. Print.

———. "The Space of Madness and Desire: Tennessee Williams and *Streetcar*". *Modern Drama* 38.04 (1995): 496-509. Print.

Fromm, Erich. *Art of Loving.* London: Unwin Paperbacks, 1978. Print.

Frye, Northrop. *Anatomy of Criticism: Four Essays.* Princeton: Princeton University Press, 1971. Print.

———. *The Secular Scripture: A Study of the Structure of Romance.* Harvard University Press, 1978. Print.

Gasset, Ortega Y. *The Revolt of the Masses.* New York: W.W. Norton & Company, 1960. Print.

Gassner, John. *Directions in Modern Theatre and Drama.* New York: Holt, Rinehart and Winston, 1965. Print.

Griffin, Alice. *Understanding Tennessee Williams.* Columbia, South Carolina: University of South Carolina Press, 1995. Print.

Gross, Robert F., ed. *Tennessee Williams: A Case Book.* New York: Routledge, 2002. Print.

Hale, Allean. "Tennessee's Long Trip". *The Missouri Review* 7.3 (1984): 201-12. Print.

———. "Tom Williams, Proletarian Playwright". *The Tennessee Williams Annual Review* 01(1998). 13-22. Print.

———. "Confronting the Late Plays of Tennessee Williams" *The Tennessee Williams Annual Review* 06 (2003): n.pag. Web. 10 March 2015.

Hart, James D., ed. *The Concise Oxford Companion to American Literature.* New York: Oxford University Press, 1986. Print.

Hauptmann, Robert. *The Pathological Vision: Jean Genet, Louis-Ferdinand Celine, and Tennessee Williams.* New York: Peter Lang, 1984. Print.

Hayman, Ronald. *Tennessee Williams: Everyone Else is an Audience.* New Haven: Yale University Press, 1993. Print.

Hesse, Hermann. *Demian.* Trans. Michael Roloff and Michael Lebeck. New York: Harper and Row, 1965. Print.

Hirsch, Foster. *A Portrait of the Artist: The Plays of Tennessee Williams.* New York: Kennikat Press, National University Publications, 1979. Print.

Hoffman, Daniel, ed. *Harvard Guide to Contemporary American Writing.* New Delhi: Oxford University Press, 1981. Print.

Holman, C. Hugh. *The Roots of Southern Writing: Essays on the Literature of the American South.* Athens: University of Georgia Press, 1972. Print.

Ionesco, Eugene. *Notes and Counter Notes.* Trans. Donald Watson. London: John Calder, 1964. Print.

Jackson, Esther Merle. *The Broken World of Tennessee Williams.* Madison: The University of Wisconsin Press, 1966. Print.

Just, Maria St., ed. *Five O'clock Angel: Letters of Tennessee Williams to Maria St. Just 1948-1982.* New York: Alfred A. Knopf, 1990. Print.

Kilgour, Maggie. *The Rise of the Gothic Novel.* London & New York: Routledge, 1995. Print.

Kolin, Philip C. "'Isolated': Tennessee Williams's First Extant Published Story". *The Tennessee Williams Annual Review* 01 (1998): 33-39. Print.

———. ed. *The Undiscovered Country: The Later Plays of Tennessee Williams.* New York: Peter Lang, 2002. Print.

Krutch, Joseph Wood. *"Modernism" in Modern Drama: A Definition and an Estimate.* Ithaca, New York: Cornell University Press, 1953. Print.

Lahr, John. *Tennessee Williams: Mad Pilgrimages of the Flesh.* New York: W.W. Norton & Company, 2014. Print.

Leavitt, Richard F., ed. *The World of Tennessee Williams (Introduction by Tennessee Williams).* New York: G.P. Putnam's 1978. Print.

Leon, Ferdinand. "Time, Fantasy, and Reality in *Night of the Iguana*". *Modern Drama* 11.1 (1968): 87-96. Print.

Leverich, Lyle. *Tom: The Unknown Tennessee Williams.* New York: Crown Publishers, 1995. Print.

Levin, Lindy. "Shadow into Light: A Jungian Analysis of *The Night of the Iguana*". *The Tennessee Williams Annual Review* 2(1999): 87-98. Print.

Levy, Eric P. "'Through Soundproof Glass': The Prison of Self-Consciousness in *The Glass Menagerie*". *Modern Drama* 36.04 (Winter 1993): 529-37. Print.

Lewis, C.S. *A Preface to Paradise Lost.* London: Oxford University Press, 1961. Print.

Londré, Felicia Hardison. *Tennessee Williams.* New York: Frederick Ungar, 1979. Print.

Martin, Robert A., ed. *Critical Essays on Tennessee Williams,* New York: G.K. Hall, 1997. Print.

Massé, Michelle A. *In the Name of Love: Women, Masochism, and the Gothic.* Ithaca: Cornell University Press, 1992. Print.

Maxwell, Gilbert. *Tennessee Williams and Friends.* Cleveland: World Publishing, 1965. Print.

Mayberry, Susan Neal. "A Study of Illusion and the Grotesque in Tennessee Williams's *Cat on a Hot Tin Roof*". *Southern Studies* 22.04 (1983): 359-65. Print.

McCann, John S. *The Critical Reputation of Tennessee Williams: A Reference Guide.* Boston: G.K. Hall, 1983. Print.

McCullers, Carson. *Reflections in a Golden Eye.* New York: Bantam Books, 1961. Print.

Murphy, Brenda. *Tennessee Williams and Elia Kazan: A Collaboration in Theatre.* Cambridge: Cambridge University Press, 1992. Print.

Nelson, Benjamin. *Tennessee Williams: The Man and His Work.* New York: Ivan Obolensky, 1961. Print.

Neumann, Erich. *The Great Mother: An analysis of the Archetype*. Trans. Ralph Manheim. New York: Pantheon, 1955. Print.

O'Connor, Jacqueline. *Dramatizing Dementia: Madness in the Plays of Tennessee Williams*. Bowling Green, Ohio: Bowling Green State University Popular Press, 1997. Print.

———. "Living in This Little Hotel: Boarders on Boarders in Tennessee Williams's Early Short Plays". *The Tennessee Williams Annual Review* 03 (2000): 101-15. Print.

Ollman, Bertell. *Alienation: Marx's Conception of Man in Capitalist Society*. Cambridge University Press, 1977. Print.

Orwell, George. *Nineteen Eighty Four*. London: Penguin Classics (Modern Classics Series), 2009. Print.

Pagan, Nicholas. *Rethinking Literary Biography: A Postmodern Approach to Tennessee Williams*. Cranbury, New Jersey: Fairleigh Dickinson University Press, 1993. Print.

Parker, Dorothy, ed. *Essays on Modern American Drama: Williams, Miller, Albee and Shepard*. Toronto: The University of Toronto Press, 1987. Print.

Parker, R. Brian. "Introduction to a One Act Version of *The Night of the Iguana*". *The Tennessee Williams Annual Review* 04 (2001): iii-v. Print.

———. Introduction. "Il Cane Incantato della Divina Costiera: A one Act Sketch for *The Rose Tattoo*." *The Tennessee Williams Annual Review* 06 (2003): n.pag. Web. 16 May 2015.

———. "The Circle Closed: A Psychological Reading of *The Glass Menagerie* and *The Two Character Play*". *Modern Drama* 28.04 (Winter 1985): 517-34. Print.

Phillips, Gene D. *The Films of Tennessee Williams*. London: Associated University Presses, 1980. Print.

Popkin, Henry. "The Plays of Tennessee Williams". *The Tulane Drama Review* 4.3 (1960): 45-64. Print.

Presley, Delma Eugene. "The Search for Hope in the Plays of Tennessee Williams". *The Mississippi Quarterly* 25 (1971): 31-43. Print.

Prosser, William. *The Late Plays of Tennessee Williams*. Lanham, MD: Scarecrow Press, 2009. Print.

Punter, David, ed. *A Companion to the Gothic*. Malden, Massachusetts: Blackwell, 2001. Print.

Rader, Dotson. *Cry of the Heart: An Intimate Memoir of Tennessee Williams*. New York: New American Library, 1985. Print.

Reck, Tom S. "The Short Stories of Tennessee Williams: Nucleus for His Drama". *Tennessee Studies in Literature* 16 (1971): 141-54. Print.

Roudané, Matthew C., ed. *The Cambridge Companion to Tennessee Williams*. Cambridge: Cambridge University Press, 1997. Print.

Russell, Bertrand. *Why I am not a Christian and Other Essays*. London: Routledge Classics, 2004. Print.

Saddik, Annette J. *Tennessee Williams and the Theatre of Excess: The Strange, The Crazed, The Queer*. Cambridge: Cambridge University Press, 2015. Print.

———. "The (Un)Represented Fragmentation of the Body in Tennessee Williams's 'Desire and the Black Masseur' and *Suddenly Last Summer*." *Modern Drama* 41.03 (Fall 1998): 347-54. Print.

———. *The Politics of Reputation: The Critical Reception of Tennessee's Later Plays*. Madison, NJ: Fairleight Dickinson UP, 1999. Print.

Sahu, Dharnidhar. *Cat on a Hot Tin Roof: A Study of the Alienated Characters in the Major Plays of Tennessee Williams*. Delhi: Academic Foundation, 1990. Print.

Schacht, Richard. *Alienation*. New York: Doubleday, 1970. Print.

Shakelford, Dean. "The Ghost of a Man": The Quest for Self-Acceptance in Early Williams". *The Tennessee Williams Annual Review* 04(2001): 49-58. Print.

Sharp, William. "An Unfashionable View of Tennessee Williams". *The Tulane Drama Review* 6.3 (1962): 160-71. Print.

Sofer, Andrew. "Self-Consuming Artifacts: Power, Performance and the Body in Tennessee Williams' *Suddenly Last Summer*". *Modern Drama* 38.03 (1995): 336-47. Print.

Spoto, Donald. *The Kindness of Strangers: The Life of Tennessee Williams.* Boston: Little, Brown & Company, 1985. Print.

Stanton, Stephen S., ed. *Tennessee Williams: A Collection of Critical Essays*. Englewood Cliffs, N.J.: Prentice-Hall, 1977. Print.

Starnes, Leland. "The Grotesque Children of *The Rose Tattoo*". *Modern Drama* 12.4 (1969): 357-69. Print.

Steinmann, Martin, ed. *Two Modern American Tragedies: Reviews and Criticism of 'Death of a Salesman'* and *'A Streetcar Named Desire'*. New York: Charles Scribner's Sons, 1961. Print.

"Tennessee Williams Stalks the Sweet Bird of His Youth in New Orleans." *People* 7.6. (14 February 1977) n.pag. Web. 10 April 2015.

Tharpe, Jac, ed. *Tennessee Williams: A Tribute* (Part 1 & 2). Jackson: The University Press of Mississippi, 1977. Print.

Thompson, Judith J. *Tennessee Williams' Plays: Memory, Myth and Symbol.* New York: Peter Lang, 1987. Print.

Tischler, Nancy Marie. *Tennessee Williams: Rebellious Puritan.* New York: Citadel Press, 1961. Print.

Traubitz, Nancy Baker. "Myth as a Basis of Dramatic Structure in *Orpheus Descending*". *Modern Drama* 19.1 (1976): 57-66. Print.

Vannatta, Dennis P. *Tennessee Williams: A Study of the Short Fiction.* Boston: Twayne Publishers, 1988. Print.

Venkateshwarulu, D., ed. *Perspectives on Post-War American Drama*. New Delhi: Prestige Books, 1996. Print.

Vidal, Gore. Introduction. *Tennessee Williams: Collected Stories.* London: Secker & Warburg, 1985. Print.

Voss, Ralph F., ed. *Magical Muse: Millennial Essays on Tennessee Williams,* Tuscaloosa: The University of Alabama Press, 2002. Print.

Vowles, Richard B. "Tennessee Williams: The World of His Imagery". *The Tulane Drama Review* 3.2 (1958): 51-56. Print.

Wager, Walter, ed. (Introduction by Harold Clurman). *The Playwrights Speak*. New York: Delacorte Press, 1967. Print.

Walker, Julia A. *Expressionism and Modernism in American Theatre: Bodies, Voices, Word*. New York: Cambridge University Press, 2005. Print.

Watson, Charles S. *The History of Southern Drama*. Lexington: The University Press of Kentucky, 1997. Print.

Weales, Gerald. *Tennessee Williams*. Minneapolis: The University of Minnesota Press, 1965. Print.

Weaver, Gordon, ed. *The American Short Story, 1945-1980: A Critical History*. Boston: Twayne Publishers, 1983. Print.

Williams, Edwina Dakin, and Lucy Freeman. *Remember Me to Tom*. New York: G.P. Putnam's, 1963. Print.

Williams, Walter Dakin, and Shepherd Mead. *Tennessee Williams: An Intimate Biography*. New York: Arbor House, 1983. Print.

"Williams Then & Now". *American Theatre* 28.7. (September 2011): 27-41. Print.

Wolff, Toni. *Structural Forms of the Feminine Psyche*. Trans. Paul Watzlawick. Zurich: C.G. Jung Institute, 1956. Print.

Zweig, Connie and Jeremiah Abrams, eds. *Meeting the Shadow*. New York: G.P. Putnam's Sons. 1991. Print.

Index